DATA BASES FOR BUSINESS

DATA BASES FOR BUSINESS

PROFILES AND APPLICATIONS

Van Mayros and D. Michael Werner

CHILTON BOOK COMPANY

Radnor, Pennsylvania

Copyright © 1982 by Van Mayros and D. Michael Werner
All Rights Reserved
Published in Radnor, Pennsylvania 19089, by Chilton Book Company and
simultaneously in Canada by Fleet Publishers,
a Division of International Thomson Limited,
1410 Birchmount Road, Scarborough, Ontario M1P 2E7

Library of Congress Cataloging in Publication Data
Mayros, Van.
    Data bases for business.

    Includes indexes.
    1. Business—Data processing.
2. Electronic data processing. I. Werner, D. Michael. II. Title.
HF5548.2.M3635 1982   650'.028'5442   82-70653
ISBN 0-8019-7255-8
ISBN 0-8019-7256-6 (pbk.)

Designed by William E. Lickfield
Manufactured in the United States of America

CONTENTS

PREFACE

THE PURPOSE OF THIS BOOK is to introduce business managers, researchers, information specialists, students, and librarians to the world of data base retrieval systems (DBRS). Until recently, data base retrieval systems were a secondary source of information for those who had difficulty locating a particular fact or piece of data. The primary method of information gathering was the search of printed materials. Prior to the availability of DBRS, we were forced to spend countless hours finding and reading journal articles, books, conference proceedings, and other periodicals just to uncover, if we were lucky, the one piece of information that we really needed. Fortunately, professional librarians were there to help. Yet, despite the skills brought to the task, the librarian would not always know how and when specific information would satisfy our needs. A communication gap often existed between the information requestor and the information gatherer. Consequently, a requestor's needs were not always met.

Today, however, new technology, indexing methods, accessing logic, and data base additions have opened up new ways of locating and using information. Data base retrieval systems have been recognized as a powerful primary resource. More and more business executives and information specialists have realized the vast extent of the information available at their fingertips. In many respects, modern computerized data bases have begun to reduce the communication gap between information requestor and information gatherer. In fact, the information requestor, searcher, and user can be the same person. Even when more than one person is involved in the process, the speed at which computerized searching can be accomplished frees all parties to focus on the most important issue—finding the right information to help solve a specific problem.

We have written this book to introduce those who are unfamiliar with DBRS to the potential usefulness of each data base. Other books already exist which provide listings of the various data bases. (The most comprehensive listing, and the most expensive, is the *Encyclopedia of Information Systems and Services,* edited by Anthony T. Kruzas and John Schmittroth, Jr. [Detroit: Gale Research, 1981]). We do not imitate them. Instead, we provide a profile of relevant business data bases with a brief description of the general ways to use them. The approach we have taken is to list, profile, and indicate the applications for those data bases which contain data and/or information that are most useful in answering business questions.

We hope you will find this book a valuable source for locating business-related data bases. Additionally, we hope it is a useful tool for understanding your own information needs and for getting the most out of DBRS in solving your business problems.

PART I

Information and the
Data Base Industry

CHAPTER 1

Introduction to Data Base Retrieval Systems

THIS BOOK is organized into three parts. Part I, Information and the Data Base Industry, contains three chapters which will introduce you to the data base industry, illuminate some aspects of the information-gathering process, tell you how to get started using computerized data bases, and give a few simple hands-on examples of data base searches. Part II, Data Base Directory, describes over 400 computerized data bases applicable to business. Part III, Indexes, provides access to the Directory via a detailed subject index. Part III also contains alphabetical directories of data base producers and vendors.

Before proceeding to the Directory and Indexes, however, you should have a basic understanding of the fundamentals of data base retrieval systems (DBRS). These concepts include:

> What DBRS are
> What DBRS can do (benefits)
> What DBRS cost
> When to use DBRS
> How DBRS are marketed

These and other subjects are covered in Chapters 1 through 3.

What DBRS Are

In its most general definition, a data base (or data bank) is a collection of data which have some common reference point. A plastic box filled with 3″ × 5″ cards containing your favorite recipes is a data base of your recipes. All of the cards have a common reference point in that they each contain a recipe which you have used or want to use. It is unlikely that you would keep your physician's address and phone number in the recipe data base. The term data

base can also take on a much broader interpretation. If we were to speak of the General Motors data base, we would be referring to all of the data maintained and used by groups and individuals within General Motors. While the historical sales data would have very little in common with the production department's data bank of inventory items, both would still pertain to some aspect of General Motors.

Data bases can be public or private. Your recipe data base would not usually be available to an outsider. Likewise, an unrelated party would not be allowed access to the General Motors data base. Public data bases, like those described in this book, are available to anyone who pays for their use.

Computerized data bases, or data base retrieval systems, are collections of data that are stored in a computer and are retrievable through access to a computer, most often via a remote terminal.

Many computerized data bases are organized much like a library's card catalog. The card catalog has drawers, index cards, and bibliographic elements. The data base has files, records, and data elements (fields). A collection of data elements (e.g., an individual's name, address, sex, and age) constitutes a record.

The organization of a data base is important to understand because it determines what you can and cannot do. You can use a library card catalog to search for a source by referring to title, author, or subject catalogs. You cannot use the card catalog to find books published by a single publisher because there is no separate card catalog for publishers, even though the publisher is printed (as a field) on each of the index cards (records). If, however, the card catalog were organized into a computerized data base, you would find fewer restrictions. Most bibliographic data bases have extensive cross-referencing capabilities. Many, in fact, have indexed each word in an entry (except words such as *the, and, or, like*).

The data in a DBRS can be in statistical form or in reference (bibliographic) form. Each form can have several different features. The statistical data base, containing numerical data, can provide time series data for an individual item, such as the monthly Consumer Price Index for the last ten years. The Evans Econometrics' data bases included in this book are good examples of time series data bases. Some statistical data bases provide data related to a single time period but include several data variables for that time period. For example, American Profile provides census/demographic data for several variables for a single census. Dun's Financial Profiles provides several data items (company financial profiles) for individual companies at one specific time period. One all-important feature of statistical data bases is that much of what they contain is not available in print. The data has been collected and formulated especially for the data base retrieval system.

The reference data base, which contains primarily written material, provides bibliographic citations and abstracts of printed literature such as books, journal articles, and newspaper features; some contain the full text of the items.

What DBRS Can Do

The number of journal articles published per year *doubled* between 1967 and 1982, and that same type of growth is occurring in other forms of communication as well. Not only are people researching, analyzing, and publishing or presenting data more frequently, but they are making it more available to an information-aware public. As a result, traditional methods of locating information, i.e., searching card catalogs, printed source directories, and periodical guides, are becoming very time-consuming and, in many cases, futile.

The primary benefit of a computerized data base retrieval system lies in its ability to search literally millions of references or data items and select only those which are most relevant to your information needs. Additionally, computerized information research provides an interactive capability which allows the user to solicit answers from the host computer within seconds of entering the question (in the form of a command). The exciting part of the search process is the computer's speed. Millions of records can be searched in less than an hour. And in that hour you might find not only what you were originally searching for, but also a tremendous amount of

supportive information you did not think to ask for. For example, if you are searching for the profit and loss statements of your primary competitor, you might easily wind up with that competitor's entire Securities and Exchange Commission financial filings or a list of its newest product innovations. In fact, you could quite easily end up with research on the competitor's size, organizational structure, and marketing practices. You would probably be able to locate journal and newspaper articles on your competitor in less than fifteen minutes. Product and related forms of technology could also be searched by checking patent and trademark data bases. In short, the use of a DBRS can become a real labor-saving device. The decreased research time and the increased thoroughness of the search process can make using a DBRS an extremely cost-effective research method. A typical ten-minute search can cost from $5.00 in a government-sponsored data base, such as ERIC (education), to $20.00 or more in the more expensive and larger commercial systems. (These charges include telecommunication and system charges, but not offline printing costs.)

Data base retrieval systems can provide information for thousands of business applications. The data and information which they provide could form the basis for management planning, research and development studies, legal research, financial analyses, chemical analyses, new technology tracking, and so on. Users of DBRS could be business managers, engineers, chemists, librarians, consultants, educators, attorneys, or physicians. Anyone who needs information is a candidate for using DBRS.

Although the list of possible application areas is virtually endless, here are a number of applications representing the comprehensive coverage of data base retrieval systems:

> Product line and pricing forecasts for consumer and industrial products
> Corporate pension and employee benefits planning
> Corporate and personal portfolio (securities) management
> Population impact on the world food supply
> Corporate and personal tax management ideas
> International product trade opportunities
> Soviet views on Third-World countries
> Mini- and microcomputer selection references
> Insurance industry data on premiums, mortality, new programs, and profits

Promotional effectiveness of various media

Air traffic safety records and analyses

Market segmentation studies

Production/manufacturing statistics by industry

Environmental studies by specific area

Domestic/international ecological comparisons

Corporate 10-k's extracts

How energy inventories and production could impact people's lifestyles

Specific molecular formulas, registry numbers, *Chemical Abstracts* indices by product type or compound

Grants and funds available to organizations in Florida, for medical care and rehabilitation, indexed by foundation and amount

Specific food distributors' pricing policies, strategies, and decisions

Private farm planning information

Break-even analysis for farm types and locations

Recent developments in education

Current flight information from London to St. Louis

Airline performance evaluations

Relationship of liquor sales to drug and alcohol rehabilitation and therapy programs

Who the leading experts in marketing information systems are

Zip code demographics by region

The prospects for a new product (market analysis)

Competitive evaluations by industry, product, or service type

Current information on genetic engineering technology

The life expectancy and care of yellow roses

Current water treatment technology

Television ratings by specific region

New architectural designs

Arctic region data and studies

Music appreciation in 16th-century Europe

Recent legal decisions in the province of Quebec

Import/export analysis for 1982 by industry type

Articles published in the last two years on the novels of James Joyce

Government sponsored inventions and research for specific applications

Current U.S. monetary policies versus those of 1977

Employment opportunities by discipline and region

Bilingual education evaluations and applications in Miami

Identifying new books or proposals dealing with computers and marketing

Credit information by company

Preschool cafeteria and nutrition programs, evaluations, and studies

Current news pertaining to the neglect and abuse of children

Current barter exchange programs in the U.S.

Construction cost estimates

Oil and gas lottery statistics for Wyoming

Foreign aid statistics for Africa

Thoroughbred blood registry and ratings

Recipes for chicken Kiev

Listing of the A-rated French restaurants in New York City

Besides instant access to thousands of subject areas, there are many other advantages to using DBRS. They can be summarized as follows:

1. *Selective Dissemination of Information (SDI).* This service, offered by many systems, conducts an automatic search of user key words or interests each time the contents of the user's data bases are updated. For example, an investment banker might have a strong interest in economic trends and conditions in selected Latin American countries. An SDI service would allow the banker to store the search logic (looking for Latin American economic trends and conditions) and to receive regular printouts of new relevant articles appearing in general news and specialty publications. In effect, the banker can keep up to date without ever opening the cover of a single publication.

2. *Easy modification of search strategies.* Data base retrieval systems allow the user to quickly see the results of his search and to take a different approach, if necessary. A manual search can go on for hours before the searcher realizes that he is looking for the "wrong" thing or discovers that the information does not exist.

3. *Up-to-date systems.* In many cases, the information is available in a data base the day it appears, allowing the user to locate information in a data base before he could find it in the printed source, even if he knew precisely where to look.

4. *Flexibility.* Data base producers and vendors continually add to and refine their systems to meet user needs. As a user's needs expand, so too might the data base(s). Producers and vendors, being in a highly competitive industry, are continually seeking

user input as to how they can serve their users more effectively.

5. *Comprehensive coverage.* Most data bases provide access to hundreds of printed sources and maintain tightly integrated cross-reference tools and indexes.

6. *Support for a manager's professional judgment.* A computer-generated research report, like an outside consultant, can help a manager substantiate his or her "gut feelings" or professional judgment.

What DBRS Cost

Although data base retrieval systems offer substantial benefits, there are costs involved in their use. One up-front cost is the purchase or lease of a remote terminal. Keep in mind, too, that special services may require the use of a specific type of terminal, one to which you may or may not have access.

Approximately a third of the data base systems require a subscription fee. These fees can vary from modest ($25) to very expensive ($5,000) and do not include the cost of any data base searches you conduct. All systems charge for the time you are connected to the computer system and for offline printing if you require printing away from your own terminal. (Offline printing of items uncovered by the search takes place at the vendor's facility, which the vendor does for a fee. You can also stay online and connect your own printer to the terminal; this can be cost-effective if the print list is short, but note that some systems charge for each record you print out on your own terminal.) Each data base has its own connect charge but most range between $20 and $125 per hour. You pay only for the fraction of the hour you spend in a data base. Many searches can be completed in under 15 minutes. If the data base you are using costs $60 per hour, you will be charged $15 for the fifteen minutes plus any offline printing you choose to have done at the vendor's facility. If you are a frequent searcher, many data base retrieval systems offer volume discount plans. These plans can substantially reduce your connect rates.

Many managers and other users ask about the cost of long distance service. Most data base services use a direct-dial telecommunications network. The two major networks are TELENET (part of the GTE system) and TYMNET (offered by Tymnet, Inc.). These networks allow you to reach the host computer anywhere in the United States for approximately $8 per hour. (This fee is in addition to the hourly connect charge for whatever data base you are using.) Foreign network charges are slightly higher. Again, you pay only for the time you are actually connected.

Most data base retrieval systems proclaim a dramatic cost effectiveness compared to traditional literature search methods. This is a fact, but with one disclaimer. Every data base retrieval system requires a certain amount of training in "easy-to-learn" English-language commands that allow you to describe your topic and manipulate the retrieval system. These commands take practice, and that practice requires some time, money, and effort. How much will, of course, vary from person to person. You probably will not become an expert searcher within three months of your first training seminar, but your proficiency will steadily improve. Moreover, your familiarity with the system will help you communicate your needs to others, because extensive searches generally should be left to those with considerably more experience. Many corporate and public librarians are trained in the art of data base searching and will therefore be familiar with the nuances of a particular system.

When to Use DBRS

With the increasing use of electronic calculators, many of us have become number lazy. We will not multiply 237 × 68 if we do not have a calculator at hand. This same phenomenon can occur with computerized data base searching. Once we have become experienced searchers, we often forget to use the more traditional methods for simple searches. This is not cost effective. To search for the possible side-effects of drug X, it would be more cost effective to look up the drug in the *Physicians' Desk Reference.* However, to identify the impact of the drug on adult males in the Caribbean, we would use a data base retrieval system. Knowing when to search and when not to search is as important as knowing how to search.

How DBRS Are Marketed

The data base industry is composed of two principal partners, the producer and the supplier (vendor). The producer is the organization that collects the data and organizes it into a usable format. The producer is often an educational group or government agency chartered with the responsibility for research in a specific area. The producer then makes the data available to a vendor for distribution to the public. The vendor either has its own telecommunications network or has access to a common network. In most cases, the vendor pays a fee to the producer for access to the producer's data base. In some cases, the producer and vendor of a data base will be the same.

In terms of the number of data bases offered,

DIALOG Information Services and Systems Development Corporation (SDC) are the two largest data base vendors in the United States. Many vendors offer a number of data bases; most producers supply just a single product. In total, there are several hundred data base producers and several hundred more data base vendors. How to select a vendor is discussed in Chapter 3.

Computer timesharing companies, such as the Business Information Services (formerly SBC) division of Control Data Corporation, have also entered the data base industry. They act as primary vendors, and, for several large and important data bases, as producers as well. Although none of the timesharing companies compares in broad scope to vendors such as DIALOG or SDC, they do have exclusive contracts with various key data base producers. Exhibit 1.1, Major Timesharing Companies, is a list of the major firms offering data base systems. Their current data base emphases are also indicated.

If a particular producer's data base is offered through both a timesharing vendor and a standard vendor, the contents of the data base will be the same. However, the timesharing vendor does offer one advantage. With the timesharing vendor, you gain immediate access to all of its data handling and statistical software packages. For example, if you were collecting demographic data through a data base offered by a timesharing vendor, you would be able to apply any statistical routines to that data that were offered by that vendor. You would also be able to save your data in a data base management system for later analysis. Typically, with a standard vendor, once you receive the data, your use of the system ends. What you do with the data once you have obtained it is independent of the vendor's system.

Information brokers are also beginning to play a major role in the data base industry. Information brokers are sellers of information. They range in size from the one-person shop specializing in a specific field (energy data, for example) to the multifaceted research organization with a staff of several hundred. We have listed several of the major business information brokers in Exhibit 1.2. One of their principal advantages is that they have access to perhaps dozens of data bases in the same field, making

Exhibit 1.1
Major Timesharing Companies Who Are Also Vendors

Company Name, Address and Phone	Primary Data Base Emphasis
Automatic Data Processing, Inc. 175 Jackson Plaza Ann Arbor, MI 48106 (313) 769-6800	Accounting and banking-related data bases. Has several exclusive financial and economic data bases and provides several other general business data bases.
Business Information Services Division of Control Data Corp. 500 West Putnam Avenue Greenwich, CT 06830 (203) 622-2000	Economic and demographics data bases. Has an exclusive contract with Evans Econometrics for several time series products and with Donnelly Marketing for its American Profile, a demographics file.
Computer Sciences Corp. (CSC) 650 North Sepulveda Boulevard El Segundo, CA 90245 (213) 615-0311	General business applications, including small business services. The sole vendor for the National Coal Resources Data System.
General Electric Information Services Company (GEISCO) 401 N. Washington Street Rockville, MD 20850 (301) 340-4000	Broad forecasting and general business offerings; particularly strong in the energy and construction fields.
National CSS, Inc. 187 Canbury Road Wilton, CT 06897 (203) 762-2511	General purpose financial and economic data bases.
Tymshare, Inc. 20705 Valley Green Drive Cupertino, CA 95014 (408) 446-6000	Has several data bases most of which are financial or economic. Plans to focus more on the banking community.

Exhibit 1.2
Major Business Information Brokers

Chemical Data Center, Inc.
3260 N. High Street
Columbus, OH 43214
(614) 261-7101

Data-Search
Box 635
Pittsboro, NC 27312
(919) 542-5114

FIND/SVP, The Information
Clearing House
500 Fifth Avenue
New York, NY 10110
(212) 354-2424

FOI Services, Inc.
12315 Wilkins Avenue
Rockville, MD 20852
(301) 881-0410

Info-Mart
Box 2400
Santa Barbara, CA 93120
(805) 965-5555

Information for Business
25 West 39 Street
New York, NY 10018
(212) 840-1220

Information Management
Specialists, Inc.
1816 Race Street
Denver, CO 80206
(303) 320-0116

Information on Demand
Box 4536
2511 Channing Way
Berkeley, CA 94704
(415) 841-1145

The Information Store, Inc.
235 Montgomery Street
Suite 800
San Francisco, CA 94104
(415) 421-9376

Packaged Facts, Inc.
274 Madison Avenue
New York, NY 10016
(212) 532-5533

PROBE
Arthur D. Little, Inc.
Acorn Park
Cambridge, MA 02140
(617) 864-5770

Warner-Edison Associates, Inc.
186 Alewife Brook Parkway
Cambridge, MA 02138
(617) 661-8124

Washington Researchers
918 16 Street, N.W.
Washington, D.C. 20006
(202) 833-2230

World Trade Information Center
One World Trade Center
Suite 86001
New York, NY 10048
(212) 466-3063

it unnecessary for the information requester to know which data base to go to. In fact, the requester does not even have to know how to access a single data base.

The primary disadvantage of using the broker for data base searching is that the broker may not have access to the data base ideally suited for your problem. Another disadvantage is that you will have to pay the broker $25 to $80 per hour on top of any data base service charges.

In Exhibit 1.3 we have listed the most common services provided by the information brokerage industry. Not all information brokers provide the same subject coverage or offer the same types of services, so you will need to interview each broker carefully before you select an information supplier.

There are several hundred timesharing companies and several thousand information brokers. For a more complete listing than we have presented here, please refer to one or more of the following publications:

1. Anthony T. Kruzas and John Schmittroth, Jr., eds., *Encyclopedia of Information Systems and Services,* 4th ed. (Detroit: Gale Research, 1981).
2. Van Mayros and D. Michael Werner, *Business Information: Applications and Sources,* in press (Radnor, Pa.: Chilton Book Co. 1983).
3. *Information Industry Market Place 1982* (New York: R. R. Bowker, 1981).

Exhibit 1.3
Typical Services of the Information Broker

Abstracting	Provides abstracts of printed publications in one or more subject areas.
Analytical reports	Sells specialized research reports on certain topics or industries.
Data base searching	Accesses one or several computerized data bases for data and information retrieval.
Document delivery	Locates and delivers copies of original articles and other printed materials.
Manual searching	Uses traditional printed sources for locating the requested information.
SDI searching	Provides "Selective Dissemination of Information" whereby special topic areas are routinely searched and information forwarded to the requestor.
Telephone interviewing	Uses telephone interviews to gather information from government and private agencies and individuals.

How to Use This Book

The Data Base Directory in Part II provides an alphabetical listing and description of over 400 computerized data bases that are used in business today. The Directory is intended to offer the reader the most extensive understanding of the major data bases with as little effort as possible. Each data base has been evaluated, profiled, and cross-referenced. The Directory tells who produces the data base, what the contents of the data base are, how the contents can be used, what subject categories are covered, and who offers it as an online service.

Although over 1,000 public data bases exist today, many are not relevant to the business organization and have not been included in the Directory. To qualify for inclusion, the data base must:

1. Provide extensive and relevant coverage of specific subject categories in a business-related discipline.
2. Be available online (i.e., be stored in a computer and available to users).
3. Have or will have English text.

Each data base profile contains the following information:

Name: The full name of the data base, with acronyms in parentheses.

Producer: The name, address, and phone number of the organization that produces the data base.

Class: Either reference or statistical. A reference data base contains citations, bibliographies, and, in some cases, abstracts or full texts of published and unpublished material. A statistical data base contains data derived from government sources, surveys, mathematical models, etc., which has been reconstructed and manipulated in some way. These data are generally in the form of time series (measurements of a single variable over time).

Data Source: The primary original source(s) of the data or information.

Size: The approximate unit or record size of the data base. The unit size indicates either the number of citations or time series. The record size indicates the total number of records as of publication date.

Maintenance: How often the data base is revised or new data entered.

Subject: Corresponds to the ten subject headings used in the Subject Index in Part III (see page 145). Each data base is identified by a primary subject and possibly a secondary subject. The term "multidisciplinary" means the data base contains data relevant to two or more of the ten major subjects.

Profile: A brief description of the data base contents. Specific field or coverage categories are listed only as a representation of the total coverage.

Application: Examples of how various users use the data base.

Subject Cross Reference: Each data base has been cross-referenced to one or more of a total of 113 business disciplines. This powerful feature will allow you to quickly interpret the wide range of applications that each data base offers. It will also help you locate related data bases via the Subject Index in Part III.

Geographic Coverage: Indicates geographical coverage, either domestic (United States), International, or a specific country or region.

Time Coverage: The time period covered in the data base.

Online Vendor: Identifies each vendor (e.g., BRS, DIALOG, SDC) through which the data base is available.

An "N/A" in the listings indicates that the category does not apply to that particular data base, or, in a few cases, that the information was not available from the producer at the time of publication.

Cost is not included in the profiles because of the volatile nature of communications charges, connect charges, and printing fees. Vendors and producers will be able to supply you with the latest cost information of a particular data base.

Access to the Data Base Directory is provided by the Subject Index in Part III. This index is divided into ten major categories, and each of these has several subcategories. The major categories are as follows:

1. Banking, economics, and finance
2. Marketing planning
3. Sales planning
4. Marketing and sales promotion
5. Legal and legislative affairs
6. Environmental, social, and political affairs
7. Industrial and manufacturing planning
8. Research and development
9. General management issues (domestic and international)
10. Long-range strategic planning

Each category and subcategory contains an alphabetical list of the data bases that pertain to that subject. To locate data bases to suit your information needs, simply read the list of data bases under the main category and subcategories most applicable to your area. Then turn to the Data Base Directory to get the profile and source of each data base.

Part III also contains alphabetical directories so you can locate and contact data base producers and vendors.

A few words of caution are in order. The data base industry is dynamic and constantly changing. Therefore, several of the data bases included here may have altered their profiles by the time you consult their descriptions. New fields may be added or entire new concepts may be included. In fact, entirely new business data bases will have become available that are not included here. Others that are included here may have been discontinued by their producers or vendors. Because of this, we suggest that you use the profiles as a guide and that you consult with the various producers and vendors for updated information on the latest versions of their products.

CHAPTER 2
The Information—Gathering Process

ALL ORGANIZATIONS depend on information in order to operate efficiently and effectively. Managers need feedback on the actions they have taken, and they need information to help in decision-making and planning for future actions. The information they need may be derived either from internal sources (sales order entries, accounts payable/receivable, production schedules, new product introduction schedules, and so on) or from external sources (competitors, customers, research firms, industry associations, and so on). Exhibits 2.1 and 2.2 give examples of the kind of data or information provided by various internal and external sources and the common types of analyses (output) that might be generated by the information system with the relevant data inputs. The information systems referred to in these exhibits are not necessarily computerized ones. We are addressing the information gathering *process*, which may or may not involve the use of a computer.

As you can see from Exhibit 2.1, internal information focuses on data or information which are routine products of the ongoing operations of the business. From these data, the business manager has access to basic sales reporting and accounting information. Most information systems were developed to serve the needs of the financial/accounting function, so it is not surprising to find that individual managers are accustomed to dealing with internal information such as expense, budget, and sales reports.

However, as you can see from Exhibit 2.2, industry comparisons, technological differences analyses, or new product developments require external information. Exhibit 2.3 illustrates the role of external information in decision-making. From a multitude of sources, information is made available to a buying public through data base retrieval systems, standard printed publications such as books, journals, and magazines, and specialized printed materials such as newsletters and expert commentaries.

It is primarily in the area of external information that today's "information explosion" has taken place. But today's business manager has generally not been in a position to explore what the information explosion has to offer because he or she has been preoccupied with the traditional ways of gathering information through libraries, encyclopedias, or texts. It is here that the computerized data base has so much to offer. All of the information sources listed in Exhibit 2.3 may be used in the development and maintenance of a data base retrieval system. To use the computer as an information resource is to link you with hundreds of millions of data records in virtually any subject, whether it be demographics by zip code or the current Soviet views on developing countries. Computerized data base retrieval systems are the key to mining the potential of the information revolution.

The Value of Information

Just how much is a particular piece of information worth? And how do we know what its long-term benefits will be?

Exhibit 2.1
Internal Input to and Output from the Information System

Source (Department)	Input	Output
Corporate Planning	Corporate objectives	Measurement of the organization's progress toward goal attainment
	Expansion plans	Data for analyses of new products or markets
Sales	Sales	Sales analysis by sales rep
	Invoices and shipments	Sales analysis of product or service lines
	Back-order status	Equivalent replacement products; communication to the sales force
Marketing	Types of new products or services with market possibilities	Data for market analyses of potential new products and customers
	Consumer response to existing products or services	Sales analysis of current products or services to current customers
	Planning and promotional campaigns	Media and lead analysis
Customer Service	Feedback from customers and sales force on product reliability and performance	Complaint file and new product ideas
Product Research and Development	New product development schedules	Proper timing for new product release and phase-in
Engineering	Engineering schedules for products	Proper timing for new product release and phase-in
Data Processing	System for organizing data files and reporting operating results	Details of what each department needs in computerized reports
Manufacturing	Inventory status	Forecasts: production and inventory updates
Personnel	Background on sales and marketing employees	Effects of a learning curve for sales force
	Salary/performance review data	Determinants for future employee selection
Corporate Financial Planning	Product pricing and costing	Profitability by product or sales rep
	Operating expenses	

Exhibit 2.2
External Input to and Output from the Information System

Source	Input	Output
Industry Reports	Corporate data and analysis	Industry growth and trend statistics
	Industry news	New technology and products
Competition	Products and product literature	Technology comparisons
	Other corporate literature	Financial comparisons
		Capitalization analysis
Distributors and Retailers	Market conditions	Special sales programs
	Consumer analysis	Sales analysis
		Pricing policy input
		Market segmentation
Customers	Profile data	Customer segmentation
	Sales data	Profile analysis
		Product history
State and Federal Statistical Data and Abstracts	Corporate statistical comparisons	Competitive analysis
	Economic/financial data	Market-segment analysis
	Securities and Exchange Commission data	Corporate financial profiles
	Department of Commerce Bureau of Census	
Data Base Retrieval Systems	Product, market, and industry news and analysis	Changes in product positions, markets, industries
		Economic influences on sales potential
	Economic news	News influences on market

Exhibit 2.3
Information Center/Directory

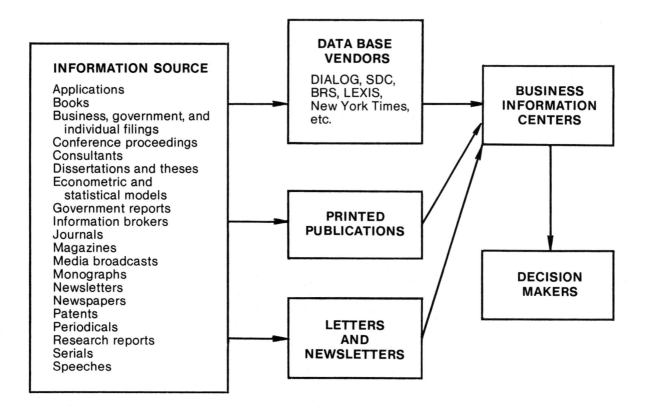

In the first question, what we are really asking is what is it worth to us to know something. Information in and of itself has no tangible economic value. In fact, if information is not used properly it can have a cost and *no* benefit. As one vice-president of a major automobile manufacturer stated:

> I am strongly opposed to the notion that the mere accumulation of information in computer files should be treated as having some general economic value apart from the specific uses to which the information may be put. The aimless accumulation of marginally useful information, in fact, strikes me as being one of the more serious economic problems associated with the computer age. (In Joel Ross, *Modern Management and Information Systems* [Reston, Va: Reston Publishing Co., 1976], p. 188).

So the dollar value of any piece of information can only be assessed if we can attach a dollar value to the benefits of that information. And this value can be determined with certainty only *after* we have found and used the information.

Let's illustrate our point with a simple example.

You are buying a new car and have narrowed your choice to Model A and Model B, both of which cost $10,000 and have identical operating costs and resale value after three years. Just as you are about to allow style and color to sway your decision in favor of Model A, you learn of a new research report, costing $650, which details the costs and benefits of owning and operating Model A. Should you spend $650 for the new research? Now, let's assume the report identifies a manufacturing problem on Model A, and that the car will require a rebuilt engine, at the cost of $1,000, after the second year. If you spend $650 for the report, you will buy Model B and save $350 ($1,000 − $650). Therefore, the value of the information is $350. If the report had cost $900, then the information would have been worth $100. On the other hand, you could decide not to purchase the report. In this case, you would go ahead with your decision to buy Model A and have to spend $1,000 after two years to rebuild the engine. Here there is an associated cost of not knowing a specific piece of information.

Hundreds of similar examples occur in the business world each day, but the value of the information may not be so readily determined. How much is it worth to you to know that your competitor will introduce a new product next year? How much is it worth to you to know how many customers will buy your Brand X next month? How much are you willing to spend in order to find out what technological developments have occurred recently that might have some impact on your existing product lines?

Although the number of situations is limitless, the theoretical value of the information will always be determined in the same way. The value to you will be the dollars saved or the incremental new revenue generated minus the cost of the information.

Andrew Garvin and Hubert Bermont approach information valuation via "failure costs":

> A good way to measure the value of information (as promulgated by *Boardroom Reports*, May 15, 1976) is to make a comparison of "failure costs." For example, if the likelihood of failure of a $100,000 project is one in three without research, the failure cost is $33,000. With research, the risk of failure is one in five, for a failure cost of $20,000. The value of the research is then the difference between the two costs, or $13,000. (Andrew P. Garvin and Hubert Bermont, *How To Win with Information or Lose Without It* [Washington, D.C.: Bermont Books, 1980], p. 52.)

No matter how we assign a dollar value to a piece of information, the valuation will always be somewhat subjective. In the Garvin and Bermont example, the risk of failure may be determined subjectively. The value of a piece of information will also vary from user to user. What is worth $10,000 to Xerox may be worth $5,000,000 to one of its competitors. In the final analysis, information worth can be estimated only by the user of the information.

Distinguishing Between Data and Information

Data are not information! Repeat: Data are not information! Unfortunately, the modern business organization usually has an overabundance of data and very little or no information. We spend most of our time collecting and reporting data and very little time analyzing and interpreting it. A company might think nothing of spending over a million dollars on new computer hardware and software in order to collect and store data. But that same company will not spend ten percent of the system cost on adequate personnel trained in information analysis. This is one of the most serious failings associated with the use of computers in business.

Information is data which have been transformed or massaged in some way that will give us specific answers to specific questions. Information is "processed" data which can provide more than just a number. Whether or not a particular item is data or information depends upon the use to which we put it—specifically, upon how well the data or information can be used to provide specific answers to specific questions. A single number can be a piece of data or information or both depending upon the use to which it is put. If the question is, "What was the company's net unit sales volume for Product A last month?" and the answer is "3,245 units," then we have data as well as information. The number 3,245 is, and always will be, a piece of data. It becomes information only when it provides an answer to our question. On the other hand, if the question is, "What is the percentage change in net unit sales for Product A from last month of one year ago to last month?", and we know that net sales of last month one year ago was 3,000 units, then we have two pieces of data but no information. We have the necessary ingredients for arriving at the answer, but until we do something else (calculate a percentage change) we do not have information. A percentage change of 8.2% is information, while 3,000 and 3,245 are data.

If you have to do something to a particular fact or number (or set of facts or numbers) before you can take action, make a decision, or answer a specific question, then you do not have information, you merely have data. If you receive a monthly computer printout which you use in your job, and if you have to manipulate the material in the printout (perform calculations, look for deviations, uncover various trends, etc.), then you are receiving data, not information.

Distinguishing between data and information is very important for two reasons. First, when you use computerized data base retrieval systems, remember that what you ultimately want is information, not data. You want answers to questions, and only relevant information can provide that. So you will need to transform the data you obtain to suit your information needs, and you want to be sure that the data you do obtain will become information when transformed. Second, because data can be very expensive, you will want to obtain the minimum amount of data to satisfy your information needs. Only by understanding the difference between data and information will you be able to save time, money, and effort.

Five Steps to Gathering Information

Defining information needs and then developing a strategy to locate those needs is a process independent of the information source. Whether you are using a specialized data base or a branch of the public library, the steps which you take to gather information are the same under any circumstances. There are five steps you will want to consider when attempting to find and use business information.

STEP 1.   *Define the business problem*

Let's use the case of a large consumer products company with a sales force which calls directly on independent retail outlets. This company is growing very rapidly and is adding new items to its product line and new sales representatives to the field. The national sales manager has noticed that there is a wide disparity in sales volume among many of the company's sales territories. This is particularly disturbing because two years ago, all territories were realigned so that sales volume and amount of customer contacts would be equal in all territories. Then last year, as the sales disparities began to show up again, the best sales reps were shifted into the low volume territories. But so far, no noticeable improvement has occurred. The low volume territories have remained stagnant and the other territories have shown varied levels of growth. The sales manager has concluded that something other than sales rep quality is contributing to the volume disparity. The problem is still misalignment of the sales territories.

STEP 2.   *Ask the right questions.*

By "right" we mean those questions which, if answered correctly, can provide solutions to the problem. From the situation outlined above, it would appear that *the* question to ask is, "What factors are causing some territories to grow rapidly, others to decline, and others to remain stagnant?" The secondary questions might include one or more of the following:

1. Is the quality of the sales rep or sales manager somehow related to sales volume? If so, to what extent?
2. Is there a substantial variation across territories in the type of retail outlets we are calling on?
3. Are there any real differences among the people (end customers) who are buying our products at retail?

STEP 3.   *Determine the data needs that
will help answer the questions*

For each question, you will have a separate set of data needs. Let's review some of the data needs which might be pertinent in answering the three secondary questions above. By answering all of the secondary questions, we will be in a good position to answer the principal question. For Question 1, you would need to gather the following types of data: identification of sales rep and manager by territory, sales history by territory, sales history by sales rep for current and all previous territories, qualitative input from sales managers on the individual sales rep, and qualitative input from individual sales reps. For Question 2, you might want to consider: identification of retail outlets by territory, sales history by outlet, and profiles of individual outlets and segments of outlets (size, type, organization, promotional strategies, product types carried, geographic areas served, etc). For Question 3, you might want to consider the types and profiles of the retail outlets' buyers (age, sex, income level, distance traveled to store, and other demographic or psychographic characteristics) and the geographic and demographic characteristics of each sales territory.

STEP 4.   *Obtain the data*

Once you have determined your data needs, you can begin searching your internal and external sources for answers. For many of the data items, particularly those related to sales history and retail outlet, you will be able to use existing internal files. But for other data items, such as customer profile and related geographic, psychographic, and demographic characteristics, you will probably need to refer to external sources. It is at this point that, depending upon your time, money, and required effort, you will be able to choose from traditional printed sources, computerized data bases, and consulting or research firms.

STEP 5.   *Analyze the data and display
the information that will
answer your questions*

The types of data analyses which you perform will, of course, be dependent upon your skills and the time you have to devote to understanding the data. Regardless of the type of analyses performed, however, you will want to ensure that what you do is consistent with your objective to provide information related to the problem at hand. It may be interesting to perform a correlation analysis between sales rep longevity in the field and sales volume, but this is of questionable value if the analysis contributes little to your overall objective. After the data have been analyzed, you are in a position to display the information. Remember that information is data which have been transformed to provide answers to specific questions. Therefore, you will need to produce and display only that information which can be used to answer your questions. The actual organization of the information display (graphs, charts, tables, etc.) is dependent upon your needs and resources.

The Information Source Directory

The information retrieval, storage, and use process is a relatively simple one when you are concerned with finding answers to only a small number of questions. You complete the process by defining the problem, translating the problem into a question (a need for specific data or information), finding the data or information, and then using that data or information to help you answer the question and solve the problem. But what do you do when you are faced with dozens or hundreds of questions which require the use of external information sources?

A good way to handle the barrage of information needs and sources is to relate the common sources to the common needs via an information source directory. An information source directory contains business discipline headings tied to a corresponding list of the sources available for finding information relative to that discipline. Exhibit 2.4 illustrates part of a

typical information source directory for a medium-sized company. This directory can include data base retrieval system sources or it can focus solely on printed reference material. In our example, the L. W. Molnar Company (LWM) has identified eight business areas which are of prime importance to the successful operation of the business. The disciplines are oriented to marketing, planning, and information processing because a directory of this type is focused on external sources. Internal sources will, of course, play a vital role in answering business questions, but they are beyond the scope of our discussion here. As you review the exhibit, note that information sources are required not only for each business area but for the functional groups within each area as well. For example, LWM has identified "Market" as one of the primary business headings. Within the Market group, there are seven specific areas of concern, identified M1 through M7. For the first Market area (M1—Market statistics and studies), the Source Matrix on the right-hand side of the exhibit shows that there are thirty-one sources of information currently available to LWM relative to that area. In the Source Matrix, a tally is kept of the number of available sources for each information

Exhibit 2.4

L. W. Molnar Company
Information Source Directory

March, 1984

MARKET	PRODUCT	CONSUMER	SOURCE MATRIX		
M1 Market statistics and studies	P1 Product specifications	C1 Direct	M1 31	P1 3	C1 1
M2 New market opportunities	P2 Product technology	C2 Indirect	M2 10	P2 4	C2 5
M3 Market change	P3 Product competition	C3 Consumer Lists	M3 3	P3 1	C3 3
M4 Market trend	P4 Product research & development	C4 Consumer Demographics	M4 1	P4 2	C4 2
M5 Market demographics	P5 Product news	C5 Consumer by SIC	M5 3	P5 11	C5 1
M6 Market technology			M6 2		
M7 Market news			M7 3		

SALES	COMPETITION	PLANNING			
S1 Revenue	CP1 Revenue	PL1 Market	S1 2	CP1 6	PL1 2
S2 Profit & Loss by competitor	CP2 Expenses	PL2 Industry	S2 2	CP2 3	PL2 12
S3 Aggregate by market	CP3 News/profiles	PL3 Marketing and/or marketing news	S3 1	CP3 8	PL3 25
S4 Aggregate by industry	CP4 Contracts activity	PL4 General management	S4 1	CP4 2	PL4 3
S5 Sales management			S5 6		

PROMOTION	INFORMATION TECHNOLOGY				
PR1 Visual advertising/ education	I1 General sources		PR1 3	I1 8	
PR2 Journal directories (health related)	I2 Office system technology, micros, minis, etc.		PR2 1	I2 8	

component. The keeper of the directory would be responsible for maintaining an accurate list (by title, function, contents, and location within the organization) of the actual sources which have been tallied in the directory.

Many organizations maintain an information source directory without including data base retrieval systems as an integral part of it. These organizations tend to rely more on printed sources and view data bases, if they use them at all, as secondary support for their information needs. There are several problems with such an approach. The information source directory which relies only on printed sources is self-limiting, because each source typically corresponds to only one discipline category. Data bases, on the other hand, can correspond to several categories. And because the directory is time consuming to maintain, the user could benefit from the automatic maintenance and updating of data base systems.

Exhibit 2.5 compares the benefits of an information source directory that does not include data bases to data base retrieval systems alone. Clearly, the most useful information source directory would be one that includes *all* available external sources of information, both printed and computerized.

Exhibit 2.5
Information Benefits Comparison

	Information Source Directory (not including data bases)	Data Base Retrieval Systems
1. Information Source		
Single	X	
Multiple		X
2. Speed		X
3. Accuracy		X
4. Quality	X	
5. Depth of Coverage		X
6. Cost	X	X
7. Cross Reference Ability		X
8. Ease of Access by Staff	X	
9. Ease of Maintenance		X

CHAPTER 3
Getting Started

USING a data base retrieval system requires less computer equipment than you might imagine and requires almost no computer or computer language experience. What it does requires, however, is access to the following:

Terminal
Modem (modulator-demodulator)
Telephone
Password
Language orientation

Your Equipment

To get started using data base retrieval systems, the user must acquire a computer terminal. This device, which usually resembles a typewriter, communicates with the data base computer through the telephone system. Data communication terminals (those that both send *and* receive information and that are required for interacting with a data base system) come in all shapes and sizes. They can vary from highly portable thermal print devices at less than $700 to very sophisticated cathode ray tube (CRT) devices costing well over $10,000. One of the most common terminals is from the Texas Instruments Silent 700 series and costs about $1,000. Most microcomputers can serve as terminals when they are connected to a modem, so if you own a micro you should check its capabilities before investing in a terminal. If you have a choice of terminals, be sure that it contains a modem so that you will be able to connect it to external computers via the telephone. We recommend that you work with the data base vendor and your data processing department to select an appropriate terminal. For a broader description of the variety of currently available terminals, you may wish to refer to *Terminal/*

Microcomputer Guide and Directory (Weston, Connecticut: Online, Inc., 1982).

You will also want to pay close attention to the baud rate of the terminals. Baud means bit per second; a bit contains up to ten characters. The baud rate is the transmission speed of bits going back and forth between the terminal and the computer. The higher the baud rate, the faster the communication. Although there are terminals which have baud rates of several thousand, the most common terminals operate around 300 or 1200 baud (30 or 120 characters per second). If you envision receiving a great many online printouts, it will be best to use a terminal operating at 120 characters per second. Remember that the primary cost to you in using a data base is your online time. The quicker you can get your information and exit from the system, the lower your cost.

To connect your terminal with the data base, you simply dial a telephone number and connect the telephone with your terminal, usually by placing the telephone into an acoustic coupler, or modem. In order to get into the data base, or LOGON, you must use the password issued to you by the data base vendor. The password is the means by which the data base vendor records your time, provides any necessary services and, of course, invoices your charges.

Signing Up

There really is very little to signing up with a vendor. If you are interested in using a data base, simply send a letter to the vendor requesting a standard agreement form. When this is returned, the data base vendor will supply you with a password. In addition, you will receive all of the basic information you need to begin using the system. An online demonstration exercise will often be included. Many data base vendors will routinely send you new information concerning their data bases, search techniques, system features, discounts, training sessions, and newsletters.

Using the Data Base Language

To use a data base retrieval system, the user must know how to enter commands to manipulate the system. The command languages are not the computer programming languages such as BASIC, FORTRAN, or COBOL. Most vendors use easy-to-learn English commands, but some command languages are easier to use than others. The number of commands will vary from fifteen to fifty depending upon the vendor's system.

Learning to search is really not very difficult. However, learning shortcuts and manipulation requires a great deal of online experience, and the ability to manipulate commands separates the beginning searcher from the experienced. Most vendors will provide you with training manuals and related search aids at a nominal cost, and some will give new subscribers free online time or a few hours of use at a minimal per-hour rate. And most also provide free access for a limited period when a new data base is offered, so that users can become familiar with it. In addition, several of the larger vendors provide system overviews and search-strategy training on specific data bases. These training seminars last from one to three days and can be held either at your organization or at a regional training center. The overview sessions cover the type of data bases offered, command requirements for the host system and the individual data bases, and examples of effective information searching. These sessions are especially beneficial in that they allow the user to experiment with all or most of the vendor's data bases at no charge. In most cases, there is a fee for the training session itself, but no additional online charges.

Defining the Information Request

Before an online search actually takes place, it is extremely important to carefully define the information request. Typically, the online research specialist who performs the data base search for a large organization receives requests like "What do you have on medical device technology?" or "Give me all you have on medical device technology." To fulfill these requests could involve tremendous amounts of time and money. This is where the pre-search interview takes place. Before any online search is conducted,

the searcher, whether a trained research specialist or an individual manager, should narrow the scope of the request. The searcher should do the following before developing an online search strategy:

1. Make the information request as specific as possible.
2. Identify the objectives of the information request.
3. Identify the data base(s) to be used.
4. Identify key word index or synonymous terms.
5. Plan search logic.
6. Determine whether output will be printed online or offline.

Applying these steps to our example, the searcher might come up with the following results:

1. Specific request: What are the current programmable features of the CMC Corporation's Alpha heart pacemakers?
2. Objective: Competitive product analysis to be used in Company X's latest situational analysis.
3. Data bases: MEDLINE, MEDOC (Medical Documents), and PNI (Pharmaceutical News Index).
4. Key words: Heart and pacemaker or Alpha and CMC.
5. Search logic: This is the actual series of steps which you will got through in order to extract the information you need. These steps will vary according to the vendor's language.
6. On- or Offline print: Offline, because there is no serious deadline for receiving the information.

This search, which has now been specifically defined, should not take more than fifteen minutes at a cost of perhaps $15.00. The results should be analyzed by both the requestor and the searcher.

To use an online data base information retrieval system efficiently and effectively, a requestor information sheet, similar to that shown in Exhibit 3.1, should be employed. These types of request forms are used in many corporate, public, and university library systems. This represents a rather formal pre-search interview procedure, but it is comprehensive and could avoid information deficiencies. Information deficiencies occur when an online search is conducted using too broad a topic. Without effective pre-search planning, it is merely coincidence if the search produces the kind of information needed.

Exhibit 3.1
The Data Base Information Request Form

1. Requestor's Name:

2. Department:

3. Address if not at Headquarters:

4. Authorization Number or Departmental Charge Number:

5. Purpose of Search (provide a general statement as to why you need the information and how you plan to use it):

6. Topic of Search (provide a statement outlining the *specific* question or series of questions you want answered):

7. Key Words (provide a list of special words or phrases that help to identify your topic):

8. Have you searched this topic before? (If so, please attach part or all of the results which you obtained):

9. Specify the languages which you will accept on output:

10. Specify the time periods which you wish covered in the search:

11. If this is a bibliographic search, do you want titles only, or abstracts?

12. Specify maximum cost of search:

13. Deadline (date and time information is needed):

_____   _____
Requestor's Signature   Date

Good data and information are a result of careful planning. A requestor information sheet like that shown in Exhibit 3.1 should eliminate such confusion.

Even if the requestor is doing his own searching, it is wise to go through the process of completing the search-request form. It is both costly and time-consuming to develop a search strategy while sitting in front of a terminal. That type of search method, which is still frequently used, is analogous to trying to find Apple Computer Company sales history information by browsing through a stack of *Business Week* magazines.

A word about key words. It is important to understand that computer systems recognize only the exact characters of a word and do not know the meaning of that word or any concepts related to it. If you are searching for the word *key*, the system looks for a string of three characters: k e y. So that when you have just spent two hours searching for current news articles on *weaponry* and have found only one source, you might have found many more if you had tried searching for *weapon*. Some systems speed up the search process through the use of a truncated entry symbol (such as a question mark) at the end of a word. The symbol tells the system to look for all words following the key word, or key word fragment. In this case, supplying the word *weapon?* or the fragment *weap?* would result in a list of all entries in the data base that begin with the word or the fragment.

The commands required to operate a data base system can be mastered in a few hours of practice. However, becoming proficient at developing effective search strategies requires months of thinking *conceptually* about search problems.

Examples of Data Base Searches

The search process is a relatively simple procedure. It involves an interaction between you (and the searcher, if someone else is doing the searching) and the data base retrieval system which you are using. Commands are the backbone of any search. Each command, or instruction, is entered at the terminal. The system will respond to each command by displaying (printing) the results of that command.

We have provided three examples of some of the typical commands which could be used in accessing three different data bases from DIALOG Information Services. The command examples used are unique to DIALOG, but they all have equivalent forms on other vendor systems. The first example, Exhibit 3.2, provides a simple illustration of the use of the NTIS (National Technical Information Service) data base to locate citations on bus fares. The commands that we entered into the system are numbered and described briefly in the Exhibit. Note that any printed item appearing after the "?" symbol indicates something which we (the user) have entered at the terminal keyboard. For the sake of simplicity, we have omitted the LOGON procedures in this example. Exhibit 3.2 shows a total of eight commands.

COMMAND 1. BEGIN 6

In this example, the search is initiated by the command BEGIN 6. This tells the system that we wish to search file (or data base) number 6, which is the NTIS data base. The system responds by telling us the date, time, and approximate cost of signing on (referred to as "logging on"). The system also confirms that we have accessed the file we intended to and then gives dates of coverage (1964-1981) provided in the file.

COMMAND 2. EXPAND FARE

At this point, we are ready to enter our second command and go into the data base to extract information. We could simply search for any occurrence of the word *fare*. However, in this case we chose to "expand" our search by asking the system for other words or phrases that are near *fare* in an alphabetic listing. Command 2, EXPAND FARE, is used to display a partial index of words and phrases around the word *fare*. The EXPAND command and its index function can be thought of as a dictionary of phrases and words that allows the user to locate a specific word and then search around it for similar words and phrases.

After we enter the command, the system responds with a list of reference numbers (E1 through E10), item numbers, and descriptions. The reference numbers are assigned to the items for the duration of this search only and are unique identifiers of the item being described. To call up an item at a later point in the search, we can use the reference number instead of the term itself. The "items" column tells us how many items of the corresponding description (set) are included in the data base. Multiple occurrences of the word *fare*, for example, in a single record (citation) is counted as only one occurrence, so that the item count represents the number of different citations included in the data base. In the example here, we can see that there are 160 separate citations containing the word *fare*, 16 citations containing the phrase *fare collection*, and so on.

Exhibit 3.2
Search of the NTIS Data Base

```
? BEGIN 6 ◄─────
        3aug81 11:28:40 User3462
   $0.32  0.008 Hrs File6
   $0.06  Tymnet
   $0.38  Estimated Total Cost
File6:NTIS - 64-81/Iss18
(Copr. NTIS)
        Set Items Description
        --- ----- -----------
```

Command 1
We begin our search by using File #6, the NTIS Data Base.

```
? EXPAND FARE ◄─────
Ref Items   Index-term
E1    1    FARCE
E2    1    FARDEAU
E3  160   *FARE
E4   16    FARE COLLECTION
E5    8    FARE COLLECTION SYSTEMS
E6    1    FARE FREE TRANSIT
E7    9    FARE FREE TRANSPORTATION
                SERVICES
E8    1    FARE INCREASES
E9   14    FARE PROJECT
E10  55    FARE STRUCTURES
                                  -more-
```

Command 2
Using the word "FARE" as a starting point, we expand upon it to determine if there are other similar words or phrases which may be of interest to us.

```
? PAGE ◄─────
Ref Items   Index-term
E11   3    FARE(FORWARD AREA
                REFUELING EQUIPMENT)
E12   1    FAREBOX
E13   5    FARED
E14   4    FARED COMPUTER CODE
E15 174    FARES
E16   1    FARES(TRANSPORTATION)
E17   7    FARET
E18   2    FAREWELL
E19  16    FARFIELD
E20   1    FARFIELD STRESSES
E21   1    FARGBILDEN
                                  -more-
```

Command 3
We want to see more, so we continue to expand further down the index page.

Command 4
No more indexing. We're ready to focus on selected word and phrase groups.

```
? SELECT E3-E10,E12,E15 ◄─────
        1   290 E3-E10,E12,E15
                E3: FARE
? SELECT BUS OR BUSES ◄─────
          1242 BUS
          1044 BUSES
        2 1831  BUS OR BUSES
```

Command 5
Let's also select from BUS or BUSES.

```
? COMBINE 1 AND 2 ◄─────
        3   128  1 AND 2
```

Command 6
And then combine the groups we're interested in.

```
? TYPE 3/6/1-2 ◄─────
3/6/1
PB81-157448   NTIS Prices: PC A02/MF A01
   Transportation for the Elderly: Happy Faces on a MARTA Bus
   Jul 79   20p


3/6/2
PB81-151375   NTIS Prices: PC A17/MF A01
   The Runaround:  User-Side Subsidies for Mass Transportation in Danville,
Illinois
   Apr 80   380p
```

Command 7
Let's type out a couple of titles in order to see if we're getting what we want.

```
? LOGOFF ◄─────
        3aug81 11:30:46 User3462
   $1.44  0.036 Hrs File6 12 Descriptors
   $0.29  Tymnet
   $1.73  Estimated Total Cost

LOGOFF 11:30:49
```

Command 8
Looks good, so we're ready to sign off.

COMMAND 3.   PAGE

At the bottom of the list under Command 2, "-more-" has been printed by the system. Since we want to see more of the index, we entered the command PAGE, which produces eleven additional index terms. Reference numbers start where they left off before, so now we have twenty-one unique reference identifiers (E1 through E21).

COMMAND 4.   SELECT E3-E10, E12, E15

The SELECT command allows us to focus on specific items, in this case reference numbers 3 through 10, 12, and 15. The system responds by informing us that there are a total of 290 citations containing one or more uses of the words or phrases identified by those reference numbers. It also creates a set number (1) that will be used throughout the remainder of the search to refer to this particular group of citations.

COMMAND 5.   SELECT BUS or BUSES

Command 5 selects all of the citations which contain the words *bus* or *buses*. The system responds by telling us how many citations contain *bus*, *buses*, and *bus* or *buses*. Any citation containing either *bus* or *buses* is included in set 2. Both sets are necessary because several citations have both terms.

COMMAND 6.   COMBINE 1 and 2

The strength of any data base retrieval system is revealed in Command 6. Here the COMBINE command is used to narrow our search to only those citations that meet the conditions of set 1 *and* set 2. The efficiency of any research topic is enhanced when you are able to qualify your exact requirements to a given group of reference documents. The result of Command 6 is a new set, set 3, which contains 128 citations.

COMMAND 7.   TYPE 3/6/1-2

At this point in our search we want to begin viewing the actual contents of the data base. The TYPE command allows us to do this. This command requires a Set Number/Format Type/Record Range format as, in this case 3/6/1-2. From set 3, we want to use format 6 (title only) to view the first two records (1-2) of the 128 total possible. Depending upon the vendor and individual data bases, several printout format options may be available. Most bibliographic data bases offer the option of title only, title with bibliographic citation, abstract, or a combination of all.

COMMAND 8.   LOGOFF

Although we have 126 additional citations that might fit our requirements, we chose to end the search at this time. It we had wanted to, we could have used a PRINT command for additional citations whereby the items would have been printed offline at the vendor's computer center and mailed to us the following day. The LOGOFF command allows us to end our search and to determine its cost.

Our second example, Exhibit 3.3, provides a different perspective on a similar search strategy. Our objective in this example is to locate special studies and reports on the microcomputer industry.

COMMAND 1.

This example contains a few housekeeping functions which were not displayed in the previous one. In Command 1 we are asked to identify the type of terminal we are using. (Our input, an "A", is not printed online and thus does not appear. The entry "-1124-005-" is the system's response.) Most systems will accommodate several types of terminals, so they must be informed as to which type we have so that the communications signals can be decoded properly.

COMMAND 2.   DIALOG

In Command 2, we indicate that we wish to use the DIALOG system.

COMMAND 3.   (*Password*)

In Command 3 we enter our password, an eight-digit code which uniquely identifies us to the system. Most systems "X out" the password so that it will remain confidential. If someone else knows your password, he can use it to access the system in your name, and you'll end up paying for his online time.

After the password is entered, the system automatically issues a NEWS command in order to give us special notices.

COMMAND 4.   B 196

The actual search begins with Command 4. We are using abbreviated commands for speedier searching, so we enter B 196, the B representing BEGIN. We want to search File 196, which is the FIND/SVP Reports and Studies Index. Again, the system responds with the date, time, and cost of signing on, and confirms that we have accessed the desired data base.

COMMAND 5.   SS MICROCOMPUTER

We use the SS command (for SELECT) and discover that the data base contains sixteen citations of special studies or reports about microcomputers.

Exhibit 3.3
Search of the FIND/SVP Data Base

```
please type your terminal identifier
-1124-005-
```
Command 1
We need to identify our terminal type.

```
please log in: DIALOG

tc> host is online
```
Command 2
We also need to indicate that we'll be working within the DIALOG system.

```
ENTER YOUR DIALOG PASSWORD
█████   LOGON File1 Thu 15apr82 13:08:11 Port02E
```
Command 3
Now, let's enter our password.

```
** FILE 25 IS NOT WORKING TODAY **

?NEWS news:
  Free time in April (half-hour):
    BIOGRAPHY MASTER INDEX (#80)
  Now Available:
    NONFERROUS METALS ABSTRACTS (#118)
    ELECTRONIC YELLOW PAGES - FINANCIAL
      SERVICES DIRECTORY (#501)
    FIND/SVP REPORTS & STUDIES (#196)
    MEDLINE reload - date changes
  Announcements:
    SDI service on DOE ENERGY (#103)
    COMPENDEX (#8) - accession# changes
    Price changes now in effect for
      Files 42, 44, and 89
? B 196
```
Command 4
Let's begin our search by using File #196, the FIND/SVP Reports and Studies Index Data Base.

```
        15apr82 13:08:44 User20529
$0.28   0.011 Hrs File1*
$0.07   Tymnet
$0.35   Estimated Total Cost

File196:FIND/SVP REPORTS AND STUDIES INDEX - 77-82/Mar
(Copr. FIND/SVP)
        Set Items Description
        --- ----- -----------
? SS MICROCOMPUTER
      1    16 MICROCOMPUTER
```
Command 5
Let's select out just those reports and studies on microcomputers.

```
? T 1/6/1-16
1/6/1
  006670
  MICROCOMPUTER MARKET STRATEGIES OF
              DIVERSIFIED MAJOR CORPORATIONS
1/6/2
  005941
  MICROPROCESSOR/MICROCOMPUTER INDUSTRY ANALYSIS

1/6/3
  004772
  PORTABLE TERMINALS

1/6/4
  004715
  DATAPRO DIRECTORY OF MICROCOMPUTER SOFTWARE
```
Command 6
Since there are only 16 records, we want to see the titles of all of them. (We show only 4 of them here.)

Exhibit 3.3 continues

? T 1/5/1,2

Command 7
*The titles of two reports look interesting—
let's see a full record on those.*

1/5/1
　006670
　MICROCOMPUTER MARKET STRATEGIES OF DIVERSIFIED MAJOR CORPORATIONS
　JUN　1981　94 p.　$1450　ONE-TIME
　Publ: CREATIVE STRATEGIES INTERNATIONAL,　SAN JOSE, CA
　Availability: PUBLISHER
　Document Type: MARKET/INDUSTRY STUDY
　Analyzes　trends　in　""Fortune　1000''　companies　involvement　in　the
microcomputer　industry　including　software　acquisition　and　publication,
high-technology　retail　stores,　and　consumer　product　orientation.　Includes
discussion　of　impact　of　such　enterprises　as　IBM,　Xerox,　Exxon　and　other　oil
companies,　McGraw Hill,　and　other　publishers,　Citicorp,　Zenith　and　other
consumer-oriented　product　companies,　Reader's Digest,　Warner Communications
and　others.　Analyzes　concepts　and　strategies　of　new　start-ups　versus
acquisitions..
　Descriptors: COMPUTERS ;　MICROCOMPUTERS;　COMPUTER SOFTWARE;　COMPUTER
STORES

1/5/2
　005941
　MICROPROCESSOR/MICROCOMPUTER INDUSTRY ANALYSIS
　1981　$16,000　ONE-TIME
　Publ: GNOSTIC CONCEPTS INC,　MENLO PARK, CA
　Availability: PUBLISHER
　Document Type: MULTICLIENT STUDY
　Analyzes　trends in the microprocessor/microcomputer industry at the chip
and board levels.　Issues covered in　depth　include　product　evaluations,
markets and applications, software, and competitive trends. Also includes a
special　analysis　on　the　strategic　marketing　of　very　small　business
computers..
　Descriptors: COMPUTERS ;　MICROPROCESSORS;　MICROCOMPUTERS;　COMPUTER
SOFTWARE; SMALL BUSINESS COMPUTERS

? LOGOFF

Command 8
*We've completed our search, so we can sign
off now.*

　　　　15apr82 13:14:58 User20529
　$6.83　0.105 Hrs File196 1 Descriptor
　$0.63　Tymnet
　$7.46　Estimated Total Cost

LOGOFF 13:15:04

Source: Reprinted with permission of FIND/SVP, New York, N.Y.

COMMAND 6.   T 1/6/1-16

We ask the system to TYPE (using the abbreviation T) the titles (format 6) for all citations (1-16) in set 1. (For the sake of brevity, Exhibit 3.3 only shows four of these citations.)

COMMAND 7.   T 1/5/1, 2

In Command 7, we use format 5 (full record) to display the information in just two of the sixteen possible reports. With this data base, we can learn each report's title, size, publication date, cost, publisher, and frequency.

COMMAND 8.   LOGOFF

As in our last example, the command LOGOFF allows us to terminate our search and determine our search time and costs.

The final example, Exhibit 3.4, applies the same basic commands to a different type of data base in a different context. In this example, we wanted to use a very specialized data base, the Career Placement Registry, in order to locate potential candidates for a job opening.

COMMANDS 1-3

Our first three commands are identical to those in the last example and get us to the point where we can begin our search. You will note that after we entered our password in Command 3, the system replied with a "RECONNECT FILE 163" notice. This indicates that we have been reconnected to File 163 and that we will not need to use the standard BEGIN command to initiate our search. We were "reconnected" because we had been using File 163 and had accidentally disconnected the system. In the DIALOG system, you can reconnect to your current file within five minutes of your disconnect (intentional or accidental).

COMMAND 4.   SS DA = 8209 and
MJ = NUCLEAR ENGR-TECH AND
LA = ARABIC

In Command 4, we want to begin searching the file. However, instead of searching (SS) for key words or phrases, we want to use special options available to us with this particular data base. Most systems have special options which vary from data base to data base. In this case, we are looking for job candidates who will be available in September 1982 (DA = 8209), who have a major in nuclear engineering technology (MJ = NUCLEAR ENGR-TECH), and who speak Arabic (LA = ARABIC). The system informs us that it contains 72 candidates who are available in September, 3 who have majored in nuclear engineering technology, and 14 who speak

Arabic. However, there is only one candidate who meets all three criteria.

COMMAND 5.   T 8/5/1

Command 5 allows us to obtain a complete profile (full record) of this one record.

COMMAND 6.   LOGOFF

We use the LOGOFF command to exit from the system.

It is beyond the scope of this book to introduce you to all of the search features of DIALOG and other systems. For superb coverage of all of the intricacies of data base searching, please refer to *Basics of Online Searching*, by Charles T. Meadow and Pauline A. Cochrane (New York: John Wiley, 1981). You can also obtain a good overview of search strategy by reviewing producer and vendor literature on specific data bases. We do want to emphasize, however, that a large portion of online searches can be successfully achieved using the simple commands illustrated in our examples. Please refer to Exhibit 3.5 for a summary of our suggested online search procedures.

Special Search Options

In addition to the standard types of commands presented in the previous examples, there are several major services which can be of tremendous help in the search process. Several of those services are outlined below.

1. *Selective Dissemination of Information* (SDI). Available for hundreds of data bases, this service allows the user to store a specified search logic in the system. Each time the data base is updated, the new entries are matched against your logic and then printed at the vendor's site and mailed to you the following day. Once you have entered your search logic, you continue to receive information without ever having to turn on the terminal again.

2. *Saved files routines*. Many systems allow you to save your search logic for future use. Many online searches are conducted repeatedly for certain types of information retrieval. By saving your logic files, you can avoid having to re-key your entries every time you wish to perform the same search.

3. *Cross data base searching*. Under various systems you can save a great deal of time by searching through several data bases simultaneously. With this type of service, you can enter one command and then determine which data base would be the most appropriate for continued searching. Many vendors with a small number of data bases provide this service across all of their files. Most of the larger ven-

Exhibit 3.4
Search of the Career Placement Registry Data Base

please type your terminal identifier ◄────
-1124-050-

> **Command 1**
> We need to identify our terminal type.

please log in: DIALOG ◄────

tc> host is online

> **Command 2**
> We need to indicate that we'll be working within the DIALOG system.

ENTER YOUR DIALOG PASSWORD ◄────
▮▮▮▮▮▮▮▮ RECONNECT File163 Thu 15apr82
                        16:03:15 Port022

> **Command 3**
> We enter our password.

** FILE 25 IS NOT WORKING TODAY **

? SS DA=8209 AND MJ=NUCLEAR ENGR-TECH AND LA=ARABIC ◄────
     5   72 DA=8209
     6   3 MJ=NUCLEAR ENGR-TECH
     7   14 LA=ARABIC
     8   1 5 AND 6 AND 7

> **Command 4**
> We narrow our search by restricting it to some specific criteria.

? T 8/5/1 ◄────
8/5/1
0001783
  FARAZ YAWAR H
  Current Address: 7901 RIGGS ROAD #207

> **Command 5**
> We look at the full record of the one relevant item in the data base.

UNIVERSITY OF MARYLAND COLLEGE PARK MD 20742   JAN 1978 TO AUG 1982
BACHELORS
  Major: NUCLEAR ENGR-TECH Minor: MECHANICAL ENGR-TECH Overall Grade: B-
  Date of Graduation: AUG 1982
  Citizenship Status: UNITED STATES
  Permanent Address: ADELPHI MD 20783   301-439-3979
  Occupational Preference: NUCLEAR ENGR-TECH/NO EXPERIENCE Function:
STANDARDS-QUALITY CONTROL; PRODUCTION-MANUFACTURING
  Occupational Preference: MECHANICAL ENGR-TECH/NO EXPERIENCE Function:
STANDARDS-QUALITY CONTROL; PRODUCTION-MANUFACTURING
  Geographical Preference: NORTHWEST; NATIONWIDE City/Area Preference: NO
PREF
  Date Available: SEP 1982
  Salary Expectation: $27,000
  Special Skills: URDU/FLUENT; ARABIC/INTERMEDIATE; FORTRAN;TYPE
  Full Resume Available: YES

? LOGOFF ◄────
        15apr82 16:05:21 User20529
  $1.80 0.036 Hrs File163 3 Descriptors
  $0.22 Tymnet
  $1.00 1 Types
  $3.02 Estimated Total Cost

> **Command 6**
> Our search is complete, so we can sign off.

LOGOFF 16:05:31

Exhibit 3.5
Online Search Procedures

1. Review topic; identify key word index and logic; select data bases.
2. Turn on terminal.
3. Dial network telephone number and listen for monotone signal.
4. Place phone handset in the acoustic coupler (on a bell modem, just depress the button).
5. The network will ask you to identify your terminal type and/or data base retrieval system.
6. Network will verify your online connection.
7. Data base retrieval system will require password identification.
8. Specify the data base file number (unless you are using a single file data base system).
9. Identify concepts (begin selecting key words).
10. Expand selected words with similar or synonymous words. (Note: This is optional; some systems do not allow you to expand.)
11. Combine several key words into one or more concept blocks.
12. Review results (type or print out identified records).
13. Logoff (end search).

dors group their data bases together into broad categories (business or energy, for example). Each group can then be cross-searched individually.

4. *Full-article delivery.* Many systems have the capability of forwarding complete articles, which you can order online.

5. *Offline print.* This service is an excellent alternative for printing when you do not wish to spend the time or money waiting at a terminal for a listing that may contain several hundred citations. The offline print is performed at the vendor's facility with a high-speed printer and is usually in the mail to you within twenty-four hours.

6. *Help commands.* Several services offer a variety of commands to assist in the search process. You can use these commands to uncover the types of information in the record (not contents, just data element names), obtain rate information, get help on the meaning and use of various commands, or get updates on new features or data bases within the vendor's system.

7. *Practice files.* Virtually all vendors provide access to special files (usually subsets of regular data bases) that you can use freely or at a nominal charge in order to improve your search techniques. Many vendors will also provide free access for a limited time, usually two weeks to a month, to new data bases.

Selecting a Vendor

When evaluating a data base retrieval system vendor, there are a number of things to consider. Exhibit

3.6 identifies the criteria you should use and gives an example comparison of three vendors. Assuming all criteria are equally important, you would go with the vendor who has the most to offer in the most categories. Here is a brief description of the criteria:

1. The number of months or years a vendor has been in business. It would obviously be unwise to pay a $2,500 subscription fee only to have the vendor fold.
2. The number of data bases and the number of records the vendor offers is one indication of the available research reservoir.
3. Choose the vendor who has the most data bases relevant to your particular research requirements. If you are interested primarily in industrial statistics, a consumer-oriented data base vendor would not be the preferred choice. Likewise, if you require general news items about particular industries, a statistical data base will not provide the necessary ammunition.
4. Understand the basic cost structure before ever using an online service. You may incur any number of the following charges: connect time/hour charges, printing charges, SDI charges, subscription charges, equipment charges, per task charges, byte charges, and charges per workspace/day.
5. Ask to see some sample searches or demonstrations. Examine the English-language

Exhibit 3.6
Vendor Selection Sample

	Vendor A	Vendor B	Vendor C
1. Length of time in operation		X	
2. Number of data bases and number of records	X		
3. Number of relevant data bases	X		
4. Cost of service	X		
5. Use of language	X		
6. Documentation		X	
7. Data base sources	X		
8. Search assistance		X	
9. Training			X
10. SDI availability	X		
11. Current users	X		
12. Discounts available by volume or nonprofit status	X		
13. Geographic coverage	X		
14. Private data base service		X	
15. Updating	X		

commands which produce the responses. Compare the level of difficulty, training offered, and the time you feel it will take to become familiar with the language.

6. Compare each vendor's system reference manual, training workbooks, file documentation, and file descriptions.

7. To the extent possible, identify the sources of the data base. Many data bases are updated only annually. If you need more timely data, select a different data base.

8. Find out whether the data base vendor provides customer support or online assistance. If so, ask whether it is on-site or via telephone and if there are any extra charges.

9. Compare each data base vendor's customer training program. Many offer in-house demonstrations, low- or no-cost seminars, and direct customer assistance.

10. Find out if the vendor offers an automatic selective dissemination of information (SDI) service. This can be important in keeping you up-to-date.

11. Obtain a list of current users; try to elicit their comments and concerns.

12. Many vendors offer discounts for high-volume users or users who perform searches for educational and other nonprofit organizations.

13. Make sure that the geographic coverage of the data base matches your specific requirements.

14. Inquire whether a private file service (data base management system) is available. This service allows a user to develop and manage his own files of information.

15. How often the data bases are updated could be crucial to the data being examined. You should identify the frequency of updates and data base maintenance.

Because of the many data bases, producers, and vendors in existence today, there is no best way to go about selecting one of them. This situation is analogous to the hardware-software dilemma which has plagued data processing professionals since the dawn of the computer age. Since all computer software is not compatible with all computer hardware, data processors have had to choose, in many cases, between innovative hardware coupled with little or no appropriate software and inadequate hardware which offered state-of-the-art software. A similar situation exists in the computer data base industry, except here the conflict is between vendors and data bases. Because it is often time-consuming and costly, it is not always possible to use several vendors. Yet, if you select a vendor who appears to offer the best "fit" to your organization's needs, you may not gain access to the ideal data bases. However, since data base vendors are pretty much the same, whereas individual data bases are not, you should first select the data bases that meet your requirements and pick the vendor accordingly.

Of course, many vendors offer the same products (or the same products with different names). If you are interested in a data base offered by several vendors, then you can apply many of the criteria we listed in Exhibit 3.5. It is perfectly possible to use different vendors for different data bases. You should remember, however, that your start-up times, maintenance of vendor relationships, and loss of volume discounts will increase in proportion to the number of vendors you use.

Terminology

Boolean Logic Used to indicate to the host computer the logical relationship between terms in "and," "or," or "not" relationships.

Connect Time Actual time the user is linked or connected to the host computer through a communications network.

CRT Cathode Ray Tube or video display; a type of terminal.

Data Base A collection of related stored data.

Data Base Retrieval Systems A host (or search) computer which contains a comprehensive collection of reference and/or statistical data and information on different fields of interest. These data and information are available to you through a user terminal and a telecommunications line.

Format Identifies the type of format output the user desires. Example: Title only or bibliographic citation and abstract.

Item Record(s) which are currently maintained in the file.

Key Word Index Subject term(s) to be used as description(s) of the topic(s) to be searched. Example: Immigrant, immigrants, immigration.

Modem Modulator-Demodulator, connects the users' terminal to the host computer by transforming telephone sounds into electrical signals which the computer understands and responds to.

Off-line An operational activity (printing and copying) which takes place at the search service's computer center.

On-line A telecommunications link between the user and the host computer. The user is, in a sense, speaking with the host computer.

Record A collection of data items pertaining to a single subject within a data file. Example: Title, author, subject, publication.

Search logic Use of key words, synonymous terms, phrases, boolean operators and English-language commands to retrieve information from the host computer's data base(s).

Set Contains all of the records which meet your search logic.

Synonymous Terms Terms or descriptors which are spelled differently but have similar meanings.

Telecommunications Link Digital communications network which transmits alphabetical and numeric characters through telephone lines between the user terminal and the host computer.

Terminal Typewriter-like device which may contain a modem to electronically link the user to a host computer.

PART II

Data Base Directory

ABI/INFORM®

Producer: Data Courier, Inc.
620 South Fifth Street
Louisville, Kentucky 40202
(502) 582-4111
(800) 626-2823

Class: Reference.

Data source: 400+ primary business publications.

Size: 143,600 records.

Maintenance: Approximately 2,000 records monthly.

Primary subject: Banking, Economics, and Finance.

Secondary subject: Marketing Planning.

Profile: Covers all areas of business management and administration. The primary emphasis is on general decision sciences information applicable to many types of businesses and industries. Also contained are specific product and industry information. Coverage includes accounting, auditing, economics, data processing (MIS), finance, law, management science, marketing, promotions, and sales. Also included but not receiving primary emphasis are public administration, government, real estate, tax, and telecommunications news.

Applications: Market segmentation analysis; new product(s) analyses; and tracking competitive comparisons (news).

Subject cross reference: 1.8, 1.9, 1.10, 1.11, 1.12, 1.17, 2.1, 2.6, 2.8, 2.10, 2.12, 2.14, 3.4, 4.3, 5.4, 6.4, 7.5, 8.1, and 9.13.

Geographic coverage: International.

Time coverage: 1971 to present.

Online vendor(s): BRS, Inc.
DATA-STAR
DIALOG Information Services, Inc.
SDC Search Service.

ACCIDENT/INCIDENT DATA SYSTEM (AIDS)

Producer: Federal Aviation Administration
Flight Standard National Field Office
800 Independence Avenue, S.W.
Washington, D.C. 20591
(202) 426-4000

Class: Reference.

Data source: FAA, the FSNFO, aircraft registrations, National Transportation Safety Board and National Flight Data Center records.

Size: 25,000 records.

Maintenance: Weekly.

Primary subject: Business (aviation).

Secondary subject: N/A

Profile: An extensive data bank of general aviation accidents and incidents and air carrier incidents, including date, type, location, aircraft involved, engine type, total airframe hours, wing code, crew, passengers, ratings, injuries, qualifications, public involvement, structural damage and factors/circumstances. National and regional statistics also are available.

Applications: Accident causal factors; flight factor analysis; accident analysis by segment (aircraft).

Subject cross reference: 5.7, 5.8, and 9.18.

Geographic coverage: Domestic.

Time coverage: 1975 to present.

Online vendor(s): United Telecom Computer Group.

ACCOUNTANTS' INDEX

Producer: American Institute of Certified Public Accountants
1211 Avenue of the Americas
New York, New York 10036
(212) 575-6326

Class: Reference.

Data source: Journals (300 total), books, pamphlets, government documents; corresponds to the printed *Accountants' Index*.

Size: 105,000 records.

Maintenance: Approximately 3,000 records quarterly.

Primary subject: Banking, Economics, and Finance.

Secondary subject: N/A

Profile: Contains international literature on accounting, auditing, data processing, financial management, investments and securities, management, and taxation. Special businesses and industries are also included.

Applications: User may locate all materials published on accounting and related subjects, i.e., new tax guidelines, accounting practices, and audit procedures.

Subject cross reference: 1.1, 1.9, 1.16, 1.17, and 9.13.

Geographic coverage: International.

Time coverage: 1974 to present.

Online vendor(s): SDC Search Service.

ACTUARIAL DATA BASE

Producer: I. P. Sharp Associates
145 King Street West
Toronto, Ontario, Canada M5H 1J8
(416) 364-5361

Class: Statistical.

Data source: Regulatory actuarial bodies.

Size: 200 actuarial tables.

Maintenance: As new requests are made.

Primary subject: Banking, Economics, and Finance.

Secondary subject: Marketing Planning.

Profile: Maintains primitive mortality information and data on the insured living, annuitants, and the general population. These data are taken from over 200 tables published by various regulatory actuarial bodies. Also supplies projection and salary scales, as well as rates of withdrawal, disability and remarriage.

Applications: Premiums adjustments and analysis.

Subject cross reference: 1.13, 2.2, and 2.4.

Geographic coverage: U.S. and Canada.

Time coverage: Latest actuarial tables.

Online vendor(s): I. P. Sharp Associates.

ADTRACK

Producer: Corporate Intelligence, Inc.
Post Office Box 16073
St. Paul, Minnesota 55116
(612) 698-3543

Class: Reference.

Data source: 148 major U.S. consumer and business magazines.

Size: 163,000 records.

Maintenance: Monthly.

Primary subject: Marketing and Sales Promotion.

Secondary subject: Marketing Planning.

Profile: A computerized index to advertisements appearing in major consumer and business magazines. Advertisements of one-fourth page size or larger are indexed by fourteen data items. Data coverage includes company name, product name, description, color, date, page number, magazine name and spokesperson.

Applications: Competitive product(s) assessments; market target analysis; promotional strategy formulations.

Subject cross reference: 2.1, 2.8, 2.10, 2.12, 2.15, 3.5, 4.1, and 4.4.

Geographic coverage: Domestic.

Time coverage: 1980 to present.

Online vendor(s): DIALOG Information Services, Inc.

ADVERTISING & MARKETING INTELLIGENCE (AMI)ˢᴹ

Producer: New York Times Information Service, Inc.
and J. Walter Thompson Company
Mount Pleasant Office Park
1719-A Route 10
Parsippany, New Jersey 07054
(201) 539-5850
(800) 631-8056

Class: Reference.

Data source: Research contents from over 60 marketing related journals.

Size: 70,000 records.

Maintenance: Daily.

Primary subject: Marketing Planning.

Secondary subject: Marketing and Sales Promotion.

Profile: Includes abstracts from advertising, media and marketing covering new products, consumer trends, people, research, media planning and buying, and sales promotions. Each entry consists of a brief statement on the subject, product, or person with the relevant bibliographic citation.

Applications: Product introduction program differentiation; sales promotion planning; media analysis; sales incentive programs; consumer segmentation analysis.

Subject cross reference: 2.2, 2.3, 2.5, 2.7, 2.8, 2.11, 2.15, 4.1, and 4.4.

Geographic coverage: Domestic.

Time coverage: 1979 to present.

Online vendor(s): The New York Times Information Service, Inc.

AGLINE

Producer: Doane-Western, Inc.
8900 Manchester Road
St. Louis, Missouri 63144
(314) 968-1000
(800) 325-9519

Class: Reference.

Data source: 300+ farm and agriculture periodicals, university and government publications, books, conference proceedings, and unpublished papers.

Size: 45,000 records.

Maintenance: 1,000 records monthly.

Primary subject: General Management (agriculture).

Secondary subject: N/A

Profile: Provides a comprehensive listing of current literature in agriculture and agribusiness. Some of the topics covered include agribusiness trade and news, farm chemicals and fuels, farmland and real estate, crop and livestock production, international trade, and government regulation and policy.

Applications: Locating information in agribusiness companies and products; identifying trend in agriculture; analysis of on-farm operations.

Subject cross reference: 9.1.

Geographic coverage: International.

Time coverage: 1977 to present.

Online vendor(s): SDC Search Service.

AGRICULTURE COMMODITIES DATA BASE (AGDATA)

Producer: Alberta Agriculture
Market Analysis Branch
3rd Floor, 9718 107th Street
Edmonton, Alberta, Canada T5K 2C8
(403) 427-5381

Class: Statistical.

Data source: Agriculture Canada, Canadian Grain Commission, Canadian Livestock Feed Board, Chicago Board of Trade, Chicago Mercantile Exchange, Kansas City Grain Exchange, Minneapolis Grain Exchange, Omaha Cattle Markets, U.S. Department of Agriculture and the Winnipeg Commodity Exchange.

Size: N/A

Maintenance: Varies according to series.

Primary subject: Banking, Economics and Finance (commodities).

Secondary subject: General Management (agriculture).

Profile: Contains information and data on agricultural commodities, spot and future pricing, volume, grains, oil seeds, cattle, hogs, broilers, eggs, fowl and related areas.

Applications: Food distributors pricing policies, strategies and decisions; food wholesalers/retailers policies.

Subject cross reference: 1.16 and 9.1.

Geographic coverage: United States and Canada.

Time coverage: Varies by series; some going back to 1961.

Online vendor(s): I. P. Sharp Associates.

AGRICULTURE DATA BANK

Producer: Data Resources, Inc.
29 Hartwell Avenue
Lexington, Massachusetts 02173
(617) 861-0165

Class: Statistical.

Data source: U.S. Department of Agriculture; U.S.
Department of Commerce; U.S. Department of Labor,
Bureau of Labor Statistics; and Weather Services
International.

Size: Multiple time series.

Maintenance: Daily, weekly, monthly, quarterly & annually.

Primary subject: General Management (agriculture).

Secondary subject: Banking, Economics, and Finance
(commodities).

Profile: Provides extensive information on historical domestic
and international commodity, supply, demand and price
information. Government policy variables and weather
information complement the data system. Coverage areas
include crop production, acreage planted and harvested,
livestock production, commodity supply and demand, prices,
receipts and income (farm), futures prices and historical
weather concepts.

Applications: Forecasting and planning product line sales;
analyzing commodity supply, demand and prices,
forecasting input prices/final product prices.

Subject cross reference: 1.8, 1.16, 6.3, and 9.1.

Geographic coverage: International.

Time coverage: Varies by time series.

Online vendor(s): Data Resources, Inc.

AGRICULTURE FORECAST

Producer: Chase Econometrics/Interactive Data Corporation
486 Totten Pond Road
Waltham, Massachusetts 02154
(617) 890-1234

Class: Statistical.

Data source: U.S. Department of Agriculture, Chase
Econometrics Agriculture Model and related government
agencies.

Size: 450 variables.

Maintenance: Bimonthly.

Primary subject: General Management (agriculture).

Secondary subject: Banking, Economics, and Finance.

Profile: Contains quarterly and annual forecasts, for ten
quarters and ten years respectively, for price, demand and
supply for animal commodities, crops, fertilizers, and
economic farm activity.

Applications: Farm cash flow analysis; commodity price
analyses.

Subject cross reference: 1.8, 1.16, and 9.1.

Geographic coverage: Domestic.

Time coverage: 1950 to forecasted period.

Online vendor(s): Chase Econometrics/Interactive Data Corp.

AGRICULTURE ON-LINE ACCESS
(AGRICOLA)

Producer: U.S. Department of Agriculture
NAL Building
Beltsville, Maryland 20705
(301) 344-3755

Class: Reference.

Data source: Journals, monographs and the holdings of the
National Agricultural Library.

Size: 1,476,000 records.

Maintenance: Approximately 12,000 records monthly.

Primary subject: General Management (agriculture).

Secondary subject: N/A

Profile: The cataloging and indexing data base of the National
Agricultural Library (NAL). The file provides
comprehensive coverage of international literature on
agriculture and related subjects. Coverage includes
agricultural economics and production; entomology, food
and human nutrition; forestry, natural resources and plant
science.

Applications: Private farm planning and development; food
management forecasts.

Subject cross reference: 1.9, 6.3, and 9.1.

Geographic coverage: International.

Time coverage: 1971 to present.

Online vendor(s): BRS, Inc.
DIALOG Information Services, Inc.
SDC Search Service.

AGRICULTURAL RESEARCH PROJECTS
(AGREP)

Producer: Commission of the European Communities
DG X111
Batiment Jean Monnet, 8
Plateau du Kirchberg, BP 1907, Luxembourg
(352) 43011

Class: Reference.

Data source: *Permanent Inventory of Agriculture Research*
from various national input centers.

Size: 22,000 records.

Maintenance: Quarterly.

Primary subject: General Management (agriculture).

Secondary subject: N/A

Profile: Data is maintained for the agricultural research
projects of the European community. Coverage includes
agriculture, natural resources, environment, food
production, fisheries, forestry, social and economic
implications.

Applications: Agricultural research.

Subject cross reference: 6.3 and 9.1.

Geographic coverage: Europe.

Time coverage: N/A

Online vendor(s): DATACENTRALEN
DIMDI
ECHO.

AIM/ARM

Producer: The National Center for Research in
     Vocational Education
     The Ohio State University
     1960 Kenny Road
     Columbus, Ohio 43210
     (614) 486-3655
     (800) 848-4815

Class: Reference.

Data source: State level project papers, professional reports and journals.

Size: 17,500 citations.

Maintenance: No longer maintained; for current data use ERIC.

Primary subject: Multidisciplinary.

Secondary subject: N/A

Profile: AIM/ARM stands for Abstracts of Instructional and Research Materials in Vocational and Technical Education. Contains citations as well as abstracts of instructional materials and research reports in the following areas of educational support: business, health occupations, home economics, industrial arts, employment, job training and vocational guidance.

Applications: Education management; career development; end-result (educational) analysis.

Subject cross reference: 6.7, 9.5, and 9.8.

Geographic coverage: Domestic.

Time coverage: 1967-1976.

Online vendor(s): DIALOG Information Services, Inc.

AIR POLLUTION TECHNICAL INFORMATION CENTER (APTIC)

Producer: U.S. Environmental Protection Agency and
     the Air Pollution Technical Information Center
     EPA (MD 18)
     Research Triangle Park, North Carolina 27711
     (919) 549-2460

Class: Reference.

Data source: *Air Pollution Abstracts*—U.S. Environmental Protection Agency (periodicals, books, and conference proceedings).

Size: 89,000 records.

Maintenance: None.

Primary subject: Environmental, Social & Political Affairs.

Secondary subject: N/A

Profile: Contains citations and abstracts of literature relating to air pollution control, effects, sources and prevention. Covers the broader areas of pollution, including the social, political, legal, and administrative aspects of the field. Some of the subjects included are atmospheric interaction, control methods, effects on human health, plants and livestock, and government participation.

Applications: Air pollution research.

Subject cross reference: 6.6.

Geographic coverage: Domestic.

Time coverage: 1966 to 1978.

Online vendor(s): DIALOG Information Services, Inc.

ALCOHOL INFORMATION RETRIEVAL SYSTEM (AIRS)

Producer: Rutgers University
     Center of Alcohol Studies
     Information Services Division
     Post Office Box 969
     Piscataway, New Jersey 08854
     (201) 932-3510

Class: Reference.

Data source: Journals, monographs, conference proceedings, and various technical reports.

Size: 40,500 records.

Maintenance: Bimonthly.

Primary subject: General Management.

Secondary subject: N/A

Profile: Maintains citations and abstracts relating to alcohol studies and alcoholism. Includes such areas/topics as aversion therapies, treatment evaluation, safety, aggression studies and disease/organ disorders. Coverage extends to multidisciplinary fields, including physiology, psychology, sociology, political science, and economics.

Applications: Liquor industry legal reference; social service program(s) analysis; alcohol-related treatment(s) reference.

Subject cross reference: 6.7, 9.7, and 9.8.

Geographic coverage: International.

Time coverage: 1950 to present.

Online vendor(s): Control Data Corporation.

ALL-CANADA WEEKLY SUMMARIES (ACWS)

Producer: Canada Law Book Limited
     240 Edward Street
     Aurora, Ontario, Canada L4G 3S9
     (416) 773-6300

Class: Reference.

Data source: Legal records (judgments) in Canadian civil cases, corresponds to the printed publication *All Canada Weekly Summaries*.

Size: 12,000 summaries.

Maintenance: Approximately 100 summaries weekly.

Primary subject: Legal and Legislative Affairs.

Secondary subject: N/A

Profile: Maintains a profile of judgments in civil cases tried in the federal and provincial supreme courts in Canada. Only maintains those cases received by the Canada Law Book Limited.

Applications: Supreme Court legal reference for cases of particular importance at the federal, provincial, and some county levels.

Subject cross reference: 5.4.

Geographic coverage: Canada.

Time coverage: 1977 to present.

Online vendor(s): QL Systems Limited.

AMERICAN BANKER INDEX (BANKER)

Producer: Bell and Howell
Old Mansfield Road
Wooster, Ohio 44691
(216) 264-6666
(800) 321-9881

Class: Reference.

Data source: *American Banker* newspaper.

Size: 27,000 citations through 1980.

Maintenance: Monthly.

Primary subject: Banking, Economics, and Finance.

Secondary subject: N/A

Profile: Maintains article and news items citations appearing in *American Banker*. Coverage includes bank news, bank stocks, marketing, automation, data processing, trust banking, mortgage industry and rate news.

Applications: Competitive practice analyses; monetary policy; marketing programs.

Subject cross reference: 1.2.

Geographic coverage: Domestic.

Time coverage: 1979 to present.

Online vendor(s): SDC Search Service.

AMERICAN MEN AND WOMEN OF SCIENCE

Producer: R. R. Bowker Company
Data Services Division
1180 Avenue of the Americas
New York, New York 10036
(212) 764-5100

Class: Reference.

Data source: Corresponds to the printed *American Men and Women of Science* and *Physical and Biological Sciences*.

Size: 130,500 records.

Maintenance: Annually.

Primary subject: Research and Development.

Secondary subject: N/A

Profile: Maintains biographies of individuals in the disciplines of physical and biological sciences. Individuals consist of scientists and engineers. Data coverage includes full names, place and date of birth, education, degrees, experience, memberships, research interests and positions. For both American and Canadian scientists.

Applications: Locating leading experts in their scientific disciplines.

Subject cross reference: 7.3, 8.9, 9.2, and 9.14.

Geographic coverage: U.S. and Canada.

Time coverage: 1979 to present.

Online vendor(s): BRS.

AMERICAN PROFILE^{SM}

Producer: Donnelley Marketing
1515 Summer Street
Stamford, Connecticut 06905
(203) 348-9999

Class: Statistical.

Data source: 1980 census data, 160 key socioeconomic studies, users.

Size: 70 million households (records).

Maintenance: Subject to new data releases.

Primary subject: Marketing Planning.

Secondary subject: Marketing and Sales Promotion.

Profile: Profiles over 70 million households. Coverage includes household population, income, dependents and other demographic variables. This data base also maintains an excellent array of socioeconomic data including number and types of businesses, number of employees in an area, banking activity, and other demographic area profiles.

Applications: Market segmentation/profiles; consumer segmentation/profiles; product introduction tests; demographics studies; market potential analyses.

Subject cross reference: 2.2, 2.3, 2.4, 2.5, 2.10, 2.13, 2.14, 2.15, and 4.4.

Geographic coverage: Domestic.

Time coverage: 1970, 1980, and 1985. Actual data and estimates.

Online vendor(s): Business Information Services (Control Data).

AQUALINE®

Producer: Water Research Centre
Communications Group
Medmenham Laboratory
Henley Road, Medmenham, Marlow
Buckinghamshire, England SL7 2HD
0491166 531

Class: Reference.

Data source: Corresponds to the printed *WRC Information* (from over 400 periodicals, research reports, legislation, conferences and other publications).

Size: 25,575 citations.

Maintenance: 550 records monthly.

Primary subject: Environmental, Social & Political Affairs.

Secondary subject: N/A

Profile: Maintains citations and abstracts on literature relating to the aquatic sciences. Areas of coverage include water (surface and groundwater), water treatment, control, testing, distribution systems, sampling, analysis, drinking water quality, river management, quality monitoring, environmental protection, sludge utilization, tidal waters, sewerage systems and water computing systems.

Applications: Water management decisions; water quality standards.

Subject cross reference: 6.3 and 6.6.

Geographic coverage: International.

Time coverage: 1974 to present.

Online vendor(s): DIALOG Information Services, Inc.
ESA-IRS.

AQUATIC SCIENCES AND FISHERIES ABSTRACTS (ASFA)

Producer: NOAA
Cambridge Scientific Abstracts
5161 River Road
Bethesda, Maryland 20816
(800) 638-8076
(301) 951-1400

Class: Reference.

Data source: *Aquatic Sciences and Fisheries Abstracts* and related books, conference proceedings and technical research reports.

Size: 76,900 records.

Maintenance: Monthly.

Primary subject: Environmental, Social & Political Affairs.

Secondary subject: N/A

Profile: Maintains a large data base of citations and abstracts of international literature on science, technology and aquatic management. Areas of coverage include aquaculture, biological oceanography, chemical oceanography, commerce, trade, economics, ecology, ecosystems, environmental studies, fisheries, fish production, geological oceanography, marine biology, policy, pollution, technology, meterology and climatology. The more immediate economic coverage includes ocean engineering, ocean resources, offshore activities, vessel data, underwater vessels and water pollution technology.

Applications: Environmental impact studies.

Subject cross reference: 6.3 and 6.6.

Geographic coverage: International.

Time coverage: 1978 to present.

Online vendor(s): DIALOG Information Services, Inc.
DIMDI
QL Systems, Ltd.

ARTBIBLIOGRAPHIES MODERN

Producer: ABC-CLIO, Inc.
Riviera Campus
2040 Alameda Padre Serra, Box 4397
Santa Barbara, California 93103
(805) 963-4221

Class: Reference.

Data source: *ARTbibliographies Modern* print (books, dissertations and articles).

Size: 51,564 records.

Maintenance: Approximately 8,000 records annually.

Primary subject: General Management.

Secondary subject: N/A

Profile: Maintains citations and abstracts of books, exhibition catalogs, dissertations, and articles related to modern art and design. Coverage period dates to the 19th century art history and media. Covers the fields of art history, biographies of artists and the various artistic media.

Applications: New corporate architectural designs; art/media planning.

Subject cross reference: 4.6, 6.8, 7.3, and 9.15.

Geographic coverage: International.

Time coverage: 1974 to present.

Online vendor(s): DIALOG Information Services, Inc.

ASIAN DATA BANK

Producer: Data Resource, Inc.
29 Hartwell Avenue
Lexington, Massachusetts 02173
(617) 861-0165

Class: Statistical.

Data source: Offical national source agencies, e.g., statistical agencies and central banks of respective countries.

Size: Several time series.

Maintenance: Monthly, quarterly and annually.

Primary subject: Banking, Economics, and Finance.

Secondary subject: N/A

Profile: Maintains primary source data detailing the economic profiles of eleven Asian countries. Data coverage includes national income and product accounts, foreign trade, prices, wages, production, balance of payments, foreign exchange, money supply, interest rates, employment and the labor force.

Applications: Evaluation of foreign aid and economic development programs; forecast key macroeconomic variables; develop interactive trade models for Asian region.

Subject cross reference: 1.8, 1.9, 2.6, and 9.12.

Geographic coverage: Australia, China, Hong King, Indonesia, Korea, Malaysia, New Zealand, The Philippines, Singapore, Taiwan, Thailand.

Time coverage: Varies by series.

Online vendor(s): Data Resources, Inc.

ASSOCIATION OF EUROPEAN AIRLINES DATA BASE (ALA)

Producer: Association of European Airlines (AEA)
B.P. 4
350 Avenue Louise
1050 Brussels, Belgium

Class: Statistical.

Data source: AEA member airlines.

Size: 175,000 time series.

Maintenance: Continuous.

Primary subject: General Management (transportation and shipping).

Secondary subject: N/A

Profile: Contains time series summarizing the results and forecasts of member airlines. Data coverage includes annual traffic and operating statistics; monthly intra-European point-to-point statistics; monthly international scheduled traffic statistics; forecasts of scheduled passenger traffic; operating economy statistics (annual revenues and costs); and monthly "on-time" statistics. The frequency and history of the data vary by series.

Applications: Air traffic management, forecasting and budgeting.

Subject cross reference: 1.12, 2.2, 2.3, and 9.18.

Geographic coverage: Europe.

Time coverage: 1965 to present.

Online vendor(s): I. P. Sharp Associates.

ASTIS ONLINE DATABASE

Producer: Arctic Institute of North America
The University of Calgary
2500 University Drive, N.W.
Calgary, Alberta, Canada T2N 1N4
(403) 284-7515

Class: Reference.

Data source: Serials, journal articles, theses, conference proceedings and research reports.

Size: 6,200 records.

Maintenance: Bimonthly.

Primary subject: Multidisciplinary.

Secondary subject: N/A

Profile: Maintains citations and abstracts on all aspects of the North which relate specifically to Arctic/cold region studies, including the physical, earth, biological, and social sciences, as well as technology, engineering, and the humanities. Geographically, the emphasis is on the North American Arctic and the Middle North; some material is also included on the USSR, Scandinavia, Antarctica, and the alpine regions. Some of the topics included are basic scientific research projects, resource development projects, transportation systems, environmental issues, native land claims, and social and economic conditions of the North.

Applications: Arctic exploration management; resource development projects analysis; native land claims reference.

Subject cross reference: 2.5, 6.3, 6.6, and 9.20.

Geographic coverage: International.

Time coverage: 1978 to present.

Online vendor(s): QL Systems Ltd.

AUERBACH COMPAR®

Producer: Auerbach
6560 North Park Drive
Pennsauken, New Jersey 08109
(609) 662-2070
(800) 257-8162

Class: Reference.

Data source: Auerbach Research.

Size: 300,000 records.

Maintenance: Daily.

Primary subject: General Management.

Secondary subject: N/A

Profile: Maintains information relating to a wide range of data processing products. Areas of coverage include price and product information, mainframe, mini-microcomputers data, software selection, application programs, operating systems, terminals, peripherals, communications equipment and purchase agreement selection criteria.

Applications: Microcomputer selection; microcomputer application ideas; mainframe decision support; current software availabilities.

Subject cross reference: 2.9, 7.11, 8.1, 8.3, and 9.11.

Geographic coverage: International.

Time coverage: Current data.

Online vendor(s): BRS, Inc.

AUSTRIALIAN BUREAU OF STATISTICS DATA BASE (ABSDATA)

Producer: I. P. Sharp Associates
145 King Street West
Toronto, Ontario, Canada M5H 1J8
(416) 364-5361

Class: Statistical.

Data source: The Australian Bureau of Statistics.

Size: 1,500 economic and financial time series.

Maintenance: Quarterly.

Primary subject: Banking, Economics, and Finance.

Secondary subject: Marketing Planning.

Profile: Maintains economic and financial time series relating to Australia. Data coverage includes agricultural production, building activity, new fixed capital expenditure by private enterprises, manpower, finance, stocks, manufacturing and mining, national accounts, overseas arrivals and departures, prices, transport, retail sales, overseas transactions; wages and salaries.

Applications: Australian product introduction analysis; Australian econometric forecasting; Australian construction planning.

Subject cross reference: 1.8, 1.15, 2.5, 2.6, 2.14, and 9.12.

Geographic coverage: Australia.

Time coverage: Depends upon series; some go back to 1953.

Online vendor(s): I. P. Sharp Associates.

AUTOMATED CITATION VERIFICATION SERVICE (AUTO-CITE)®

Producer: Lawyer's Co-operative Publishing Company
50 Broad Street
Rochester, New York 14603
(716) 546-5530

Class: Reference.

Data source: Federal case (litigation records) opinions.

Size: 3,500,000 records.

Maintenance: Daily (approximately 25,000 records per year).

Primary subject: Legal and Legislative Affairs.

Secondary subject: N/A

Profile: Maintains Federal case law opinions from 50 states. Coverage includes title of case, official citation, the court, place and date of decision, parallel citations and citations to any subsequent decisions (legal history of reported court opinions) which directly influence the legal status of the cited case.

Applications: Check of case-law citations; verification of case-law research.

Subject cross reference: 5.9.

Geographic coverage: Federal/State court opinions.

Time coverage: Early 1700's to present.

Online vendor(s): Lawyer's Co-operative
Mead Data Central.

BANCOMPARE®

Producer: Cates, Lyons and Company
74 Trinity Place
New York, New York 10006
(212) 964-7002

Class: Statistical.

Data source: Annual report filings, call reports, and 10-K reports.

Size: 250 banks and bank holding companies.

Maintenance: Annually.

Primary subject: Banking, Economics and Finance.

Secondary subject: N/A

Profile: Maintains financial data on 250 publicly held financial institutions, primarily banks and bank holding companies. These data cover over 800 key financial data items for each institution. In addition, 17 preselected peer groups are broken down by size, region, type and credit quality.

Applications: Financial planning; forecasting; competitive analysis; acquisition or merger analysis; credit analysis.

Subject cross reference: 1.2, 2.1, and 10.1.

Geographic coverage: Domestic.

Time coverage: Current data.

Online vendor(s): ADP Network Services, Inc.

BANK ANALYSIS SYSTEM (BANKANAL)

Producer: Robinson-Humphrey Company, Inc.
2 Peachtree Street, N.W.
Atlanta, Georgia 30303
(404) 581-7176

Class: Statistical.

Data source: Questionnaire surveys.

Size: 208 major banks time series.

Maintenance: Quarterly.

Primary subject: Banking, Economics and Finance.

Secondary subject: N/A

Profile: Maintains financial profiles of 208 of the top bank holding companies in the U.S. Annual data, on over 100 items, are available for 1969 to 1980; quarterly data are available on selected banks from the first quarter 1974 through the most recent quarter.

Applications: Forecast balance sheet/income statements items; comparative analyses of banking organizations.

Subject cross reference: 1.2, 1.11, and 2.1.

Geographic coverage: Domestic.

Time coverage: Depends upon series; most either from 1969 or 1974.

Online vendor(s): Business Information Services (Control Data).

BANK OF CANADA WEEKLY FINANCIAL STATISTICS

Producer: I. P. Sharp Associates
145 King Street West
Toronto, Ontario, Canada M5H 1J8
(416) 364-5361

Class: Statistical.

Data source: Bank of Canada.

Size: 153 weekly time series.

Maintenance: Weekly.

Primary subject: Banking, Economics, and Finance.

Secondary subject: N/A

Profile: Maintains records of 153 weekly financial statistics. Areas of coverage include assets and liabilities (Bank of Canada), balances and securities outstanding for the Government of Canada, money supply, money market rates, bond yield data and chartered bank liquidity.

Applications: Financial (capitalization) decisions.

Subject cross reference: 1.1, 1.2, 1.3, 1.8, 1.12, and 10.7.

Geographic coverage: Canada.

Time coverage: 1976 or 1977 (depending upon series) to present.

Online vendor(s): I. P. Sharp Associates.

BEST EXECUTIVE DATA SERVICE (BEDS)

Producer: A. M. Best Company
Ambest Road
Oldwick, New Jersey 08858
(201) 439-2200

Class: Statistical.

Data source: Insurance industry statistics.

Size: 1,000 + insurance companies.

Maintenance: Annually.

Primary subject: Banking, Economics and Finance (insurance).

Secondary subject: N/A

Profile: This data base is sometimes referred to as the Bible of insurance data. Maintains annual data for over 1,000 property and casualty insurance companies for each of 38 lines of insurance. Single company as well as consolidated group coverage is provided. Data items include written premiums, earned premiums, dividends paid on policies, losses incurred, losses paid, adjusted loss ratios, and market shares.

Applications: Insurance company comparisons/selection; insurance company standards; rate scheduling reference; profitability analysis.

Subject cross reference: 1.13, 1.15, 2.1, 10.4, and 10.7.

Geographic coverage: Domestic.

Time coverage: 1977 to present.

Online vendor(s): Data Resources, Inc.

BHRA FLUID ENGINEERING

Producer: British Hydromechanics Research Association Fluid Engineering
Cranfield, Bedford
England MK43 0AJ
(0234) 750422

Class: Reference.

Data source: Over 550 journal reports and magazines of a scientific and technical nature, conference papers, technical reports, theses and United Kingdom patents.

Size: 63,640 records.

Maintenance: Quarterly.

Primary subject: Industrial and Manufacturing Planning.

Secondary subject: Research and Development.

Profile: Maintains indexing and abstracting of international literature covering the behavior and applications of fluids in engineering. Areas of coverage include statistics and dynamics, fluid control and instrumentation, mixing and separation, laminar and turbulent flow, energy storage and conversion, fluid mechanics, pumping and pipeline technology, industrial aerodynamics, sealing technology, fluid power, jet cutting and cleaning, and mathematical techniques and computations.

Applications: Reviewing fluid flow technology; research and development assistance (new product technology).

Subject cross reference: 7.3, 8.3, 8.4, and 8.8.

Geographic coverage: International.

Time coverage: 1974 to present.

Online vendor(s): DIALOG Information Services, Inc.

BI/DATA®

Producer: Business International Corporation (BI)
One Dag Hammerskjold Plaza
New York, New York 10017
(212) 750-6300

Class: Statistical.

Data source: United Nations, The Organization for Economic Cooperation and Development, The International Monetary Fund and country statistical reporting.

Size: 20,000 time series.

Maintenance: Daily.

Primary subject: Banking, Economics, and Finance.

Secondary subject: Marketing Planning.

Profile: Maintains annual time series (historical data) on national accounts, labor statistics, foreign trade, consumption and production, price trends, balance of payments, and demographics for 131 countries.

Applications: Country economic analysis; foreign trade statistics. Using General Electric, the user can convert data to a common currency, use constant prices from base year exchange rates, use growth rates calculations and aggregate data (countries) for baseline forecasting and planning.

Subject cross reference: 1.7, 1.8, 2.3, 2.4, 2.6, 2.13, and 9.6.

Geographic coverage: International.

Time coverage: Varies by series; many from 1960.

Online vendor(s): General Electric Information Services Co. (BI/DATA through I. P. Sharp Associates and BI/DATA ITS through DIALOG Information Services, Inc.).

BIIPAM℠

Producer: Centre de Recherches de Pont-A-Mousson
Service de Documentation Industrielle
BP No. 28—Maidieres
54700 Pont-a-Mousson, France
(8) 381 60 29

Class: Reference.

Data source: *Diffusion Hebdomodiare Systematique.*

Size: 42,000 records.

Maintenance: Approximately 450 records monthly.

Primary subject: Science and Technology (engineering-metallurgy).

Secondary subject: N/A

Profile: Maintains citations and abstracts on French, English and German engineering literature. Coverage includes metallurgy; industrial foundry processes; standards, controls, testing, regulations; gas mains; mechanics; plastics; pollution and pollution prevention. Entries include original language of the document.

Applications: Industrial processes; product development and applications analyses.

Subject cross reference: 6.6, 7.3, and 8.4.

Geographic coverage: Europe and the United States.

Time coverage: 1970 to present.

Online vendor(s): Spidel.

BILLBOARD MAGAZINE/INFORMATION NETWORK (BIN)

Producer: Billboard
1515 Broadway
New York, New York 10036
(212) 764-7300

Class: Statistical.

Data source: Participating radio stations and record stores.

Size: 1,500 records.

Maintenance: Daily.

Primary subject: Marketing Planning.

Secondary subject: N/A

Profile: Over 400 participating radio stations maintain data on the number of times a record is played, popularity standards, selection patterns and programming formats by geographical area. Data fields include label, station (radio), title, artist and format. Also includes data from record stores.

Applications: Promotional decisions; programming decisions.

Subject cross reference: 2.11 and 2.12.

Geographic coverage: Domestic.

Time coverage: N/A

Online vendor(s): Billboard.

BIOETHICSLINE

Producer: Georgetown University, Kennedy Institute for Ethics
Washington, D.C. 20057
(202) 625-2371

Class: Reference.

Data source: Journals, other data bases and selected references. Corresponds to the annual *Bibliography of Bioethics.*

Size: 11,867 records.

Maintenance: 450 records quarterly.

Primary subject: Multidisciplinary.

Secondary subject: N/A

Profile: Maintains citations of literature relating to abortion, genetic intervention, reproductive technologies, population control, organ transplants, euthanasia, human experimentation, and recombinant DNA research. Also covered are issues (moral and ethical) concerning the medical community.

Applications: Bioethics research; social problems analyses.

Subject cross reference: 5.4, 5.8, 6.7, 8.6, and 9.7.

Geographic coverage: International.

Time coverage: 1973 to present.

Online vendor(s): BLAISE.
National Library of Medicine.

BIOGRAPHY MASTER INDEX

Producer: Gale Research Company
Book Tower
Detroit, Michigan 48226
(313) 961-2242

Class: Reference.

Data source: *Who's Who*-type publications, biographical dictionaries and directories.

Size: 2,000,000 indexed name entries.

Maintenance: Irregular.

Primary subject: Multidisciplinary.

Secondary subject: N/A

Profile: A master index for over 600 biographic source publications. Fields covered are person's name, birth date, death date, and source of publication. Coverage ranges from members of the scientific community to stage celebrities and sports figures.

Applications: Historical reference; personal data reference.

Subject cross reference: 6.4.

Geographic coverage: International.

Time coverage: N/A

Online vendor(s): DIALOG Information Services, Inc.

BIOSIS PREVIEWS

Producer: Biosciences Information Service (BIOSIS)
2100 Arch Street
Philadelphia, Pennsylvania 19103
(215) 568-4016
(800) 523-4806

Class: Reference.

Data source: 8,000 periodicals, books, conference proceedings, research findings, symposia, reviews and selected institutional and government reports.

Size: 3,000,000 + records.

Maintenance: Approximately 35,000 records semi-monthly.

Primary subject: Research and Development.

Secondary subject: N/A

Profile: Maintains citations of international research in the following life sciences: agriculture, biochemistry, ecology, biophysics, pharmacology, bioengineering and experimental medicine. Coverage includes research reporting, reviews of these reports, biomedicine and biological history and philosophy and documentation and retrieval of biological information.

Applications: Biological analysis; comparative analyses; life science research.

Subject cross reference: 8.3, 8.6, 8.8, and 9.7.

Geographic coverage: International.

Time coverage: 1969 to present.

Online vendor(s): BRS, Inc.
CISTI
DATA-STAR
DIALOG Information Services, Inc.
DIMDI
ESA-IRS
SDC Search Services.

BOECKH BUILDING COST SYSTEM

Producer: E. H. Boeckh Company
Post Office Box 664
615 East Michigan Street
Milwaukee, Wisconsin 53202
(414) 271-5544
(800) 558-8650

Class: Statistical.

Data source: Boeckh *Building Valuation Manual*.

Size: 30,000 cost items.

Maintenance: Monthly.

Primary subject: General Management (real estate and building trends).

Secondary subject: N/A

Profile: Provides access to cost estimating reports for residential, commercial, industrial, and institutional buildings. For a residential report, the user inputs zip code location, basement availability, ground floor area, number of stories, material for exterior walls, and construction quality. For all other reports, the user inputs zip code locations, material for exterior walls, occupancy type, number of stories, and gross floor area. Includes both current and historical costs.

Applications: Construction valuations; cost reporting.

Subject cross reference: 1.12, 7.10, and 9.15.

Geographic coverage: U.S. and Canada.

Time coverage: Latest ten years.

Online vendor(s): ADP Network Services, Inc.
E. H. Boeckh Company
General Electric Information Services Co.

BOOK EXPRESS®

Producer: Brodart Inc.
On-Line Services
1609 Memorial Avenue
Williamsport, Pennsylvania 17705
(717) 326-2461
(800) 233-8467

Class: Reference.

Data source: U.S. and foreign trade book publishers.

Size: 800,000 + records.

Maintenance: Weekly.

Primary subject: Multidisciplinary.

Secondary subject: N/A

Profile: Maintains references for over 800,000 English-language publications. Fields covered include title, author, publisher, date, International Standard Book Number (ISBN), Library of Congress card number, publication status and price (if available). Includes juvenile books, textbooks, and serial monographs.

Applications: Technical support to librarians; library acquisitions.

Subject cross reference: 9.20.

Geographic coverage: International.

Time coverage: 1950's to present.

Online vendor(s): Brodart, Inc.
BRS, Inc.

BOOK REVIEW INDEX (BRI)

Producer: Gale Research Company
Book Tower
Detroit, Michigan 48226
(313) 961-2242

Class: Reference.

Data source: *Book Review Index* from over 380 journals.

Size: 1,000,000 citations.

Maintenance: Bimonthly.

Primary subject: General Management.

Secondary subject: N/A

Profile: BRI indexes all reviews of books and periodicals in over 380 journals. Coverage includes social science and humanities, literature, history, library science, fine arts and education. Each record includes author, book or periodical being reviewed, document type code, and the source of the review.

Applications: Library acquisition analysis; personal acquisition analysis; source/reference guide of published reviews.

Subject cross reference: 6.8, 9.5, 9.8, 9.13, and 9.20.

Geographic coverage: Domestic.

Time coverage: 1969 to present.

Online vendor(s): DIALOG Information Services, Inc.

BOOKS IN PRINT (BBIP)

Producer: R. R. Bowker Company
Data Services Division
1180 Avenue of the Americas
New York, New York 10036
(212) 764-5100

Class: Reference.

Data source: Books in print from data supplied by publishers and the U.S. Library of Congress.

Size: 640,000 records.

Maintenance: Monthly.

Primary subject: Multidisciplinary.

Secondary subject: N/A

Profile: Maintains citations covering books in current print or recently declared out of print. Also maintains up to 60,000 forthcoming publications. Government publications, bibles and free books are excluded. Included are scholarly, popular, reprint and subject types.

Applications: Book acquisitions; book proposal analysis.

Subject cross reference: 2.1, 2.12, and 6.4.

Geographic coverage: Domestic.

Time coverage: Current books in print.

Online vendor(s): BRS, Inc.

BRIDGE DATA STOCK & OPTIONS REAL TIME INFORMATION SYSTEM

Producer: Bridge Data Company
10050 Manchester Road
St. Louis, Missouri 63122
(314) 821-5660

Class: Statistical.

Data source: N.Y.S.E. (New York Stock Exchange), A.S.E. (American Stock Exchange), and N.A.S.D.A.Q.

Size: 5,300 + records.

Maintenance: Continuous.

Primary subject: Banking, Economics, and Finance.

Secondary subject: N/A

Profile: Maintains a current data base of common stock listings, Over-The-Counter (NASDAQ) stocks, commodities, futures and all listed options. Some proprietary data items are available. This coverage includes individual securities, options, stock groupings and the market as a whole.

Applications: Stock analysis; portfolio management.

Subject cross reference: 1.16.

Geographic coverage: Domestic plus Canada, Australia and Europe.

Time coverage: Most current data.

Online vendor(s): ADP Network Services, Inc.
Bridge Data Company
Market Data Systems, Inc.

BRITANNICA 3

Producer: Encyclopaedia Britannica, Inc.
425 N. Michigan Avenue
Chicago, Illinois 60611
(312) 321-7000

Class: Reference.

Data source: *The Encyclopaedia Britannica 3*, 15th edition.

Size: 10 volume micropaedia, 19 volumes macropaedia.

Maintenance: N/A

Primary subject: Multidisciplinary.

Secondary subject: N/A

Profile: Covers the full-text of the ten volume *Britannica 3* encyclopaedia set and the nineteen volume macropaedia. Both sets provide a most comprehensive range of subjects and information. Material from future editions will be included. Part of the overall LEXIS system available through Mead Data Central.

Applications: General research; educational reference.

Subject cross reference: 1.19, 2.16, 3.6, 4.6, 5.9, 6.8, 7.12, 8.9, 9.20, and 10.8.

Geographic coverage: International.

Time coverage: 15th edition.

Online vendor(s): Mead Data Central.

BROADCAST ADVERTISERS REPORTS (BAR)

Producer: Broadcast Advertiser Reports, Inc.
500 5th Avenue
New York, New York 10036
(212) 221-2630

Class: Statistical.

Data source: BAR sound recordings and video installations in major U.S. markets.

Size: N/A

Maintenance: Monthly.

Primary subject: Marketing and Sales Promotion.

Secondary subject: Marketing Planning.

Profile: Maintains monthly data on network television commercial activities and expenditures by product, network, parent company and mean cost per commercial minute. Includes the relationship between a particular commercial and the others aired in the preceding and succeeding time slots.

Applications: Promotional comparison analyses; promotional budgeting/planning.

Subject cross reference: 2.1, 2.2, 2.10, 2.11, 2.15, 4.1, and 4.4.

Geographic coverage: Domestic.

Time coverage: 1979 to present.

Online vendor(s): Interactive Market Systems, Inc.
Management Science Associates, Inc.
Market Science Associates, Inc.
Telmar Media Systems, Inc.

BUSINESS CONDITIONS DIGEST (BCD)

Producer: U.S. Department of Commerce: Bureau of Economic Analysis
1401 K Street, N.W.
Washington, D.C. 20230
(202) 523-0777

Class: Statistical.

Data source: U.S. Department of Commerce *Business Conditions Digest*; some surveys.

Size: 750 business cycle measurements from the *Business Conditions Digest*. Much of these data are obtained from the Bureau of Labor Statistics.

Maintenance: Monthly.

Primary subject: Banking, Economics, and Finance.

Secondary subject: N/A

Profile: Maintains measurements (monthly) on important economic activity, business indicators and diffusion indexes. Coverage includes business and government expenditures, capital appropriations, aggregate national accounts, housing starts, personal statistics, manufacturing trade and inventories, production statistics, contracts, orders, earnings, imports, exports, earnings, stock price index and producer/consumer price indexes.

Applications: Economic analysis of leading indicators; product forecasts; sales potential analysis.

Subject cross reference: 1.5, 1.8, 1.9, 5.3, 7.6, and 10.7.

Geographic coverage: Domestic.

Time coverage: 1946 to present.

Online vendor(s): ADP Network Services, Inc.
Chase Econometrics/Interactive Data Corp.

BUSINESS CREDIT SERVICES

Producer: TRW, Inc.
Business Credit Services Division
1 City Boulevard
Orange, California 92668
(714) 937-2700

Class: Reference.

Data source: Contributing companies and Standard & Poor's.

Size: 8,000,000+ records.

Maintenance: Continuous.

Primary subject: Banking, Economics, and Finance.

Secondary subject: N/A

Profile: A broad-based business credit and financial information system containing payment information on individual business locations. Coverage includes company descriptions, location(s), payment trends, bank information, and key financial data. The data base is searchable by name, address, state, and zip code.

Applications: Competitive analysis; market segmentation studies; credit evaluation; contracts administration.

Subject cross reference: 1.6, 1.8, 2.1, 2.5, 7.11, and 10.8.

Geographic coverage: Domestic.

Time coverage: Current data.

Online vendor(s): TRW, Inc.

CALIFORNIA DATA BANK®

Producer: Security Pacific National Bank (SPNB)
SPNB California Data Bank, H8-3
Post Office Box 2097, Terminal Annex
Los Angeles, California 90051
(213) 613-5381

Class: Statistical.

Data source: Federal Home Loan Board; Federal Reserve Bank of San Francisco; private research agencies; U.S. Department of Agriculture; U.S. Department of Commerce; U.S. Department of Labor; and State of California government agencies.

Size: 35,000 time series.

Maintenance: Weekly, monthly, quarterly and annually.

Primary subject: Banking, Economics, and Finance.

Secondary subject: Marketing Planning.

Profile: Maintains macroeconomic time series data. Coverage includes population and other vital statistics, income, prices, labor force and employment, building and real estate activity, trade, transportation, agriculture and finance. Other data included are business indexes, contract activity, business failures, help wanted index and finance. Data are by SMSA, SCSA, counties and cities.

Applications: Plant location comparisons; control and budget planning; geographical sales potential analysis; local economy monitoring; regional consumer budget analysis; market potential forecasting.

Subject cross reference: 1.8, 2.3, 2.5, 2.8, 2.10, 5.3, 7.4, and 10.7.

Geographic coverage: California.

Time coverage: Varies by series; some from 1920's.

Online vendor(s): Chase Econometrics/Interactive Data Corp.
Data Resources, Inc.
National CSS, Inc.

CALIFORNIA UNION LIST OF PERIODICALS (CULP)

Producer: California Library Authority for Systems and
Services (CLASS)
1415 Koll Circle
Suite 101
San Jose, California 95112
(408) 289-1756

Class: Reference.

Data source: Library research and data.

Size: 72,000 titles.

Maintenance: N/A

Primary subject: Multidisciplinary.

Secondary subject: N/A

Profile: Maintains references to serial holdings and titles for
approximately 75% of the libraries in California.

Applications: Book research and library reference.

Subject cross reference: 2.10 and 6.8.

Geographic coverage: California.

Time coverage: Current holdings.

Online vendor(s): BRS, Inc.

CANADIAN BONDMARKET

Producer: Wood Gundy Limited
Royal Trust Tower
Post Office Box 274, T-D Center
Toronto, Ontario, Canada M5K 1M7
(416) 362-4433

Class: Statistical.

Data source: Wood Gundy research.

Size: 1,000 government bonds time series.

Maintenance: Weekly.

Primary subject: Banking, Economics, and Finance.

Secondary subject: N/A

Profile: Maintains price and yield data for Canadian
government, provincial, provincial guaranteed, municipal,
corporate and foreign government bonds. Fields included
are bid, ask, yield, maturity date and currency type. Some of
the bond types involved are convertibles, extendibles,
retractables, Euro-Canadian, and Euro-U.S. issues.

Applications: Capitalization decisions; merger and acquisitions
analysis.

Subject cross reference: 1.11, 1.16, and 10.1.

Geographic coverage: Canada.

Time coverage: 1977 to present.

Online vendor(s): I. P. Sharp Associates.

CANADIAN BUSINESS PERIODICALS INDEX (CBPI)

Producer: Micromedia Limited
144 Front Street, West
Toronto, Ontario, Canada M5J 1G2
(416) 593-5211

Class: Reference.

Data source: Business and Trade publications as well as the
Financial Post, Financial Times and *Globe and Mail.*

Size: 232,511 records.

Maintenance: 4,500 records monthly.

Primary subject: Banking, Economics, and Finance.

Secondary subject: N/A

Profile: Maintains citations to 170 Canadian English-language
business, industry, and trade publications. Included are the
Globe and Mail Report on Business, Financial Post and
The Financial Times. Coverage includes new product
introductions, corporate activities, finance, computer
science, real estate, taxation, general management, service
industries and utilities.

Applications: Corporate profiles and comparisons; new market
analysis.

Subject cross reference: 1.10, 1.11, 1.17, 2.1, 2.8, 2.10, 8.1, and
10.7.

Geographic coverage: Canada.

Time coverage: 1975 to present.

Online vendor(s): QL Systems Limited
SDC Search Service.

CANADIAN CHARTERED BANKS

Producer: I. P. Sharp Associates
145 King Street West
Toronto, Ontario, Canada M5H 1J8
(416) 364-5361

Class: Statistical.

Data source: Canadian Department of Finance, Chartered Banks of Canada.

Size: 13 banks.

Maintenance: Quarterly and annually.

Primary subject: Banking, Economics, and Finance.

Secondary subject: N/A

Profile: Maintains financial information for each of Canada's chartered banks. This data base is composed of three segments: monthly assets and liabilities, quarterly financial information, and annual financial information. The monthly data consists of 27 asset items and 17 liability items. The quarterly data consists of balance sheet, revenue, expense and dividend statistics. The annual data consists of 87 data items. Coverage includes revenue statements, expense profiles, profits, statements of accumulated appropriations for losses, statements of rest account, earnings per share data, statements of assets and liabilities and capital stock information.

Applications: Chartered bank comparisons; banking industry statistics.

Subject cross reference: 1.2, 1.11, and 2.1.

Geographic coverage: Canada.

Time coverage: 1966 to present.

Online vendor(s): I. P. Sharp Associates.

CANADIAN DEPARTMENT OF INSURANCE

Producer: Department of Insurance (Canada)
L'es Planade Laurier
140 O'Conner Street
Ottawa, Ontario, Canada K1A 0H2
(613) 996-8587

Class: Statistical.

Data source: Questionnaires and financial statement submissions from individual companies to the Canadian Department of Insurance.

Size: Data on approximately 600 federally registered companies.

Maintenance: Annually.

Primary subject: Banking, Economics, and Finance (insurance).

Secondary subject: N/A

Profile: Maintains financial information for over 600 federally registered insurance companies, trust companies, loan companies and cooperative credit associations. Data

originate from the companies' financial statements submitted yearly by each company to the Department of Insurance. Some of the same data are published in the "blue book" annual reports of the Superintendent of Insurance for Canada.

Applications: Competitive comparisons, profiles and analyses; insurance selection.

Subject cross reference: 1.11 and 1.13.

Geographic coverage: Canada.

Time coverage: Three most recent years of data.

Online vendor(s): I. P. Sharp Associates.

CANADIAN ENVIRONMENT (CENV)

Producer: Environment Canada, Watdoc, Inland Waters
Directorate
Ottawa, Ontario, Canada K1A 0E7
(819) 997-1238

Class: Reference.

Data source: Reports, publications and journal articles relative to Canadian environmental issues.

Size: 43,000 records.

Maintenance: Approximately 600 records monthly.

Primary subject: Environmental, Social, and Political Affairs.

Secondary subject: N/A

Profile: Maintains citations and abstracts of Canadian environmental literature. Coverage includes water quality, pollution, wildlife, marine technology, water research, regulations, irrigation, aquatic life, offshore resources, flooding and scientific and technical socioeconomic aspects.

Applications: Environmental research and analysis pertinent to Canadian matters.

Subject cross reference: 6.3 and 6.6.

Geographic coverage: Canada.

Time coverage: 1970 to present.

Online vendor(s): QL Systems Limited.

CANADIAN NEWS INDEX (CNI)

Producer: Micromedia Limited
144 Front Street, West
Toronto, Ontario, Canada M5J 2L7
(416) 593-5211

Class: Reference.

Data source: The following major Canadian newspapers: *The Calgary Herald, Halifax Chronicle-Herald, Montreal Star, Toronto Globe & Mail, Toronto Star, Vancouver Sun and The Winnipeg Free Press.*

Size: 53,000 citations.

Maintenance: Monthly.

Primary subject: Multidisciplinary.

Secondary subject: N/A

Profile: Maintains citations to items in the above named newspapers. The CNI also covers 27 national, regional and public affairs magazines. Selected subjects include: national and international news, provincial affairs and activities, politics, labor news, editorials, reviews, biographies and obituaries.

Applications: News analysis; news research support.

Subject cross reference: 1.19, 2.16, 3.6, 4.6, 5.9, 6.8, 7.12, 8.9, 9.20, and 10.8.

Geographic coverage: Canada.

Time coverage: 1977 to present.

Online vendor(s): QL Systems Limited
SDC Search Service.

CANADIAN PRESS NEWSTEX (CPN)

Producer: QL Systems Limited
797 Princess Street
Kingston, Ontario, Canada K7L 1G1
(613) 549-4611

Class: Reference.

Data source: Canadian Press News Wires, Broadcast News Limited, Associated Press, and The Agence France-Presse.

Size: 1+ million records.

Maintenance: Approximately 1,000 records daily.

Primary subject: Multidisciplinary.

Secondary subject: N/A

Profile: Provides full-text coverage of both English and French-language news articles and reports covering all aspects of business.

Applications: News search and research activities.

Subject cross reference: 1.19, 2.16, 3.6, 4.6, 5.9, 6.8, 7.12, 8.9, 9.20, and 10.8.

Geographic coverage: International.

Time coverage: English-1974 to present, French-1976 to present.

Online vendor(s): QL Systems Limited.

CANADIAN SOCIO-ECONOMIC INFORMATION MANAGEMENT SYSTEM (CANSIM)®

Producer: Statistics Canada
User Services
Ottawa, Ontario, Canada K1A 0V7
(613) 992-3151

Class: Statistical.

Data source: Bank of Canada, Statistics Canada.

Size: 20,000 indicators and 55,000 time series.

Maintenance: Daily.

Primary subject: Banking, Economics and Finance.

Secondary subject: Marketing Planning.

Profile: Presents socio-economic indicators at both the macro- and microeconomic levels. Maintains overall Canadian economic, financial, and demographic statistics. Data are updated daily by a direct computer-to-computer link between Ottawa and DRI.

Applications: Historical macro- and microeconomic analyses; demographic studies; long-term analysis; forecasting.

Subject cross reference: 1.8, 2.4, 2.5, 2.8, and 9.6.

Geographic coverage: Canada.

Time coverage: Varies by series; some from early 1900's.

Online vendor(s): Data Resources, Inc.
I. P. Sharp Associates.

CANADIAN STOCK OPTIONS

Producer: I. P. Sharp Associates
145 King Street West
Toronto, Ontario, Canada M5H 1J8
(416) 364-5361

Class: Statistical.

Data source: Trans Canada Options, Inc. (TCO).

Size: N/A

Maintenance: Daily.

Primary subject: Banking, Economics, and Finance (securities).

Secondary subject: N/A

Profile: Maintains trading data for both put and call options issued by TCO. These data include puts and calls traded on the Toronto and Montreal Stock Exchanges. Data fields include dollar value traded, volumes, prices and open interest data, high, low, close, bid and ask. There are 16 data items in all.

Applications: Securities analysis and decisions.

Subject cross reference: 1.16.

Geographic coverage: Canada.

Time coverage: Most recent 200 trading days.

Online vendor(s): I. P. Sharp Associates.

CA SEARCH

Producer: Chemical Abstracts Service (CAS)
American Chemical Society
Post Office Box 3012
Columbus, Ohio 43210
(614) 421-6940
(800) 848-6533

Class: Reference.

Data source: Various chemical literature (journals, conference proceedings, research, etc.).

Size: 5,090,000 records.

Maintenance: BRS and CISTI; 4,000 records monthly; DIALOG, ESA-IRS, Infoline and SDC, 19,000 records biweekly.

Primary subject: Research and Development.

Secondary subject: N/A

Profile: Maintains an elaborate array of basic bibliographic (citations and abstracts) information from the following chemical literature disciplines: organic, analytical, physical, applied, macromolecular, biochemical and chemical engineering. Includes CAS registry numbers.

Applications: Chemical (subject and index) analyses; chemical terminology and research.

Subject cross reference: 6.8, 7.3, 8.2, and 8.6.

Geographic coverage: International.

Time coverage: 1967 to present.

Online vendor(s): BRS, Inc. (CHEM)
CISTI (CAS)
DIALOG Information Services, Inc. (CA Search)
ESA-IRS (CHEMABS)
Pergamon-Infoline (CA Search)
SDC Search Service (CAS)
Telesystems-Questel (EURECAS).

CAS ONLINE

Producer: American Chemical Society/Chemical Abstracts Service (CAS)
Post Office Box 3012
Columbus, Ohio 43210
(614) 421-6940
(800) 848-6533

Class: Reference.

Data source: Chemical Abstracts' *The CAS Chemical Registry File.*

Size: 5,500,000 substances.

Maintenance: Weekly.

Primary subject: Research and Development.

Secondary subject: N/A

Profile: For chemical substances, provides CAS registry numbers, molecular formula, structural diagram, index name, and synonyms.

Applications: Chemical substance analysis.

Subject cross reference: 8.2 and 8.6.

Geographic coverage: International.

Time coverage: 1977 to present.

Online vendor(s): Chemical Abstracts Service.

CAS SOURCE INDEX (CASSI)

Producer: Chemical Abstracts Service (CAS)
Post Office Box 3012
Columbus, Ohio 43210
(614) 421-6940
(800) 848-6533

Class: Reference.

Data source: 50,000 serial/non-serial publications in over 400 libraries and 28 countries.

Size: 50,000 + records.

Maintenance: 1,250 records quarterly.

Primary subject: Research and Development.

Secondary subject: N/A

Profile: A compilation of bibliographic and library holdings information for scientific and technical literature relevant to the chemical sciences, engineering, biology and related technical areas.

Applications: Chemical science research (source of research and literature).

Subject cross reference: 6.8, 8.2, and 8.6.

Geographic coverage: International.

Time coverage: 1907 to present.

Online vendor(s): SDC Search Service.

CATLINE (CATALOG ONLINE)

Producer: U.S. National Library of Medicine (NLM)
8600 Rockville Pike
Bethesda, Maryland 20209
(301) 496-6217

Class: Reference.

Data source: NLM *Current Catalog.*

Size: 207,000 + citations.

Maintenance: Weekly.

Primary subject: General Management (health care and medicine).

Secondary subject: N/A

Profile: Maintains citations, monographs, books, serials, and technical reports catalogued by the NLM on medicine, the life sciences and related topics.

Applications: Biomedical applied research techniques and data reference.

Subject cross reference: 9.7.

Geographic coverage: International.

Time coverage: 1965 to date.

Online vendor(s): National Library of Medicine (MEDLARS Online Network).

CHEMICAL DATA BANKS

Producer: Data Resources, Inc.
29 Hartwell Avenue
Lexington, Massachusetts 02173
(617) 861-0165

Class: Statistical.

Data source: Chlorine Institute, U.S. Department of Commerce, U.S. International Trade Commission, Rubber Manufacturers Association, McGraw-Hill, Inc., Textile Economics Bureau, and American Chemical Society.

Size: Several time series.

Maintenance: Monthly, quarterly and annually.

Primary subject: Multidisciplinary.

Secondary subject: N/A

Profile: Covers the economic, market, and financial aspects of the chemical industry. Contains data on production, sales, prices, and foreign trade of chemical products by type. Also contains data on plant capacities by product, process, company, and location. Data are available at the product, company, and national levels.

Applications: Monthly monitoring reports for chemical reports; forecasts of demand and price for key chemicals; analysis of energy policies affecting chemical producers.

Subject cross reference: 1.11, 2.1, 2.12, and 10.3.

Geographic coverage: Domestic.

Time coverage: Varies by series.

Online vendor(s): Data Resources, Inc.

CHEMICAL INDUSTRY NOTES (CIN)

Producer: American Chemical Society
Chemical Abstracts Service
Post Office Box 3012
Columbus, Ohio 43210
(614) 421-6940
(800) 848-6533

Class: Reference.

Data source: *Chemical Industry Notes* and periodicals.

Size: 368,300 records.

Maintenance: Biweekly (DIALOG), weekly (SDC).

Primary subject: Banking, Economics, and Finance.

Secondary subject: Multidisciplinary.

Profile: Maintains extracted articles from over 78 international business-oriented periodicals which cover the chemical processing industries. Coverage includes products, processes, production, revenue, facilities, pricing, people and governmental and corporate activities.

Applications: Industry analysis; corporate situational analysis.

Subject cross reference: 1.11, 2.1, 2.8, 2.10, 4.3, 4.4, 5.8, and 8.4.

Geographic coverage: International.

Time coverage: 1974 to present.

Online vendor(s): DIALOG Information Services, Inc.
SDC Search Service.

CHEMLAW

Producer: The Bureau of National Affairs, Inc. (BNA)
1231 25th Street, N.W.
Washington, D.C. 20037
(202) 452-4200

Class: Reference.

Data source: *U.S. Code of Federal Regulations (CFR)* and *Federal Register (FR)*.

Size: N/A

Maintenance: N/A

Primary subject: Legal and Legislative Affairs.

Secondary subject: Research and Development.

Profile: Maintains information covering the regulations of U.S. agencies such as the Department of Agriculture, Commerce, Consumer Product Safety Commission, Energy, Environmental Protection Agency, Federal Aviation Administration, Food and Drug Administration, Railroad Administration, Mine Safety and Health Administration, Occupational Safety and Health Administration, Nuclear Regulatory Commission, and the Department of Transportation. Record field coverage consists of full text regulations, published publisher-prepared summaries, word length, trade names, chemical abstracts registry numbers, chemical names and synonyms, FR publication dates, CFR and FR citations, statutory authorities for each regulation and agencies. Spans 23 CFR titles and more than a dozen federal agencies.

Applications: Chemical applications analyses; new product (legalities) analyses; product liability decisions.

Subject cross reference: 5.7, 5.8, 5.9, 6.8, 7.1, 7.7, 8.2, and 8.6.

Geographic coverage: Domestic.

Time coverage: Current data.

Online vendor(s): CIS, Inc.
DIALOG Information Services, Inc. (1982).

CHEMSEARCH®

Producer: DIALOG Information Services, Inc.
3460 Hillview Avenue
Palo Alto, California 94304
(800) 227-1927 (U.S.)
(800) 982-5838 (California)

Class: Reference.

Data source: *Chemical Abstracts* Service (CAS).

Size: 183,876 chemical substances.

Maintenance: Biweekly.

Primary subject: Research and Development.

Secondary subject: N/A

Profile: A dictionary listing of the most recently cited substances in CA Search and is a companion file to Chemname. Coverage includes CAS Registry Number, molecular formula and CA Substance Index Names. Includes all new substances cited in the latest issues of *Chemical Abstracts* (CA).

Applications: Chemical(s) research and applications; users may generate chemical substance search terms and retrieve information from only the most recent issues of CA.

Subject cross reference: 8.2, 8.3, and 8.6.

Geographic coverage: N/A

Time coverage: 1967 to present.

Online vendor(s): DIALOG Information Services, Inc.

CHEM SINGLY INDEXED SUBSTANCES (CHEMSIS)®

Producer: DIALOG Information Services, Inc. (From CAS)
3460 Hillview Avenue
Palo Alto, California 94304
(800) 227-1927 (U.S.)
(800) 982-5838 (California)

Class: Reference.

Data source: *Chemical Abstracts* Service (CAS).

Size: 1,320,880 records.

Maintenance: Irregular.

Primary subject: Research and Development.

Secondary subject: N/A

Profile: A dictionary, non-bibliographic file of chemical substances cited only once in either the 9th collective index period (1972-1976) or the 10th CI period (1977-1981) of *Chemical Abstracts*. Coverage includes CAS Registry Number, molecular formula, CA Substance Index Name, available synonyms, ring data and other chemical substance data are included.

Applications: Chemical(s) Search and Analysis; Chemsis is an important access point to chemical information as 75% of the chemicals cited appear only once.

Subject cross reference: 8.2, 8.3, and 8.6.

Geographic coverage: N/A

Time coverage: 1977 to present for the "open" file.

Online vendor(s): DIALOG Information Services, Inc.

CHILD ABUSE AND NEGLECT

Producer: U.S. Department of Health and Human Services, National Center on Child Abuse and Neglect Children's Bureau
Post Office Box 1182
Washington, D.C. 20013
(202) 343-8435

Class: Reference.

Data source: Child abuse and neglect programs and reportings, child abuse research centers.

Size: 10,301 citations.

Maintenance: Semiannually.

Primary subject: Environmental, Social & Political Affairs.

Secondary subject: N/A

Profile: Maintains citations and abstracts relative to the definition, prevention, identification and treatment of child abuse and neglect. Coverage includes current law literature, current research projects, general child abuse literature, bibliographic references and service program listings.

Applications: Child abuse information support; child abuse direction for social workers; family planners, sociologists, educators, criminologists and legal researchers.

Subject cross reference: 6.7.

Geographic coverage: Domestic.

Time coverage: 1965 to present.

Online vendor(s): DIALOG Information Services, Inc.

CHRONOLOG NEWSLETTER

Producer: DIALOG Information Retrieval Service
3460 Hillview Avenue
Palo Alto, California 94304
(800) 227-1927 (U.S.)
(800) 982-5838 (California)

Class: Reference.

Data source: DIALOG monthly newsletter.

Size: 500 records.

Maintenance: Monthly.

Primary subject: Multidisciplinary.

Secondary subject: N/A

Profile: The online version of the monthly publication of the DIALOG Information Retrieval Service. This online service provides information on new data bases, reloaded data files, special DIALOG features, search tips and examples and search aids.

Applications: Full text article search examples.

Subject cross reference: 1.19, 2.16, 3.6, 4.6, 5.9, 6.8, 7.12, 8.9, 9.20, and 10.8.

Geographic coverage: International.

Time coverage: 1981 to present.

Online vendor(s): DIALOG Information Services, Inc.

CIS/INDEX

Producer: Congressional Information Service, Inc. (CIS)
7101 Wisconsin Avenue, Suite 900
Washington, D.C. 20014
(301) 654-1550

Class: Reference.

Data source: All U.S. Congressional publications except the *Congressional Record*.

Size: 143,800 records.

Maintenance: Monthly.

Primary subject: Legal and Legislative Affairs.

Secondary subject: Multidisciplinary.

Profile: Provides citations and abstracts of virtually every publication (including Congressional reports, committee prints, hearing documents, and executive branch documents) produced by approximately 300 House, Senate, and Joint Committees and sub-committees of Congress since 1970. Subject areas include almost all business, economic, and technology topics.

Applications: Management planning and analysis; legislative news analysis; subject matter tracking and research.

Subject cross reference: 1.19, 2.16, 3.6, 4.6, 5.9, 6.8, 7.12, 8.9, 9.20, and 10.8.

Geographic coverage: Domestic.

Time coverage: 1970 to present.

Online vendor(s): DIALOG Information Services, Inc.
SDC Search Service.

CITIBASE®

Producer: Citibank, Citibase Economic Database
Post Office Box 5294 FDS Station
New York, New York 10150
(212) 559-5312

Class: Statistical.

Data source: Bureau of Economic Analysis (e.g., from Survey of Current Business and Business Conditions Digest), various other macroeconomic series.

Size: 4,500 time series.

Maintenance: Daily to Monthly depending on on-line economic service.

Primary subject: Banking, Economics, and Finance.

Secondary subject: Multidisciplinary.

Profile: Maintains time series pertaining to the U.S. economy. Coverage includes national income; product accounts; U.S. international transactions (e.g., imports and exports); plant and equipment expenditures; capacity utilization rates; manufacturing and trade; industrial production index; housing and construction starts; price structures (e.g., producer price index and consumer price index); population, earnings, employment; finance (e.g., interest rates, money supply, foreign exchange rates and profit statistics).

Applications: Economic market analyses; forecasting modeling; various industry-segment analyses.

Subject cross reference: 1.2, 1.6, 1.7, 1.8, 1.9, 1.10, 1.14, 2.8, 7.5, 9.13, 9.15, 10.2 and 10.7.

Geographic coverage: Domestic.

Time coverage: 1947 to present.

Online vendor(s): ADP Network Services, Inc.
Citishare
CompuServe, Inc.
Computer Sciences Corporation
COMSHARE, Inc.
The Conference Board of Canada
Control Data Corporation
Datacrown, Inc.
G. CAM
General Electric Information Services Co.
Informatics, Inc.
Massachusetts Institute of Technology
Proprietary Computer Systems, Inc.
Rapidata, Inc.
SIA Computer Services
STSC, Inc.
Sun Information Services
Time Sharing Resources, Inc.
Tymshre, Inc.

CITIBASE — WEEKLY

Producer: Citibank, Citibank Economic Data Base
Post Office Box 5294
FDR Station
New York, New York 10022
(212) 559-5312

Class: Statistical.

Data source: Federal Reserve, American Metal Markets, U.S. Department of Commerce and U.S. Department of Labor.

Size: 400 time series.

Maintenance: Daily.

Primary subject: Banking, Economics, and Finance.

Secondary subject: N/A

Profile: Maintains approximately 400 weekly time series pertaining to the U.S. financial, economic, and employment data. Coverage includes large commercial banks (e.g., money supplies, financial condition, reserves and deposits and other components); Federal Reserve bank credit, yields on government securities, yields on corporate and some utility bonds, N.Y.S.E. daily volume index, Standard & Poor's 500 composite index and index of 400 industrials. This data base also maintains related data on commodities, production and unemployment rates, numbers, and claims.

Applications: Market analysis; economic and/or product forecasting.

Subject cross reference: 1.2, 1.6, 1.7, 1.8, 1.14, 2.8, 9.13, 9,15, and 10.7.

Geographic coverage: Domestic.

Time coverage: 1980 to present.

Online vendor(s): Citishare
CompuServe, Inc.
Rapidata, Inc.

CLAIMS/CHEM®

Producer: IFI/Plenum Data Company
302 Swann Avenue
Arlington, Virginia 22301
(703) 683-1085

Class: Reference.

Data source: U.S. Patent and Trademark Office.

Size: 116,000 citations.

Maintenance: Not updated.

Primary subject: Research and Development.

Secondary subject: N/A

Profile: Maintains citations for chemical and chemical-related patents in the United States. Equivalent patents for several European countries are also included in many cases.

Applications: New product research; new technology tracking.

Subject cross reference: 8.1 and 8.7.

Geographic coverage: Primarily Domestic.

Time coverage: 1950-1970.

Online vendor(s): DIALOG Information Services, Inc.

CLAIMS/CITATION®

Producer: IFI/Plenum Data Company
302 Swann Avenue
Alexandria, Virginia 22301
(703) 683-1085

Class: Reference.

Data source: U.S. Patent and Trademark Office.

Size: 1,757,000 records.

Maintenance: 32,000 records per quarter.

Primary subject: Research and Development.

Secondary subject: N/A

Profile: Maintains information for over 10 million patent numbers records between 1947 and 1979. Each patent record contains the patent number of each patent (U.S. and International) that is contained in patents it cites.

Applications: Product research and development; product opportunity research.

Subject cross reference: 2.1, 2.12, 8.1, 8.5, and 8.7.

Geographic coverage: Domestic.

Time coverage: 1947 to present.

Online vendor(s): DIALOG Information Services, Inc.

CLAIMS/UNITERM®

Producer: IFI/Plenum Data Company
302 Swann Avenue
Arlington, Virginia 22301
(703) 683-1085

Class: Reference.

Data source: U.S. Patent and Trademark Office.

Size: 497,600 records.

Maintenance: Approximately 4,500 records quarterly.

Primary subject: Research and Development.

Secondary subject: N/A

Profile: Provides user access to chemical and chemical-related patents. This data base has the special feature of subject indexing for each chemical patent from a controlled vocabulary designed to facilitate retrieval of chemical structures and polymers. Uniterm is a set of at least 20 descriptors used to describe each patent in the system.

Applications: Chemical product research; new product opportunities.

Subject cross reference: 2.1, 2.12, 8.1, 8.5, and 8.7.

Geographic coverage: Primarily Domestic.

Time coverage: 1950 to present.

Online vendor(s): DIALOG Information Services, Inc.

CLAIMS/U.S. PATENTS

Producer: IFI/Plenum Data Company
302 Swann Avenue
Arlington, Virginia 22301
(703) 683-1085

Class: Reference.

Data source: U.S. Patent and Trademark Office.

Size: 483,300 records.

Maintenance: Not updated. However, Claims/U.S. Patents Abstracts (a continuation of this data base) is updated monthly.

Primary subject: Research and Development.

Secondary subject: N/A

Profile: Maintains citations for all patents listed in general, chemical, electrical and mechanical sections of the *Official Gazette* of the U.S. Patent Office. Foreign equivalents from Belgium, France, Great Britain, West Germany and The Netherlands are included for approximately 20% of the U.S. patents in this file.

Applications: Product research and development; product opportunity research.

Subject cross reference: 2.1, 2.12, 8.1, 8.5, and 8.7.

Geographic coverage: Primarily Domestic.

Time coverage: 1971 to 1977.

Online vendor(s): DIALOG Information Services, Inc.

CLINICAL TOXICOLOGY OF COMMERCIAL PRODUCTS (CTCP)

Producer: University of Rochester
Department of Pharmacology
601 Elmwood Avenue
Rochester, New York 14642
(716) 275-3146

Class: Reference.

Data source: Journals, manufacturers, and primary research.

Size: 20,000 records.

Maintenance: Quarterly.

Primary subject: Research and Development.

Secondary subject: N/A

Profile: Maintains chemical and toxicological data for over 20,000 commercial products but this excludes food products. Data fields include trade name, manufacturer name, chemical names of ingredients, product use category, formulas, abstracts registry number, toxicity, symptoms and treatments.

Applications: Brand comparisons; marketing programs—product introductions; toxicity research.

Subject cross reference: 2.12, 8.1, 8.2, and 8.6.

Geographic coverage: Domestic.

Time coverage: Most current data.

Online vendor(s): CIS, Inc.

COAL DATA BANK

Producer: U.S. Department of Energy (DOE)
12th Street and Pennsylvania Avenue, N.W.
Washington, D.C. 20461
(202) 556-6061

Class: Statistical.

Data source: Federal Energy Data Systems (FEDS), the National Coal Association, and U.S. Department of Energy.

Size: 4,000 time series.

Maintenance: Monthly and Annually.

Primary subject: General Management (agriculture and mining).

Secondary subject: N/A

Profile: Provides coverage of the U.S. coal industry. Data coverage includes average Btu content of coal burned by state, demand of electric utilities by state, number and type of mines by state, mine employment by state and type, productivity by state and mine type, import/export of coal, and average stocks of coal by consuming sector. These data are generally available at the state, regional, and national levels.

Applications: Industry analysis and forecast; identification of potential coal markets; examining the impact of fiscal and environmental legislation on the coal industry.

Subject cross reference: 9.1 and 10.5.

Geographic coverage: Domestic.

Time coverage: Varies by series.

Online vendor(s): Data Resources, Inc.

COAL DATA BASE

Producer: International Energy Agency (IEA)
Technical Information Service
14/15 Lower Grosvenor Place
London, England SW1W 0EX
(01) 828-4661

Class: Reference.

Data source: Reports, periodicals, monographs, dissertations and conference proceedings of the IEA.

Size: 40,000 records.

Maintenance: Monthly.

Primary subject: General Management (mining).

Secondary subject: Long-Range Strategic Planning (energy).

Profile: Maintains an extensive coverage of international literature on the scientific and technical aspects of the coal industry. Coverage includes coal preparation, processing, properties, handling, management, transport, exploration and reserves data.

Applications: Industry analysis; product line forecasting; coal processing technology.

Subject cross reference: 6.3, 9.1, and 10.5.

Geographic coverage: International.

Time coverage: 1978 to present.

Online vendor(s): CISTI.

COLD REGIONS

Producer: Library of Congress, Science and Technology Division
Cold Regions Bibliography Project
Washington, D.C. 20541
(202) 287-5668

Class: Reference.

Data source: Journals, technical reports, conference papers, monographs, patents, maps and related articles.

Size: 74,000 citations.

Maintenance: Quarterly.

Primary subject: Industrial and Manufacturing Planning.

Secondary subject: N/A

Profile: Maintains citations and abstract coverage of the social, political and natural aspects of international cold regions. Coverage includes data pertaining to the relationships of snow, ice and frozen ground to civil engineering and management; navigation on ice and equipment in cold temperatures.

Applications: Cold region management assistance; operational strategies.

Subject cross reference: 6.3 and 7.3.

Geographic coverage: Antarctica, The Antarctica Ocean and Subantarctic Islands.

Time coverage: 1962 to present.

Online vendor(s): SDC Search Service.

COMMODITIES MARKET DATA BANK

Producer: Data Resources, Inc.
29 Hartwell Avenue
Lexington, Massachusetts 02173
(617) 861-0165

Class: Statistical.

Data source: Bunker Ramo, Commodity Systems, Inc., Reuters News Services, and many commodity exchanges.

Size: 18,000 time series.

Maintenance: Daily.

Primary subject: Banking, Economics, and Finance.

Secondary subject: N/A

Profile: Maintains time series for the following futures markets' commodities categories: feed grains, livestock, products, foreign currency, fiber, financial instruments, wood, metals and foods. Fields include high, low, closing, volume, cash and total open interest. Data are available by commodity by exchange.

Applications: Commodities management, risk and opportunities associated with changing commodities prices.

Subject cross reference: 1.16.

Geographic coverage: U.S. and Canada.

Time coverage: 20 years for U.S. markets and 10 years for Canadian.

Online vendor(s): Data Resources, Inc.

COMMODITY DATA INFORMATION SYSTEM (CDIS)

Producer: MJK Associates
122 Saratoga Avenue, #11
Santa Clara, California 95050
(408) 247-5102

Class: Statistical.

Data source: Chicago Board of Trade, Chicago Mercantile Exchange, New York Mercantile Exchange, New York Cotton Exchange, Commodity Exchange, Inc., New York CoCoa Exchange, Kansas City Exchange, Minneapolis Wheat Exchange, New York Coffee and Sugar Exchange and the Winnipeg Exchange.

Size: 40 major commodities.

Maintenance: Daily.

Primary subject: Banking, Economics, and Finance.

Secondary subject: N/A

Profile: Contains daily futures and cash prices and data such as open, high, low, close, volume and open interest for each of several major commodities.

Applications: Users can derive quotations, compute weekly to annual moving averages, summary tables, graphs, etc.

Subject cross reference: 1.16.

Geographic coverage: United States and Canada.

Time coverage: 1960's to present.

Online vendor(s): MJK Associates.

COMMONWEALTH AGRICULTURAL BUREAUX ABSTRACTS: NUTRITION ABSTRACTS AND REVIEWS (NAR)

Producer: Commonwealth Agricultural Bureaux
Farnham House
Farnham Royal
Slough, England SL2 3BN
2814 2281

Class: Reference.

Data source: Journals, books, and special reports.

Size: 1,713,817 records.

Maintenance: Approximately 12,000 records monthly.

Primary subject: General Management (agriculture).

Secondary subject: N/A

Profile: A comprehensive file of agricultural and biological information containing all records in the 26 main abstract journals published by Commonwealth Agricultural Bureaux. Coverage includes breeding data, bees, crops, dairy science, economics, forestry, helminthology, horticulture, nutrition, protozoology, plant pathology, rural development, sociology, soils and fertilizer, and weed study.

Applications: Agricultural studies and programs.

Subject cross reference: 9.1.

Geographic coverage: International.

Time coverage: 1973 to present.

Online vendor(s): DIALOG Information Services, Inc. (CAB Abstracts)
DIMDI (CAB Abstracts)
ESA-IRS (CAB Abstracts)
GID-SIT (NAR)
SDC Search Service (CAB Abstracts)

COMPREHENSIVE DISSERTATION INDEX
(CDI)

Producer: University Microfilms International, Inc.
300 North Zeeb Road
Ann Arbor, Michigan 48106
(313) 761-4700
(800) 521-0600

Class: Reference.

Data source: Doctoral dissertations from accredited U.S. educational institutions and over 200 non-U.S. institutions.

Size: 756,300 citations.

Maintenance: Approximately 3,000 records monthly.

Primary subject: Multidisciplinary.

Secondary subject: N/A

Profile: A definitive subject, title, and author guide to virtually every American dissertation accepted by an accredited institution since 1861. Also includes citations for Canadian dissertations. International dissertation records are increasing and now represent over 200 institutions.

Applications: Basic research in any business discipline.

Subject cross reference: 1.19, 2.16, 3.6, 4.6, 5.9, 6.8, 7.12, 8.9, 9.20, and 10.8.

Geographic coverage: International.

Time coverage: 1861 to present.

Online vendor(s): BRS, Inc.
DIALOG Information Services, Inc.
SDC Search Service.

COMPUBOND®

Producer: Paine, Webber, Jackson & Curtis, Inc.
140 Broadway
New York, New York 10005
(212) 437-2121

Class: Statistical.

Data source: Securities & Exchange Commission.

Size: 800+ money market instrument profiles.

Maintenance: Daily.

Primary subject: Banking, Economics, and Finance.

Secondary subject: N/A

Profile: A bond market analysis system which combines historical data with analytical capabilities. Covers industrial, utility, telephone, finance, treasury, agency, GNMA-FMAC. BOA pass through, T-bill and GNMA futures, various money market, and foreign bonds. Primarily designed for the institution investor (banks, pension funds, and insurance companies).

Applications: Industrial analysis (financial); portfolio management.

Subject cross reference: 1.3, 1.8, 1.12, and 1.16.

Geographic coverage: Domestic.

Time coverage: Latest four years.

Online vendor(s): ADP Network Services, Inc.

COMPUSERVE

Producer: CompuServe, Inc.
Information Services Division
5000 Arlington Centre Blvd.
Columbus, Ohio 43220
(614) 457-8600

Class: Reference and Statistical.

Data source: Newspapers, journals, reference documents and other data base services.

Size: Information coverage on 40,000 stocks, 1,600 companies, over 16 recreational games.

Maintenance: Varies according to data base.

Primary subject: Multidisciplinary.

Secondary subject: N/A

Profile: A multifaceted information service providing full text news retrievals from an assortment of wire services and newspapers; international, national, regional, and local news; family service information (recipes, personal health, gardening tips, etc.); electronic mail; financial information; entertainment; and, personal computing.

Applications: Personal recreation advice; stock/portfolio management; discount purchasing.

Subject cross reference: 1.16, 6.4, and 9.20.

Geographic coverage: Domestic.

Time coverage: Varies by series and data base.

Online vendor(s): CompuServe, Inc.

COMP*U*STAR

Producer: Comp-U-Card of America, Inc.
777 Summer Street
Stamford, Connecticut 06901
(203) 324-9261

Class: Reference and Statistical.

Data source: National advertising data.

Size: 30,000+ items (producers).

Maintenance: Continuous.

Primary subject: Marketing and Sales Promotion.

Secondary subject: N/A

Profile: Provides a shop-at-home discount shopping service. Lists many nationally advertised consumer products. Coverage includes such items as appliances, cameras, musical instruments, and home entertainment and video products. Special sale items are listed and can be ordered online.

Applications: Shop-at-home service; consumer products price monitoring.

Subject cross reference: 2.1, 2.14, 4.1, and 4.4.

Geographic coverage: Domestic.

Time coverage: Current products.

Online vendor(s): CompuServe
Source Telecomputing Corporation (THE SOURCE).

COMPUSTAT®

Producer: Standard & Poor's Compustat Services, Inc.
7400 S. Alton Court
Englewood, Colorado 80112
(303) 771-6510

Class: Statistical.

Data source: Company annual reports (10K and 10Q).

Size: 6,000 + companies.

Maintenance: Quarterly and Annually.

Primary subject: Banking, Economics, and Finance.

Secondary subject: Marketing Planning.

Profile: Provides access to 170 annual and 65 quarterly balance sheet and income statement items for 6,000 + industrial companies. Data items include assets, liabilities, net worth, sources and uses of funds, and common stock. Data are stored at the company level and composites are available for 120 SIC industry classifications.

Applications: Business segment analysis; financial trends; acquisition analysis; investment candidates; credit analysis.

Subject cross reference: 1.8, 1.11, 1.12, 1.16, 2.1, 2.5, 2.9, 10.1, 10.2, and 10.7.

Geographic coverage: United States and Canada.

Time coverage: Annual data for 20 years; quarterly data for ten years.

Online vendor(s): ADP Network Services, Inc.
Business Information Services (Control Data)
Chase Econometrics/Interactive Data Corp.
CompuServe, Inc.
Data Resources, Inc.
Time Sharing Resources, Inc.
United Telecom Computer Group
Warner Computer Systems, Inc.

COMPUTERIZED ENGINEERING INDEX (COMPENDEX)

Producer: Engineering Index, Inc.
345 East 47th Street
New York, New York 10017
(212) 644-7600
(800) 221-1044

Class: Reference.

Data source: Over 3500 journals, symposia proceedings, and government and private agency reports.

Size: 1,001,000 records.

Maintenance: Approximately 9,000 records monthly.

Primary subject: Industrial and Manufacturing Planning.

Secondary subject: Research and Development.

Profile: Maintains an extensive coverage of world literature (citations and abstracts) in engineering and technology. Coverage includes bioengineering, aerospace, automotive, agriculture, electronics, communications, geology, marine, railroad, petroleum, medicine, mechanical, heat and thermodynamics, sound and acoustics, food science, fluid flow, measurements and optics.

Applications: Industrial analysis and opportunities; technology and engineering research comparisons.

Subject cross reference: 7.3, 7.5, 8.3, 8.4, and 8.8.

Geographic coverage: International.

Time coverage: 1969 to present.

Online vendor(s): BRS, Inc.
CISTI
DIALOG Information Services, Inc.
ESA-IRS
ESA-QUEST
SDC Search Service.

CONFERENCE BOARD (CBDB)

Producer: The Conference Board
Informational Services Department
845 3rd Avenue
New York, New York 10022
(212) 759-0900

Class: Statistical.

Data source: The Conference Board's Research Division.

Size: 819 time series.

Maintenance: 10-day, monthly, bimonthly, quarterly, and annually.

Primary subject: Banking, Economics, and Finance.

Secondary subject: Marketing Planning.

Profile: Provides historical and forecasted economic data. Historical data include surveys of consumer and business sentiment, capital appropriations, expenditures, cancellations, and backlogs for manufacturers and utilities, household budgetary patterns, and measures of direct impact of the Federal budget. Forecasted data includes detailed forecast for all major GNP components, summary forecasts from major economic forecasting companies, consensus and secteral forecasts of GNP components, and forecasts of capital appropriations and expenditures.

Applications: Macroeconomic modeling; industrial analyses.

Subject cross reference: 1.4, 1.8, 2.3, 9.16, and 10.7.

Geographic coverage: Domestic.

Time coverage: Varies by series, some from the 1950's.

Online vendor(s): ADP Network Services, Inc.
Chase Econometrics/Interactive Data Corp.
Cornell University
Data Resources, Inc.
Rapidata, Inc.

CONFERENCE PAPERS INDEX (CPI)®

Producer: Cambridge Scientific Abstracts
5161 River Road
Bethesda, Maryland 20816
(800) 638-8076
(301) 951-1400

Class: Reference.

Data source: Current research papers (conferences and meetings) in science, engineering, and technology.

Size: 895,700 records.

Maintenance: Approximately 8,000 records monthly.

Primary subject: Research and Development.

Secondary subject: N/A

Profile: Provides citations of more than 100,000 scientific and technical papers presented at over 1,000 major regional, national and international meetings each year. Coverage includes the physical sciences, medicine, engineering, geosciences, and chemistry. Records include author name, address, paper title, conference title, location, date, sponsors, and paper ordering information.

Applications: Research studies and analysis (various disciplines).

Subject cross reference: 7.3, 8.3, 8.6, 8.8, and 9.7.

Geographic coverage: International.

Time coverage: 1973 to present.

Online vendor(s): DIALOG Information Services, Inc.
ESA-IRS.

CONGRESSIONAL RECORD ABSTRACTS (CRECORD)

Producer: Capitol Services Inc. (CSI)
415 Second Street, N.E.
Washington, D.C. 20002
(202) 546-5600

Class: Reference.

Data source: Abstracts prepared from citations in the *Congressional Record*.

Size: 205,000 records.

Maintenance: Approximately 1,000 records weekly.

Primary subject: Legal and Legislative Affairs.

Secondary subject: Multidisciplinary.

Profile: Maintains a comprehensive coverage of the *Congressional Record*, the offical journal of the U.S. Congress including the Senate, House, extension of remarks and digest sections. Coverage includes reference to various bills, resolutions, amendments to bills and resolutions, floor actions, committee/subcommittee reports, recent legislation, schedules of committees and floor hearings, Executive communications, speeches, participation in debates and other materials by members of Congress.

Applications: Industry analysis; government influence analyses.

Subject cross reference: 1.19, 2.16, 3.6, 4.6, 5.4, 5.6, 5.8, 6.8, 7.12, 8.9, 9.20, and 10.8.

Geographic coverage: Domestic.

Time coverage: 1976 to present.

Online vendor(s): DIALOG Information Services, Inc.
SDC Search Service.

CONSUMER ECONOMIC SERVICE DATA

Producer: Data Resources, Inc.
29 Hartwell Avenue
Lexington, Massachusetts 02173
(617) 861-0165

Class: Statistical.

Data source: Simmons Market Research Data; Social Security Administration; U.S. Department of Commerce, U.S. Department of Labor.

Size: Multiple data banks and time series.

Maintenance: One-time surveys, quarterly, and annually.

Primary subject: Marketing Planning.

Secondary subject: Banking, Economics and Finance.

Profile: Offers a vast amount of detailed demographic and economic data in five report areas: (1) Current Population Survey Annual Demographic File; (2) Consumer Expenditures Survey—a diary and interview of 40,000 households; (3) Target Group Index—Brand-specific purchasing and media penetration data; (4) Longitudinal Retirement History Survey; and (5) Consumer Markets Services—Personal consumption, retail sales, and associated prices.

Applications: Analysis of consumption patterns; demographic trend studies.

Subject cross reference: 1.5, 2.2, 2.3, 2.4, 2.5, 2.8, 2.10, and 2.14.

Geographic coverage: Primarily Domestic.

Time coverage: Varies by specific data base and series.

Online vendor(s): Data Resources, Inc.

CONSUMER PRICE INDEX/PRODUCER PRICE INDEX (CPI/PPI)

Producer: U.S. Department of Labor, Bureau of Labor Statistics (BLS)
441 G Street, N.W.
Washington, D.C. 20212
(202) 523-1092

Class: Statistical.

Data source: Government economic statistics.

Size: 10,000 + time series for CPI; 5,000 + time series for PPI.

Maintenance: Monthly.

Primary subject: Banking, Economics and Finance.

Secondary subject: Marketing Planning.

Profile: As part of the overall BLS Data Bank, CPI/PPI maintains historical time series for consumer goods and commodities expressed in percentages against base year or in standard points. The CPI maintains data on over 10,000 time series relating to cost of living standards and changes. Data are available by SMSA, region or population class. The PPI maintains data for approximately 5,000 monthly time series related to the commodities market. CPI field coverage includes food prices, clothes, transportation and housing. PPI coverage includes farm products, textiles, processed foods and chemicals.

Applications: Industry and market forecasts; production planning; pricing decision.

Subject cross reference: 1.5, 1.8, 1.16, 2.2, 2.3, 2.5, and 2.14.

Geographic coverage: Domestic.

Time coverage: Varies, but some from early 1900's to present.

Online vendor(s): ADP Network Services, Inc.
Business Information Services (Control Data)
Chase Econometrics/Interactive Data Corp.
I. P. Sharp Associates
Time Sharing Resources, Inc.
Uni-Coll, Inc.

COST FORECASTING DATA BANKS

Producer: Data Resources, Inc. (DRI)
29 Hartwell Avenue
Lexington, Massachusetts 02173
(617) 861-0165

Class: Statistical.

Data source: DRI costs forecasting data from several journals and government publications.

Size: Several time series.

Maintenance: Monthly, quarterly, and annually.

Primary subject: Banking, Economics, and Finance.

Secondary subject: N/A

Profile: Maintains a set of data bases designed to offer data on construction and other industries earnings, production, expenses, salaries, labor statistics, inventories, import/export price indices by commodity, lead-times, and related concepts of construction and other industries. The international data banks contain wholesale price, import price, export price and earnings indices by country for Japan and four European nations: Germany, France, Italy and the United Kingdom.

Applications: Industry projections and analysis; estimating new capacity expansion costs; timing orders for long-term projections.

Subject cross reference: 1.8, 1.9, and 9.15.

Geographic coverage: United States, United Kingdom, France, Germany, Italy and Japan.

Time coverage: Varies by series.

Online vendor(s): Data Resources, Inc.

COST PROGRAMS

Producer: Marshall and Swift Publication Company
1617 Beverly Boulevard
Post Office Box 26307
Los Angeles, California 90026
(213) 624-6451
(800) 421-8042

Class: Statistical.

Data source: The Marshall and Swift *Residential Cost Handbook*, Marshall Valuation Service, and the Valuation Quarterly.

Size: 100 + various building occupancies.

Maintenance: Monthly.

Primary subject: General Management (real estate and building trends).

Secondary subject: N/A

Profile: Maintains data for residential building costs (components) on approximately 100 building types. These costs cover a wide range of residential, commercial, industrial, and government buildings. Cost reports can be generated for buildings in each type of occupancy using simple square foot or a segregated cost format. Data may be adjusted to fit different local areas and depreciation schedules.

Applications: Users may enter proposed residential building characteristics and the data base system will format a valuation and replacement cost report.

Subject cross reference: 1.12, 7.4, 7.10, and 9.15.

Geographic coverage: Domestic.

Time coverage: Most current month.

Online vendor(s): Marshall and Swift Publication Company.

CREDIT DATA

Producer: TRW Information Services Division,
Credit Data Service
505 City Parkway West, Suite 100
Orange, California 92668
(714) 937-2000

Class: Statistical.

Data source: Court records, credit grantors, individuals.

Size: 80 + million consumers.

Maintenance: Continuously.

Primary subject: Banking, Economics, and Finance.

Secondary subject: N/A

Profile: Collects and stores credit information on consumers for use by those bona fide credit grantors limited by Federal law. Users must have a contract with TRW in order to use the service. The individual profiles include positive and negative information on retail credit card accounts, bank charge card accounts, lines of credit, secured loans, finance company accounts, and selected public record information limited to tax liens, judgments, and bankruptcies.

Applications: Credit management; sales consignment decisions.

Subject cross reference: 1.6 and 1.11.

Geographic coverage: Domestic.

Time coverage: Data maintained for seven years.

Online vendor(s): TRW Information Services Division.

CSS/QUOTES+

Producer: National CSS, Inc.
187 Danbury Road
Wilton, Connecticut 06897
(203) 762-2511

Class: Statistical.

Data source: Stock exchanges and government agencies.

Size: 42,000 + securities.

Maintenance: Daily.

Primary subject: Banking, Economics, and Finance.

Secondary subject: N/A

Profile: Lists both current and historical data on securities, including daily pricing, descriptive information, dividend history, and market indexes. Securities covered include common and preferred stocks, bonds and notes, mutual funds, options, government securities, municipal bonds, equipment trusts, and U.S. savings bonds.

Applications: Corporate portfolio management; securities market analysis—historical reference.

Subject cross reference: 1.16.

Geographic coverage: United States and Canada.

Time coverage: Latest four years.

Online vendor(s): National CSS, Inc.

CURRENCY

Producer: I. P. Sharp Associates, Ltd.
145 King Street West
Toronto, Ontario, Canada M5H 1J8
(416) 364-5361

Class: Statistical.

Data source: Provided by the national banking systems of major North American and European countries.

Size: Varies by exchange; from 12 to 58 currencies per exchange.

Maintenance: Daily.

Primary subject: Banking, Economics, and Finance.

Secondary subject: N/A

Profile: Maintains daily time series of exchange rates for major world currencies on the London, New York, Toronto, Zurich, Copenhagen, Melbourne, Paris, Frankfurt and Vienna exchanges. The number of currencies covered and the amount of data history vary among exchanges. The exchange rates are expressed in the currency of the country in which the exchange is located.

Applications: Financial statement consolidation.

Subject cross reference: 1.1, 1.3, 1.7, 1.9, and 2.6.

Geographic coverage: International.

Time coverage: Time series vary by country, most begin in early 1970's to present.

Online vendor(s): I. P. Sharp Associates, Ltd.

CURRENCY EXCHANGE DATA BASE

Producer: International Marine Banking Co., Ltd. and International Monetary Fund
Bureau of Statistics
700 19th Street, N.W.
Washington, D.C. 20431
(202) 477-3206

Class: Statistical.

Data source: Currency exchange rates.

Size: 120 time series.

Maintenance: Daily.

Primary subject: Banking, Economics, and Finance.

Secondary subject: N/A

Profile: Maintains current and historical (daily, monthly, and yearly) exchange rate data for over 40 world currencies and related economic data.

Applications: Corporate consolidations and currency exchange values.

Subject cross reference: 1.1 and 1.7.

Geographic coverage: International.

Time coverage: Varies by series; generally last 3 months.

Online vendor(s): General Electric Information Services Co.

CURRENT RESEARCH INFORMATION SYSTEM (CRIS)

Producer: U.S. Department of Agriculture (USDA)
National Agriculture Library Building
Beltsville, Maryland 70705
(301) 344-3755

Class: Reference.

Data source: USDA research agencies, state agricultural departments, and various forestry schools.

Size: 50,900 citations.

Maintenance: Approximately 1,500 citations quarterly.

Primary subject: General Management (agriculture).

Secondary subject: N/A

Profile: A current-awareness data service for agriculturally-related research projects. The projects described in CRIS cover current research in agriculture and related sciences. Coverage includes biological, physical, social and behavioral sciences. Specific areas of coverage include natural resource conservation, management, marketing and economics, food and nutrition, consumer health and safety, family life, housing and rural development, environmental protection, forestry and regional development.

Applications: Tracking of agricultural projects.

Subject cross reference: 6.3 and 9.1.

Geographic coverage: Domestic.

Time coverage: 1974 to present.

Online vendor(s): DIALOG Information Services, Inc.
SDC Search Service, Inc.

DATA BASE INDEX (DBI)

Producer: System Development Corporation (SDC)
2500 Colorado Avenue
Santa Monica, California 90406
(213) 820-4111

Class: Reference.

Data source: SDC Search Service data bases.

Size: 80+ data bases.

Maintenance: Quarterly.

Primary subject: Multidisciplinary.

Secondary subject: N/A

Profile: DBI is the master index to all SDC Search Service's data bases. Data bases are printed in a ranked order with the associated number of occurrences for a chosen term.

Applications: Users may select or obtain a listing of appropriate data bases for a given subject area.

Subject cross reference: 1.19, 2.16, 3.6, 4.6, 5.9, 6.8, 7.12, 8.9, 9.20, and 10.8.

Geographic coverage: International.

Time coverage: Current data bases.

Online vendor(s): SDC Search Service.

DECHEMA THERMOPHYSICAL PROPERTIES DATA BANK—DATA RETRIEVAL SYSTEMS (DETHERM-SDR)

Producer: Dechema
Deutsche Gesellschaft fur Chemisches Apparatewessen e.v.
Informationssysteme und Datenbanken (IUD)
Theodor Heuss Allee 25
Postfach 970146
D-6000 Frankfurt
Federal Republic of Germany
0611/75641

Class: Reference.

Data source: Data collections; handbooks, journals, and data bases.

Size: 3,000 industrial chemicals.

Maintenance: 400 records bimonthly.

Primary subject: Research and Development.

Secondary subject: N/A

Profile: Maintains citations and abstracts in English of literature relating to the thermophysical properties of industrially significant chemicals and mixtures. Used for searching literature within a given range of properties.

Applications: Physical science, kinetics and thermodynamic analysis.

Subject cross reference: 8.4 and 8.8.

Geographic coverage: International.

Time coverage: 1976 to present.

Online vendor(s): GID-SIT.

DEFENSE MARKET MEASURES SYSTEM
(DM2)

Producer: Frost & Sullivan, Inc.
106 Fulton Street
New York, New York 10038
(212) 233-1080

Class: Reference.

Data source: U.S. Government award announcements.

Size: 327,925 records.

Maintenance: Approximately 20,000 records quarterly.

Primary subject: Multidisciplinary.

Secondary subject: Marketing Planning.

Profile: The DM2 bata base provides access to announcements about U.S. Government contract awards, requests for proposals, research and development sources sought, sole-source negotiations, long-range planning estimates and advanced planning procurement information for the engineered systems and services market. Specifically, this data base provides a measurement of: (a) the systems being studied, developed, engineered, produced, installed, operated and retrofitted; (b) the companies producing these systems; and (c) the agencies entrusted with their conception, development and utilization. Product groups covered include aircraft, communications, data processing, transportation, medical instrumentation, management services, missiles and space, navigation and basic research.

Applications: Analysis of Government contracts; forecasting government activity.

Subject cross reference: 2.1, 2.8, 3.2, 3.5, 5.3, 5.8, 6.2, 8.1, and 10.4.

Geographic coverage: Domestic.

Time coverage: 1960 to present.

Online vendor(s): DIALOG Information Services, Inc.

DEVELOPING COUNTRIES PRIMARY SOURCE DATA BANK

Producer: Data Resources, Inc.
29 Hartwell Avenue
Lexington, Massachusetts 02173
(617) 861-0165

Class: Statistical.

Data source: Country bulletins; government news releases, central banks, and various statistical institutions.

Size: Several time series.

Maintenance: Monthly, quarterly, and annually.

Primary subject: Miltidisciplinary.

Secondary subject: N/A

Profile: Maintains economic profiles of leading economic indicators for the developing countries of Africa and Middle East. Coverage includes balance of payments, commercial bank statistics, employment statistics, industrial production data, foreign exchange data, imports and exports, price indexes, national accounts data, prices and wages and related financial statistics.

Applications: Third World Country comparisons and development (expansion) analysis; credit and investment decisions.

Subject cross reference: 5.9, 6.8, 9.12, 9.20, and 10.8.

Geographic coverage: Africa and the Middle East.

Time coverage: Varies by series.

Online vendor(s): Data Resources, Inc.

DISCLOSURE II

Producer: Disclosure, Inc.
5161 River Road
Bethesda, Maryland 20816
(301) 951-1300
(800) 638-8076

Class: Statistical and Reference.

Data source: 7-Q, 8-K, 10-C, 10-K, 10-Q, 12-K, proxy statements, prospectus, annual report, and other SEC-required filings of public U.S. corporations and foreign corporations trading stock in the United States.

Size: 14,198 records.

Maintenance: Weekly.

Primary subject: Banking, Economics and Finance.

Secondary subject: Long-Range Strategic Planning.

Profile: Provides extracts of reports filed with the Securities and Exchange Commission by publicly owned companies. These filings of over 11,000 companies provide an extremely reliable and detailed summary of public financial and administrative data. The user may profile company data by name, address, SIC, balance sheet data, income statement data, and full text summaries highlighting the management of each company.

Applications: Marketing intelligence; competitive profiles; legal and accounting research; corporate planning and development.

Subject cross reference: 1.1, 1.10, 1.11, 1.12, 2.1, 9.13, 10.1, 10.2, 10.4, and 10.7.

Geographic coverage: Domestic.

Time coverage: Maintains current data only.

Online vendor(s): Business Information Services (Control Data)
DIALOG Information Services, Inc.
Dow Jones & Company, Inc.
Mead Data Central/LEXIS
The New York Times Information Service, Inc.

DODGE CONSTRUCTION ANALYSIS SYSTEM

Producer: McGraw-Hill Information Systems Company
F. W. Dodge Division
1221 Avenue of the Americas
New York, New York 10020
(212) 997-1221

Class: Statistical.

Data source: Dodge Division field surveys, reports and contacts.

Size: One-half million cross-classifications of construction data.

Maintenance: Monthly.

Primary subject: General Management (real estate and building trends).

Secondary subject: Industrial and Manufacturing Planning.

Profile: Maintains a wide variety of highly specific building statistics. Coverage is provided for over a half-million cross classifications of construction data based on 209 structure types, two ownership categories (public or private) and location by over 3,000 counties. Data coverage includes the number of projects, square footage, contract value and the number of dwelling units for each cross-classification.

Applications: Product line analysis; market share and sales territory analysis; distribution planning.

Subject cross reference: 2.5, 3.4, 7.4, 7.5, 7.9, 7.10, 7.11, and 9.15.

Geographic coverage: Domestic.

Time coverage: 1970 to present.

Online vendor(s): Data Resources, Inc.

DOE ENERGY DATA BASE (EDB)

Producer: U.S. Department of Energy (DOE)
Technical Information Center
Post Office Box 62
Oak Ridge, Tennessee 37830
(615) 576-1188

Class: Reference.

Data source: Journals, conference papers, books, patents, government reports, dissertations and translations.

Size: 640,000 records.

Maintenance: Approximately 13,000 records monthly.

Primary subject: Research and Development.

Secondary subject: Long-Range Planning (energy).

Profile: Maintains citations and abstracts on international literature pertaining to all aspects of energy and related topics. All manner of energy topics are included: nuclear, wind, fossil, geothermal, tidal, and solar. Also covered are the related topics of environment, policy and conservation.

Applications: Advanced energy research; policy decisions and regulations affecting energy planning.

Subject cross reference: 6.3, 6.6, and 10.5.

Geographic coverage: International.

Time coverage: Late 1800's to present; however, most is from early 1970's to present.

Online vendor(s): BRS, Inc.
DIALOG Information Services, Inc.
SDC Search Service.

DOW JONES NEWS/RETRIEVAL SERVICE AND STOCK QUOTE REPORTER

Producer: Dow Jones & Company, Inc.
Post Office Box 300
Princeton, New Jersey 08540
(800) 257-5114
(609) 452-2000

Class: Reference and Statistical.

Data source: *Barron's* and *Dow Jones News Service*, and all major stock exchanges.

Size: 6,000 companies.

Maintenance: Continuous (news age ranges from 60 seconds to 90 days).

Primary subject: Banking, Economics, and Finance.

Secondary subject: Multidisciplinary.

Profile: The News/Retrieval Service maintains full-text news and articles from major financial publications such as the *Wall Street Journal, Dow Jones News* and *Barron's*. Coverage is for 6,000 + companies, 30 industries, major government agencies, and foreign countries. The Stock Quote Reporter maintains price quotations for most stock exchange companies (6,000 +). Also covered are preferred issues, warrants, options, bonds, mutual funds and some U.S. Treasury issues.

Applications: User may retrieve news and stock activity by corporate stock symbol, industry or government codes and DJ miscellaneous codes.

Subject cross reference: 1.8, 1.9, 1.10, 1.11, 1.12, 1.14, 1.16, 2.1, and 10.7.

Geographic coverage: Domestic.

Time coverage: Latest 90 days of news.

Online vendor(s): BRS, Inc.
Dow Jones & Company, Inc.

DRI CAPSULE: EEI CAPSULE

Producer: Data Resources, Inc. (DRI) and Evans Economics, Inc. (EEI)
Data Resources, Inc.
29 Hartwell Avenue
Lexington, Massachusetts 02173
(617) 861-0165

Evan's Economics, Inc.
1211 Connecticut Ave. N.W.
Suite 710
Washington, D.C. 20036
(202) 342-0050

Class: Statistical.

Data source: International Monetary Fund, Standard & Poor's, Investor Management Sciences, and private research firms.

Size: 3,700 time series.

Maintenance: Monthly.

Primary subject: Banking, Economics, and Finance.

Secondary subject: N/A

Profile: DRI and EEI capsule data bases contain U.S. socio-economic data, and consist of over 3,700 monthly, quarterly and annual time series. Data coverage includes money supply, money market rates, balance of payments, population, labor force, employment, earnings, national income, forecasts and producer prices.

Applications: Economic forecasting; analysis of time series data as related to budgeting, revenue, expenses and planning.

Subject cross reference: 1.5, 1.8, 2.13, and 10.7.

Geographic coverage: Domestic.

Time coverage: 1947 to present.

Online vendor(s): Business Information Services (EEI)
I. P. Sharp Associates (DRI)
United Telecom Computer Group (DRI).

DRI FINANCIAL AND CREDIT STATISTICS (DRI-FACS)

Producer: Data Resources, Inc.
29 Hartwell Avenue
Lexington, Massachusetts 02173
(617) 861-0165

Class: Statistical.

Data source: Federal Reserve releases, U.S. Department of the Treasury.

Size: N/A

Maintenance: Daily, Weekly, Monthly, and Quarterly.

Primary subject: Banking, Economics, and Finance.

Secondary subject: N/A

Profile: A collection of financial data which are maintained by DRI. The coverage area is broad for both current and historical data. Areas covered include daily/weekly interest rates covering domestic money and bond markets; U.S. Government security issues; international money and foreign exchange rates; daily financial futures data; weekly and monthly financial operating statistics of banks, including supply factors in domestic capital markets, Federal Reserve Bank reserves and credit, U.S. Treasury holdings, weekly conditions of large commercial banks and thrift institutions' activity; quarterly flow of U.S. funds accounts.

Applications: Monitoring world financial and commodity markets; investment and borrowing decisions.

Subject cross reference: 1.2, 1.3, 1.4, 1.5, 1.6, 1.7, 1.8, 1.9, 1.12, 1.14, 9.13, 10.2, and 10.7.

Geographic coverage: International.

Time coverage: 1973 to present.

Online vendor(s): Data Resources, Inc.

DRI INDUSTRY FINANCIAL SERVICE DATA BANK (DRIFS)

Producer: Data Resources, Inc.
29 Hartwell Avenue
Lexington, Massachusetts 02173
(617) 861-0165

Class: Statistical.

Data source: Company quarterly and annual reports.

Size: 600 company records.

Maintenance: Annually, quarterly and monthly.

Primary subject: Banking, Economics, and Finance.

Secondary subject: N/A

Profile: Maintains company and industry data and forecasts that are structured for use by the investment, financial and corporate communities. Sales, income, balance sheet data and forecasts are available for user software routines. Data are available for 81 industries and approximately 600 individual companies.

Applications: Examination of industry growth potential; investment planning (risk analysis); alternative economic growth path(s).

Subject cross reference: 1.8, 1.9, 1.11, 7.5, and 10.7.

Geographic coverage: Domestic.

Time coverage: Most current data.

Online vendor(s): Data Resources, Inc.

DRILLING ACTIVITY ANALYSIS SYSTEMS (DAAS)®

Producer: Petroleum Information Corporation
Box 2612
Denver, Colorado 80201
(303) 825-2181

Class: Statistical.

Data source: Data are provided by producer.

Size: N/A

Maintenance: Monthly.

Primary subject: Long-Range Strategic Planning (energy).

Secondary subject: N/A

Profile: A sophisticated time-share system designed to allow quick compilation, comparison and analysis of drilling data, nationwide. Coverage includes well identification, location, permit, spud and completion data, well class, well potential, formation, status, field name, geologic province, drill depth and costs. Over 30 standard report formats are available.

Applications: Well profit and loss analysis; expense breakouts; well analysis.

Subject cross reference: 10.5.

Geographic coverage: Domestic.

Time coverage: 1974 to present.

Online vendor(s): General Electric Information Services Co.

DRI-SEC (SECURITIES DATA BANK)

Producer: Data Resources, Inc.
29 Hartwell Avenue
Lexington, Massachusetts 02173
(617) 861-0165

Class: Statistical.

Data source: Telestat Systems, Inc., Merill Lynch.

Size: 55,000 security issues.

Maintenance: Daily, weekly, monthly, quarterly & annually.

Primary subject: Banking, Economics, and Finance.

Secondary subject: N/A

Profile: A securities data bank which maintains current and historical trading, financial, and descriptive information for over 55,000 security issues. Dri-Sec is broken out into three principal parts: (1) The master data base contains descriptive and status information, and current fundamental data on all securities; (2) the price data base maintains an extensive historical record of daily volumes, highs, lows, and closing prices; (3) the dividend data base maintains complete dividend and stock distribution statistics for equity issues and bond interest payment for debt issues.

Applications: Short-term quantitative and qualitative investment decisions.

Subject cross reference: 1.3, 1.12, 1.16, 10.2, and 10.7.

Geographic coverage: Domestic.

Time coverage: Mostly current, but with selective time series.

Online vendor(s): Data Resources, Inc.

DRUG INFO AND ALCOHOL USE/ABUSE

Producer: Drug Information Service Center (DISC)
University of Minnesota
College of Pharmacy
Minneapolis, Minnesota 55455
(612) 376-7190

Class: Reference.

Data source: Journals, conference papers, instructional guides, films, governmental documents, and data bases.

Size: 4,000 records.

Maintenance: Quarterly.

Primary subject: General Management (health care).

Secondary subject: N/A

Profile: Two separate data collections: Drug Info maintains citations and abstracts which deal primarily with the sociological and psychological aspects of alcohol and drug use/abuse. Alcohol Use/Abuse maintains primarily with research in the area of chemical dependency.

Applications: Drug rehabilitation information and sources; treatment evaluations.

Subject cross reference: 6.7 and 9.7.

Geographic coverage: Domestic.

Time coverage: 1968 to present.

Online vendor(s): BRS, Inc.

DUN'S FINANCIAL PROFILES®

Producer: Dun & Bradstreet, Inc.
99 Church Street
New York, New York 10007
(212) 285-7000

Class: Statistical.

Data source: Company financial statements.

Size: 400,000 companies.

Maintenance: Weekly.

Primary subject: Banking, Economics, and Finance.

Secondary subject: N/A

Profile: Maintains annual financial (balance sheet and profit/loss statement) data for public and private companies. Data is by name, address, and SIC code. Purpose is to provide information on new business candidates.

Applications: Company financial profiles, comparisons and market analysis; user may produce a company market and intelligence directory.

Subject cross reference: 1.11.

Geographic coverage: Domestic.

Time coverage: Most current data.

Online vendor(s): DIALOG Information Services, Inc.
National CSS, Inc.

DUNSPRINT

Producer: Dun & Bradstreet, Inc.
99 Church Street
New York, New York 10007
(212) 285-7669

Class: Statistical and Reference.

Data source: Dun's *Business Information Reports.*

Size: 4,000,000 reports.

Maintenance: Daily.

Primary subject: Banking, Economics, and Finance.

Secondary subject: N/A

Profile: Provides basic company profile information on U.S. companies. Data items include company name and address, principal officers and responsibilities, SIC number, various pieces of financial statement data, number of employees, bill-payment history, and operating facts.

Applications: Company profiles; history for competitive advantage analyses; opportunity management.

Subject cross reference: 1.11, 1.12, 2.1, 2.10, 3.4, 4.2, and 10.3.

Geographic coverage: Primarily domestic, and some protectorates.

Time coverage: Current data.

Online vendor(s): Dun & Bradstreet, Inc.

DWIGHT'S ENERGYDATA

Producer: Dwight's Energydata, Inc.
1201 Exchange Drive
Richardson, Texas 75081
(214) 783-8002
(800) 224-4784

Class: Statistical.

Data source: State and federal regulatory agencies.

Size: 400,000+ records.

Maintenance: Quarterly.

Primary subject: Long-Range Strategic Planning (energy).

Secondary subject: N/A

Profile: Covers monthly and annual production data for gas wells and oil leases. Coverage includes descriptive data on each well or lease, operator name, location, county, reservoir, name and number of field, pressure, depth, API number, completion date, and first production date.

Applications: Oil and lease management; lottery decisions; land management.

Subject cross reference: 10.5.

Geographic coverage: Wyoming, Gulf Coast, Utah, North Dakota, Kansas, Texas, Louisiana, New Mexico, Arkansas and Oklahoma.

Time coverage: Past seven years.

Online vendor(s): General Electric Information Services Co.

ECONOMICS ABSTRACTS INTERNATIONAL

Producer: Learned Information Ltd.
Besselsleigh Road
Abingdon, Oxford, England 0X13 6EF
Oxford (0865) 730275

Class: Reference.

Data source: International literature, e.g., journals, books, directories, corporate records, and reports.

Size: 107,663 records.

Maintenance: 1,250 records monthly.

Primary subject: Banking, Economics and Finance.

Secondary subject: Marketing Planning.

Profile: Provides coverage of the World's literature on markets, industries, country; specific economic data and research in the fields of economic science and management. Also covered is information specific to certain industries, regulations, investments, distribution channels and economic structures.

Applications: International marketing research and analysis; economic trends by country.

Subject cross reference: 1.8, 1.9, 1.12, 1.15, 2.5, 2.6, 2.10, and 9.12.

Geographic coverage: International.

Time coverage: 1974 to present.

Online vendor(s): BELINDIS
DIALOG Information Services, Inc.

ECONOMIST'S STATISTICS®

Producer: James R. Lymburner & Sons Limited
20 Victoria Street
Toronto, Ontario, Canada M5C 1Y1
(416) 862-0595

Class: Statistical.

Data source: World-wide currency and commodity exchanges.

Size: Number of currencies varies by exchange.

Maintenance: Daily.

Primary subject: Banking, Economics, and Finance.

Secondary subject: N/A

Profile: Contains daily time series of exchange rates for the major world currencies. The number of currencies covered and the amount of data history vary among exchanges. The currency rate is expressed in the currency of the country in which the exchange is located.

Applications: Financial reporting analysis and consolidations; contracts administration (international).

Subject cross reference: 1.7, 1.9, 1.15, and 9.12.

Geographic coverage: North America, Western Europe and Far East.

Time coverage: Most current with varying degrees of history.

Online vendor(s): I. P. Sharp Associates.

EDUCATIONAL RESOURCES INFORMATION CENTER (ERIC)®

Producer: U.S. Department of Education
National Institute of Education
ERIC Processing and Reference Facility
4833 Rugby Avenue, Suite 303
Bethesda, Maryland 20014
(301) 656-9723

Class: Reference.

Data source: Journals and special reports.

Size: 421,925 citations.

Maintenance: Approximately 2,500 citations monthly.

Primary subject: General Management (education).

Secondary subject: N/A

Profile: A comprehensive data base on educational materials. It consists of two main files: *Research in Education,* which is concerned with identifying the most significant and timely educational research reports and projects, and *Current Index to Journals in Educations,* which indexes more than 700 publications of interest to every segment of the educational profession.

Applications: Educational research and decision support reference.

Subject cross reference: 9.5.

Geographic coverage: Domestic.

Time coverage: 1966 to present.

Online vendor(s): BRS, Inc.
DIALOG Information Services, Inc.
SDC Search Service.

EIS DIGESTS OF ENVIRONMENTAL IMPACT STATEMENTS®

Producer: Information Resources Press—Horner & Company
1700 North Moore Street
Suite 700
Arlington, Virginia 22209
(703) 558-8270

Class: Reference.

Data source: All environmental impact statements issued or received by the Department of Interior and other federal agencies.

Size: 1,400 EIS statements yearly.

Maintenance: Monthly.

Primary subject: Environmental, Social & Political Affairs.

Secondary subject: N/A

Profile: Maintains abstracts from various governmental departments which summarize environmental impact studies on proposed major projects of various industries and other organizations. Coverage includes the environmental aspects of transportation, defense programs, energy, hazardous waste, land use, water resources, and other areas. Digests of both draft and final statements are included.

Applications: Project management and development; project budget and forecast estimates; project research (legal implications).

Subject cross reference: 5.6, 5.8, 6.3, and 6.6.

Geographic coverage: Domestic.

Time coverage: 1970 to present.

Online vendor(s): BRS, Inc.

EIS INDUSTRIAL PLANTS

Producer: Economic Information Systems, Inc. (EIS)
310 Madison Avenue
New York, New York 10017
(212) 697-6080

Class: Statistical.

Data source: Census Bureau statistics, financial reports, journals, books, and directories.

Size: 130,000 records.

Maintenance: Approximately 60,000 revisions annually.

Primary subject: Multidisciplinary.

Secondary subject: Marketing Planning.

Profile: Offers information on a broad range of questions pertaining to the U.S. industrial economy. Coverage includes information on 130,000 establishments, representing 67,000 firms, which have annualized sales of more than $500,000 and have more than 20 employees. Data items include name, address, telephone number of each plant, SIC code, shipment values, employment size, market share estimate, and parent company identification.

Applications: Market share analysis; market potential studies; line of business identification; company profiles; SIC code comparisons.

Subject cross reference: 1.11, 2.1, 2.10, 3.4, 3.5, 7.4, 7.11, and 10.3.

Geographic coverage: Domestic.

Time coverage: Most current data.

Online vendor(s): Business Information Services (Control Data)
Control Data Corporation—Cybernet
DIALOG Information Services, Inc.

EIS NON-MANUFACTURING ESTABLISHMENTS

Producer: Economic Information Systems, Inc. (EIS)
310 Madison Avenue
New York, New York 10017
(212) 697-6080

Class: Statistical.

Data source: Census Bureau statistics, financial reports, journals, books, and directories.

Size: 200,000+ records.

Maintenance: Annual or as needed.

Primary subject: Multidisciplinary.

Secondary subject: Marketing Planning.

Profile: Similar to EIS Industrial Plants (see separate profile listing) except focus is on agriculture, construction, transportation, utilities, finance, and service businesses.

Applications: Market share analysis; market potential studies; line of business identification; company profiles; SIC code comparisons.

Subject cross reference: 1.11, 2.1, 2.10, 3.4, 3.5, 7.11, 9.1, 9.15, 9.16, 9.17, and 10.3.

Geographic coverage: Domestic.

Time coverage: Most current data.

Online vendor(s): Business Information Services (Control Data)
Control Data Corporation—Cybernet
DIALOG Information Services, Inc.

ELCOM DATA BASE (ELECTRONICS AND COMPUTERS)

Producer: Cambridge Scientific Abstracts (CSA)
6611 Kenilworth Avenue
Suite 307
Riverdale, Maryland 20840
(301) 951-1327

Class: Reference.

Data source: "Electronics and Communications Abstracts Journal" and "Information Systems (CISA) Abstracts Journal."

Size: 60,000+ records.

Maintenance: Approximately 3,000 monthly.

Primary subject: General Management (information processing technology).

Secondary subject: N/A

Profile: Maintains information on the following: electronic physics, electronic systems and applications, electronic circuits, communications, electronic devices; computer software, computer applications, computer math and computer electronics. Data base includes periodicals, government reports, conference proceedings, books, dissertations and patents.

Applications: Hardware and software selection; hardware and software applications and analysis; computer system enhancement ideas.

Subject cross reference: 2.9, 8.2, 8.3, 8.4, 8.7, 8.8, 8.9, and 9.11.

Geographic coverage: International.

Time coverage: 1977 to present.

Online vendor(s): SDC Search Service.

ELECTRONIC MATERIALS INFORMATION SERVICE (EMIS)

Producer: Institution of Electrical Engineers (IEF)
Station House Hitchin
Nightengale Road
Herts, England SG5 1RJ
(0462) 53331

Class: Reference.

Data source: Published documents and scientific submissions to EMIS.

Size: 1 million+ abstracts.

Maintenance: Daily.

Primary subject: Research and Development.

Secondary subject: N/A

Profile: Maintains references to information on properties of selected solid state materials (e.g., silicon, gallium arsenide, indium phosphide, and lithium niobate). Also maintains information on commercial suppliers of solid state electronic materials.

Applications: Electronics supplier identification; basic electronics research.

Subject cross reference: 7.11 and 8.2.

Geographic coverage: International.

Time coverage: 1898 to present.

Online vendor(s): General Electric Information Services Co.

ELECTRIC POWER INDUSTRY ABSTRACTS (EPIA)

Producer: Edison Electric Institute
c/o Utility Data Institute, Inc.
1225 Nineteenth Street, N.W., Suite 250
Washington, D.C. 20036
(202) 887-1922

Class: Reference.

Data source: Technical reports and studies prepared by electric utilities and federal/state agencies.

Size: Over 20,000 citations.

Maintenance: Five times yearly.

Primary subject: Long-Range Strategic Planning (energy).

Secondary subject: N/A

Profile: Provides access to literature on electric power plants and related facilities. Topics include the environmental effects of electric power plants and associated transmission lines; power plant siting methodologies; fuel transportation, storage and use; licensing and permit information, energy resources; monitoring programs, safety and risk management, waste disposal facilities; coastal zone management and land-use studies.

Applications: Nuclear power plant management and technical comparisons.

Subject cross reference: 6.3, 6.6, 7.1, 7.3, 7.4, 7.5, 7.9, 7.10, and 10.5.

Geographic coverage: Domestic.

Time coverage: 1975 to present.

Online vendor(s): SDC Search Service.

ENCYCLOPEDIA OF ASSOCIATIONS (EA)

Producer: Gale Research Company
Book Tower
Detroit, Michigan 48226
(313) 961-2242

Class: Reference.

Data source: *Encyclopedia of Associations* via questionnaires and telephone contacts.

Size: 14,724 records.

Maintenance: Annual updates.

Primary subject: Multidisciplinary.

Secondary subject: N/A

Profile: Provides detailed information on several thousand trade associations, professional societies, labor unions, fraternal and patriotic organizations and similar types of groups consisting of voluntary members. Data items include name, address, phone number, size, scope or purpose of the organization, publications available and the location and date of annual conference.

Applications: Fund raising and development; public relations; information needs identification.

Subject cross reference: 2.10, 4.6, 9.2, 9.4, and 9.20.

Geographic coverage: Domestic.

Time coverage: Most current data.

Online vendor(s): DIALOG Information Services, Inc.

ENERGY

Producer: Chase Econometrics/Interactive Data Corporation
486 Totten Pond Road
Waltham, Massachusetts 02154
(617) 890-1234

Class: Statistical.

Data source: American Petroleum Institute, U.S. Bureau of Mines, U.S. Department of Energy, and Edison Electric Institute.

Size: 40,000 time series.

Maintenance: Continuous.

Primary subject: Long-Range Strategic Planning (energy).

Secondary subject: N/A

Profile: Provides state, national, and international energy statistics for petroleum, natural gas, coal, and electricity. Data items include demand, supply, world energy supplies, state energy consumption, and various institutes and government agency statistics.

Applications: Energy management decisions.

Subject cross reference: 10.5.

Geographic coverage: Primarily domestic.

Time coverage: Approximately 1950 to present; varies by series.

Online vendor(s): Chase Econometrics/Interactive Data Corp.

ENERGY BIBLIOGRAPHY & INDEX (EBI)

Producer: Gulf Publishing Company and Texas A&M
University Library
P.O. Box 2608
3301 Allen Parkway
Houston, Texas 77001
(713) 529-4301
Reference Division
College Station, Texas 77843
(713) 845-5741

Class: Reference.

Data source: Non-journal literature: books, serials, periodicals, government documents, and some technical reports.

Size: 14,000 records (held in the Texas A&M Library).

Maintenance: Periodically.

Primary subject: Long-Range Strategic Planning (energy).

Secondary subject: N/A

Profile: Maintains citations and abstracts of worldwide literature on energy from the Texas A&M library. Subject coverage includes conservation, production, utilization, fuels, energy storage, alternative energy sources, power plants, transmission systems. Economic, political, environmental and statistical aspects of energy-related issues and aspects are covered as well.

Applications: Energy research and management; energy use forecasts.

Subject cross reference: 6.3, 6.6, 8.8, and 10.5.

Geographic coverage: International.

Time coverage: Many references from mid-1800's. Most from 1919 to present.

Online vendor(s): SDC Search Service.

ENERGY CALENDAR (ENC)

Producer: Energy, Mines and Resources (Canada)
CANMET, Technology Information Division
555 Booth Street
Ottawa, Ontario, Canada K1A 0G1
(613) 995-4029

Class: Reference.

Data source: Sponsors of the various events described.

Size: N/A

Maintenance: Monthly.

Primary subject: Long-Range Strategic Planning (energy).

Secondary subject: N/A

Profile: Provides a listing of energy conferences and seminars, both Canadian and international, with descriptions of the location, sponsors, abstract of the event(s), and contacts.

Applications: Energy research.

Subject cross reference: 10.5.

Geographic coverage: International.

Time coverage: Current and near future events only.

Online vendor(s): QL Systems Ltd.

ENERGY DATA BANK

Producer: Data Resources, Inc.
29 Hartwell Avenue
Lexington, Massachusetts 02173
(617) 861-0165

Class: Statistical.

Data source: American Gas Association, American Petroleum Institute, Canadian Petroleum Association, Edison Electric Institute, U.S. Department of Energy, and U.S. Department of Commerce.

Size: 20,000+ time series.

Maintenance: Weekly, monthly, quarterly and annually.

Primary subject: Long-Range Strategic Planning (energy).

Secondary subject: N/A

Profile: This data base details energy sources and uses for all major fuels. This includes information on fossil fuel, supplies, demands, utility industry inputs, and motor vehicle consumption and usage. Coverage detail consists of prices and costs, reserves, production, imports/exports, supply and distribution, operating data of refineries and utilities.

Applications: Analysis of future market demands; current market monitoring and analysis; governmental impact analysis.

Subject cross reference: 7.10 and 10.5.

Geographic coverage: Domestic.

Time coverage: Varies depending on time series; most from 1960's to present.

Online vendor(s): Data Resources, Inc.

ENERGYLINE®

Producer: Environment Information Center, Inc.
292 Madison Avenue
New York, New York 10017
(212) 949-9494

Class: Reference.

Data source: The *Energy Index* produced from periodicals, books, films, speeches, symposia, and corporate reports.

Size: 32,509 citations.

Maintenance: Approximately 500 monthly.

Primary subject: Long-Range Strategic Planning (energy).

Secondary subject: N/A

Profile: Provides a primary source for information relating specifically to energy. The data are drawn from fields such as chemistry or engineering, but only as they relate to energy issues or problems. Coverage includes congressional committee prints, books, journals, conference proceedings, speeches and statistics.

Applications: User information on scientific, technical, socio-economic, governmental policy and planning and current affairs aspects of energy.

Subject cross reference: 10.5.

Geographic coverage: International.

Time coverage: 1971 to present.

Online vendor(s): BRS, Inc.
DIALOG Information Services, Inc.
ESA-IRS
SDC Search Service.

ENERGYNET®

Producer: Environment Information Center, Inc.
292 Madison Avenue
New York, New York 10017
(212) 949-9494

Class: Reference.

Data source: *The Energy Directory*.

Size: 3,500 records.

Maintenance: Quarterly.

Primary subject: Long-Range Strategic Planning (energy).

Secondary subject: N/A

Profile: Maintains information on over 3,000 organizations who have any energy-related connection. The following organizations are included: federal and state energy offices, congressional committees and subcommittees, professional associations, research groups or centers, public interest groups, utilities; oil, gas, coal companies; consulting companies and other energy consuming companies. Data fields include organization's name, address, phone, parent and subsidiary names, product or service lines, chief officers and a profile description of the organization.

Applications: Energy management and planning; energy use analysis by organization.

Subject cross reference: 10.5.

Geographic coverage: Domestic.

Time coverage: 1982 to present.

Online vendor(s): DIALOG Information Services, Inc.

ENERGY PROGRAMS (ENP)

Producer: Energy, Mines and Resources (Canada)
CANMET, Technology Information Division
555 Booth Street
Ottawa, Ontario, Canada K1A 0G1
(613) 995-4029

Class: Reference.

Data source: Canadian government energy legislation records.

Size: N/A

Maintenance: Irregularly.

Primary subject: Long-Range Strategic Planning (energy).

Secondary subject: N/A

Profile: Descriptions of current Canadian government energy-related programs. Each entry provides a title, ministry responsible for program, contact name and address, and abstract.

Applications: Energy management and opportunity analysis.

Subject cross reference: 10.5.

Geographic coverage: Canada.

Time coverage: Current programs.

Online vendor(s): QL Systems Ltd.

ENERGY PROJECTS (ENG)

Producer: Energy, Mines and Resources (Canada)
CANMET, Technology Information Division
555 Booth Street
Ottawa, Ontario, Canada K1A 0G1
(613) 995-4029

Class: Reference.

Data source: Federal Office of Energy Research and Development of Canada, with assistance from other federal and provincial agencies.

Size: N/A

Maintenance: Infrequently and irregularly.

Primary subject: Long-Range Strategic Planning (energy).

Secondary subject: N/A

Profile: Consists of abstracts concerning energy projects in Canada. Covers conservation, fossil fuels, nuclear energy, renewable energy, energy transportation, and transmission. Each entry includes project name and location, project management responsible, funding agencies, cost, start date, completion date, description (abstract), status, and jurisdiction.

Applications: Energy management and research.

Subject cross reference: 6.3, 6.8, and 10.5.

Geographic coverage: Canada.

Time coverage: Current programs only.

Online vendor(s): QL Systems Limited.

ENVIRODOQ

Producer: Ministere De L'Environnement Du Quebec
Place Innovation
2360 Chemin Ste Foy
Ste Foy, Quebec, Canada G1V 6H2
(418) 643-2795

Class: Reference.

Data source: Monographs, government reports, statistics, maps and impact studies.

Size: 2,000 records.

Maintenance: Monthly.

Primary subject: Environmental, Social, and Political Affairs.

Secondary subject: N/A

Profile: Maintains citations and abstracts of literature pertaining to Quebec's environment. Coverage areas include environmental impact studies, biophysical studies, environmental planning, geological, legal and social science aspects.

Applications: Quebec environmental analysis, programs and decision support.

Subject cross reference: 5.8, 6.3, and 6.6.

Geographic coverage: Quebec, Canada.

Time coverage: 1970 to present.

Online vendor(s): Informatech.

ENVIROLINE®

Producer: Environment Information Center, Inc.
292 Madison Avenue
New York, New York 10017
(212) 949-9494

Class: Reference.

Data source: Industry reports, periodicals, government documents, meeting proceedings, articles and films.

Size: 86,126 citations.

Maintenance: Approximately 600 citations monthly.

Primary subject: Environmental, Social & Political Affairs.

Secondary subject: N/A

Profile: Covers the world's environmental information. It is a comprehensive, interdisciplinary approach providing indexing and abstracting of more than 5,000 international primary and secondary source publications reporting on all aspects of the environment. Field coverage includes: economics, biology, technology, law, political science, management and chemistry.

Applications: Environmental research studies.

Subject cross reference: 6.3, 6.4, 6.5, and 6.6.

Geographic coverage: International.

Time coverage: 1971 to present.

Online vendor(s): BRS, Inc.
DIALOG Information Services, Inc.
SDC Search Service.

ENVIRONMENTAL PERIODICALS BIBLIOGRAPHY (EPB)

Producer: International Academy at Santa Barbara
Environmental Studies Institute
2074 Alameda Padre Sierra
Santa Barbara, California 93103
(805) 965-5010

Class: Reference.

Data source: 300 international journals.

Size: 169,397 records.

Maintenance: Approximately 5,000 records bimonthly.

Primary subject: Environmental, Social and Political Affairs.

Secondary subject: N/A

Profile: Covers the fields of general human ecology, atmospheric studies, land resources, nutrition and health, water resources, energy and related environmental research topics.

Applications: Environmental research for librarians, chemists, land-use planners, government officials and corporate executives.

Subject cross reference: 6.3, 6.6, and 10.5.

Geographic coverage: Domestic.

Time coverage: 1973 to present.

Online vendor(s): DIALOG Information Services, Inc.

EPILEPSYLINE

Producer: U.S. National Institutes of Health
National Institute of Neurological and
Communicative Disorders and Stroke
9000 Rockville Pike
Bethesda, Maryland 20014
(301) 496-9271

Class: Reference.

Data source: Journal articles from 3,500+ periodicals.

Size: 30,000 records.

Maintenance: Approximately 650 records quarterly.

Primary subject: Multidisciplinary.

Secondary subject: N/A

Profile: Maintains citations and abstracts of International
literature (which have been abstracted by Excerpta
Medica) relative to all aspects and implications of epilepsy.
Areas covered include physiology, biochemistry, seizures,
etiology, genetics, systemic changes, diagnostic aids,
treatments, psychology, sociology and epidemiology.

Applications: Epileptic research and decision support service.

Subject cross reference: 4.7, 8.6, 9.7.

Geographic coverage: International.

Time coverage: 1945–1978.

Online vendor(s): National Library of Medicine.

EURABANK

Producer: European-American Bank & Trust Company
10 Hanover Square
New York, New York 10016
(212) 437-4300

Class: Statistical.

Data source: Annual reports.

Size: 1,500 banks.

Maintenance: Annually.

Primary subject: Banking, Economics, and Finance.

Secondary subject: N/A

Profile: Maintains financial profiles of banks in 100+
countries in Europe, North America, South America and
Australia. Data coverage includes address, country, deposit
statistics, capital, prime assets, net income and loans
activity.

Applications: User may prepare special ranking reports and
comparisons by geographical segmentation.

Subject cross reference: 1.2, 1.3, 1.11, and 2.1.

Geographic coverage: International.

Time coverage: Most recent five years.

Online vendor(s): Business Information Services (Control
Data).

EUROCHARTS COMMODITIES

Producer: Eurocharts Ltd.
Plantation House, 2nd Floor, E Section
10/15 Mincing Lane
London, England EC3M 3DB
(01) 626-8765

Class: Statistical.

Data source: London, New York and Chicago futures market.

Size: N/A

Maintenance: Daily.

Primary subject: Banking, Economics and Finance
(commodities).

Secondary subject: N/A

Profile: The Commodities data base contains daily and
monthly time series of prices and volumes for all
commodities traded on the London, New York and Chicago
futures markets. Data items include open, high, low, close,
volume and open interest for both metals and soft
commodities.

Applications: Commodities management and investment.

Subject cross reference: 1.16.

Geographic coverage: U.S. and the United Kingdom.

Time coverage: Daily data, 1973 to present; monthly data, 1960
to present.

Online vendor(s): I. P. Sharp Associates.

EUROFILE (FILE OF FILES)

Producer: European Association of Information Services
(EUSIDIC)
Post Office Box 85566
The Hague, The Netherlands

Class: Reference.

Data source: EUSIDIC Data Base Guide.

Size: N/A

Maintenance: Quarterly.

Primary subject: Multidisciplinary.

Secondary subject: N/A

Profile: Maintains references to data bases or data banks
available to the public in Europe. Coverage includes those
data bases available either online or offline (batch) or those
data bases not in Europe which are accessible through a
telecommunications network. Contains data on each data
base's brokers, originators, and operators.

Applications: Guide to European data base retrieval systems.

Subject cross reference: 1.19, 2.16, 3.6, 4.6, 5.9, 6.8, 7.12, 8.9,
9.20, and 10.8.

Geographic coverage: Europe.

Time coverage: Current data.

Online vendor(s): ECHO Services (EUSIDICFILE)
ESA-IRS.

EUROPEAN NATIONAL SOURCE

Producer: Data Resources, Inc.
29 Hartwell Avenue
Lexington, Massachusetts 02173
(617) 861-0165

Class: Statistical.

Data source: Central statistical agencies (various countries), government ministries, central banks, and trade organizations.

Size: Eleven countries.

Maintenance: Weekly, monthly, quarterly and annually.

Primary subject: Banking, Economics, and Finance.

Secondary subject: N/A

Profile: Covers a wide range of macroeconomic, microeconomic and financial variables which were designed to provide an economic profile of several European countries. Coverage includes: industrial production, national income and product accounts, wage and prices by sector, labor force and unemployment by sector, consumer and retail trade behavior, money supply and components, interest and exchange rates, balance of payments and trade and construction sector indicators.

Applications: Econometric modeling.

Subject cross reference: 1.8, 1.9, 1.12, 2.5, 9.6, and 9.16.

Geographic coverage: Belgium, Denmark, France, Germany, Ireland, Italy, The Netherlands, Spain, Sweden, Switzerland and the United Kingdom.

Time coverage: N/A

Online vendor(s): Data Resources, Inc.

EUROPEAN PATENT REGISTER (EPR)

Producer: European Patent Office (EPO)
Post Box 5818 Patentlaan 2
NL-2280 HV Rijswijk
Netherlands
(070) 906-789

Class: Reference.

Data source: European Patent Office information.

Size: 6,000.

Maintenance: Weekly.

Primary subject: Research and Development.

Secondary subject: N/A

Profile: Maintains bibliographic information on European patents issued and/or applied for.

Applications: European technology comparisons; product differentiation analysis.

Subject cross reference: 2.12 and 8.7.

Geographic coverage: Europe.

Time coverage: 1978 to present.

Online vendor(s): European Patent Office (European Patents Register)
Telesystemes—Questel (INPI-2).

EUROPROSPECTS-EUROPEAN ECONOMIC INDICATORS

Producer: ADP Network Services, Inc.
175 Jackson Plaza
Ann Arbor, Michigan 48106
(313) 769-6800

Class: Statistical.

Data source: European government agencies (central banks, statistical offices, and official country publishers).

Size: 1,400 time series.

Maintenance: Daily.

Primary subject: Banking, Economics, and Finance.

Secondary subject: N/A

Profile: Offers data on capital accounts, employment, exchange rates, housing, industrial production, interest rates, trade balances, money stock, official financing and reserves, population, private investment, retail sales, and wages.

Applications: Optimization of planning and decisions for corporate development; performance analysis; forecasting.

Subject cross reference: 1.3, 1.5, 1.6, 1.7, 1.8, 1.14, and 10.7.

Geographic coverage: Europe.

Time coverage: 1970 to present.

Online vendor(s): ADP Network Services, Inc.

EVANS ECONOMICS AGRICULTURE DATA BASE

Producer: Evans Economics, Inc.
1211 Connecticut Avenue, N.W.
Suite 710
Washington, D.C. 20036
(202) 342-0050

Class: Statistical.

Data source: U.S. Department of Agriculture, Agriculture Marketing Service, Commodity Research Bureau, Inc., U.S. Census Bureau.

Size: 900 time series.

Maintenance: Continuous.

Primary subject: General Management (agriculture).

Secondary subject: N/A

Profile: Provides national-level data on supply and utilization for major agricultural commodities (barley, beef, chickens, corn, cotton, dairy products, eggs, feed grains, hogs, oats, sorghum, soybean, turkeys, and wheat), prices, farm income, farm marketing, consumer and producer prices, and average hourly earnings.

Applications: Agricultural management and planning.

Subject cross reference: 1.16 and 9.1.

Geographic coverage: Domestic.

Time coverage: Varies by series; most from 1958 to present.

Online vendor(s): Business Information Services (Control Data).

EVANS ECONOMICS CONSUMER PRICE INDEX DATA BASE*

Producer: Evans Economics, Inc.
1211 Connecticut Avenue, N.W.
Suite 710
Washington, D.C. 20036
(202) 342-0050

Class: Statistical.

Data source: Bureau of Labor Statistics (U.S. Department of Labor).

Size: 8,000 + time series.

Maintenance: Monthly.

Primary subject: Banking, Economics, and Finance.

Secondary subject: Marketing Planning.

Profile: Provides time series data on regional (including 28 major cities) and national Consumer Price Indexes supplied by the Bureau of Labor Statistics. Provides both non-seasonally adjusted and seasonally adjusted data.

Applications: Analysis of consumer spending patterns.

Subject cross reference: 1.8, 2.3, 2.5, and 2.14.

Geographic coverage: Domestic.

Time coverage: 1947 to present.

Online vendor(s): Business Information Services (Control Data).

*Note: Chase Econometrics/Interactive Data Corp. has a similar data base.

EVANS ECONOMICS FINANCIAL DATA BASE*

Producer: Evans Economics, Inc.
1211 Connecticut Avenue, N.W.
Suite 710
Washington, D.C. 20036
(202) 342-0050

Class: Statistical.

Data source: Federal Reserve Board, The Bond Buyer, Federal Home Loan Bank Board, Standard & Poor's and U.S. Department of the Treasury.

Size: 2,000 time series.

Maintenance: Continuous.

Primary subject: Banking, Economics, and Finance.

Secondary subject: N/A

Profile: Provides series data on money stock measures, consumer credit, commercial and industrial loans, interest rates, assets and liabilities of commercial banks, indices for stocks/bonds, and various other factors affecting the Federal Reserve Banks System. Data are by both U.S. totals and Federal Reserve District.

Applications: Long-term financial management analysis, decisions and forecasts.

Subject cross reference: 1.2, 1.3, 1.4, 1.6, 1.8, 1.14, 1.15, and 1.16.

Geographic coverage: Domestic.

Time coverage: Varies by series, most data from 1955 to present.

Online vendor(s): Business Information Services (Control Data).

*Note: Chase Econometrics/Interactive Data Corp. has a similar data base.

EVANS ECONOMICS FLOW OF FUNDS DATA BASE*

Producer: Evans Economics, Inc.
1211 Connecticut Avenue, N.W.
Suite 710
Washington, D.C. 20036
(202) 342-0050

Class: Statistical.

Data source: Federal Reserve Board.

Size: 1940 records.

Maintenance: Continual.

Primary subject: Banking, Economics, and Finance.

Secondary subject: N/A

Profile: Contains the complete Flow of Funds National Accounts as published by the Federal Reserve Board. For over 40 sectors in the economy, these accounts measure the aggregate stock and flow of transactions between the financial and non-financial markets. Nonfinancial transactions include sources for savings and investment and receipts for wages, goods and services, taxes, and transfers. Financial transactions include credit market instruments, monetary reserves, and deposit claims on financial institutions.

Applications: Flow of funds accounting; aggregate economic analyses.

Subject cross reference: 1.2, 1.8, and 1.19.

Geographic coverage: Domestic.

Time coverage: 1952 to present.

Online vendor(s): Business Information Services (Control Data).

*Note: Chase Econometrics/Interactive Data Corp. has a similar data base.

EVANS ECONOMICS FORECAST DATA BASE

Producer: Evans Economics, Inc.
1211 Connecticut Avenue, N.W.
Suite 710
Washington, D.C. 20036
(202) 342-0050

Class: Statistical.

Data source: Evans Econometric Models.

Size: 1,000 time series per data base.

Maintenance: Monthly.

Primary subject: Banking, Economics, and Finance.

Secondary subject: N/A

Profile: Comprised of eight separate forecast data bases generated from Evans Economics, Inc. (EEI) models: Standard Macro, Macro Long-Term, Agriculture Model, International Model, Industrial Production, PPI, and short and long-term industry employment. The Macro and Industrial Production forecast data bases provide annual forecast data for ten years; all others provide quarterly data for two years. Historical data is included for all models.

Applications: Econometric forecasting.

Subject cross reference: 1.4, 1.8, 1.19, and 2.14.

Geographic coverage: International.

Time coverage: See profile above.

Online vendor(s): Business Information Services (Control Data).

EVANS ECONOMICS IMF INTERNATIONAL FINANCIAL STATISTICS*

Producer: Evans Economics, Inc.
1211 Connecticut Avenue, N.W.
Suite 710
Washington, D.C. 20036
(202) 342-0050

Class: Statistical.

Data source: International Monetary Fund.

Size: 45,000 series.

Maintenance: Continual.

Primary subject: Banking, Economics, and Finance.

Secondary subject: N/A

Profile: Provides time series data on over 210 countries and geographic areas of the world. Data items include international payments, exchange rates, international liquidity, money and banking, international trade, prices, production, government finances, interest rates, wages and employment and population.

Applications: Country financial studies.

Subject cross reference: 1.2, 1.7, 1.8, 1.14, 2.13, and 9.6.

Geographic coverage: International.

Time coverage: 1957 to present.

Online vendor(s): Business Information Services (Control Data).

*Note: Chase Econometrics/Interactive Data Corp. has a similar data base.

EVANS ECONOMICS INDUSTRY PRICE INDEX DATA BASE

Producer: Evans Economics, Inc.
1211 Connecticut Avenue, N.W.
Suite 710
Washington, D.C. 20036
(202) 342-0050

Class: Statistical.

Data source: Bureau of Labor Statistics (U.S. Department of Labor).

Size: 800 time series.

Maintenance: Monthly.

Primary subject: Banking, Economics, and Finance.

Secondary subject: N/A

Profile: Provides Industry Price Indexes as calculated by the Bureau of Labor Statistics. Organized by the 1972 SIC (Standard Industrial Classification) System, these indices are calculated from series which closely match an industry or industry sector.

Applications: Industry-by-industry analysis; forecasting.

Subject cross reference: 1.8 and 2.14.

Geographic coverage: Domestic.

Time coverage: Varies by series; most from 1947 to present.

Online vendor(s): Business Information Services (Control Data).

EVANS ECONOMICS INTERNATIONAL DATA BASE

Producer: Evans Economics, Inc.
1211 Connecticut Avenue, N.W.
Suite 710
Washington, D.C. 20036
(202) 342-0050

Class: Statistical.

Data source: Various international statistical publications from the various countries.

Size: 3,000 + time series.

Maintenance: Continuous.

Primary subject: Banking, Economics, and Finance.

Secondary subject: N/A

Profile: Provides time series profiles of selected major foreign countries. Data items include national income accounts, government finances, banking and finance, exchange rates, labor force statistics, prices, and production.

Applications: International economic analyses.

Subject cross reference: 1.2, 1.4, 1.6, 1.7, 1.8, 1.14, 2.14, and 9.12.

Geographic coverage: U.K., France, Italy, West Germany, Japan and Canada.

Time coverage: 1960 to present.

Online vendor(s): Business Information Services (Control Data).

EVANS ECONOMICS METALS DATA BASE

Producer: Evans Economics, Inc.
1211 Connecticut Avenue, N.W.
Suite 710
Washington, D.C. 20036
(202) 342-0050

Class: Statistical.

Data source: U.S. Department of the Interior, The Bureau of Mines, the *Wall Street Journal*.

Size: 35 time series.

Maintenance: Continuous.

Primary subject: Banking, Economics, and Finance.

Secondary subject: N/A

Profile: Maintains time series covering the precious metals—gold, silver, copper and platinum. Data is by month, quarter and year. Data coverage includes import and export statistics, consumption, production, and stocks.

Applications: Metals buying and selling.

Subject cross reference: 1.8 and 1.15.

Geographic coverage: Domestic.

Time coverage: 1960 to present.

Online vendor(s): Business Information Services (Control Data).

EVANS EVONOMICS PRODUCER PRICE DATA BASE*

Producer: Evans Economics, Inc.
1211 Connecticut Avenue, N.W.
Suite 710
Washington, D.C. 20036
(202) 342-0050

Class: Statistical.

Data source: Bureau of Labor Statistics (U.S. Department of Labor).

Size: 4,000 time series.

Maintenance: Continual.

Primary subject: Banking, Economics, and Finance.

Secondary subject: N/A

Profile: Formerly known as Wholesale Prices Indexes, this data base contains production price indices for nearly 2,800 commodities. The indices are by processing (crude materials, intermediate materials, and finished goods) stage and by commodity grouping.

Applications: Commodity price trends and analyses.

Subject cross reference: 1.16 and 2.14.

Geographic coverage: Domestic.

Time coverage: 1947 to present.

Online vendor(s): Business Information Services (Control Data).

*Note: Chase Econometrics/Interactive Data Corp. has a similar data base.

EVANS ECONOMICS REGIONAL FORECASTING SERVICE DATA BASE

Producer: Evans Economics, Inc.
1211 Connecticut Avenue, N.W.
Suite 710
Washington, D.C. 20036
(202) 342-0050

Class: Statistical.

Data source: Multiple federal agencies, The University of Maryland, Evans Economics, Inc. and Urban Systems Research and Engineering, Inc.

Size: 780,000 + time series.

Maintenance: Annually.

Primary subject: Banking, Economics, and Finance.

Secondary subject: N/A

Profile: Provides historical and forecasted macroeconomic and industry data by state, and 585 sub-state regions, including 266 separate SMSA's. Data items include domestic output, personal consumption expenditures, employment, total demand, payrolls, and federal, state, and local government expenditures by function.

Applications: Forecasting; geographic economic analyses.

Subject cross reference: 1.8, 2.3, and 2.5.

Geographic coverage: Domestic.

Time coverage: 1970 to 1990.

Online vendor(s): Business Information Services (Control Data).

EVANS ECONOMIC REGIONAL HOUSING SERVICE DATA BASE

Producer: Evans Economics, Inc.
1211 Connecticut Avenue, N.W.
Suite 710
Washington, D.C. 20036
(202) 342-0050

Class: Statistical.

Data source: Department of Commerce, Bureau of the Census, and Economic Intelligence Associates.

Size: 7,000 + time series.

Maintenance: Continuous.

Primary subject: Multidisciplinary.

Secondary subject: N/A

Profile: Provides monthly, quarterly and annual time series data on housing statistics at the SMSA, state, regional, and national levels. Data items include the number of housing permits and starts, mobile home shipments and production, non-agricultural employment, personal income, wage and salary disbursements, and average house price.

Applications: Construction/housing industry trend analysis.

Subject cross reference: 1.8, 1.19, and 9.15.

Geographic coverage: Domestic.

Time coverage: Varies by series; most from 1970 to present.

Online vendor(s): Business Information Services (Control Data).

EVANS ECONOMICS USA DATA BASE

Producer: Evans Economics, Inc.
1211 Connecticut Avenue, N.W.
Suite 710
Washington, D.C. 20036
(202) 342-0050

Class: Statistical.

Data source: Bureau of Economic Analysis, The Census Bureau, U.S. Department of Energy, Federal Reserve Board, Federal Trade Commission, Bureau of Labor Statistics, U.S. Department of Housing and Urban Development, U.S. Department of the Treasury, The Bond Buyer, New York Stock Exchange, and a variety of private trade associations.

Size: 20,000+ time series.

Maintenance: Monthly, quarterly, and annually.

Primary subject: Banking, Economics and Finance.

Secondary subject: Multidisciplinary.

Profile: These time series describe macroeconomic and industry-level economic activity. The macroeconomic data include national income and product accounts, employment, construction, housing starts, exports, imports, balance of payments, production, and wholesale/retail items. The industry data include industrial production indices, shipments, inventories, orders, and the annual survey of manufacturers.

Applications: Econometric modeling and forecasting.

Subject cross reference: 1.5, 1.8, 2.8, 7.6, 9.9, 9.15, and 9.16.

Geographic coverage: Domestic.

Time coverage: Varies by series; most data from 1947 to present.

Online vendor(s): Business Information Services (Control Data).

EXCERPTA MEDICA (EMBASE)®

Producer: Excerpta Medica Foundation
Post Office Box 1126
Keizergracht 305
Amsterdam, The Netherlands
(020) 264438

Class: Reference.

Data source: Over 3,500 biomedical journals, books, symposia, and special reports.

Size: 1,346,913 records.

Maintenance: Approximately 20,000 records monthly.

Primary subject: Research and Development.

Secondary subject: N/A

Profile: Maintains abstracts and citations of articles from over 3,500 biomedical journals published throughout the world. This online file corresponds to the 43 separate specialties abstract journals and two literature indices which make up the printed Excerpta Medica, plus an additional 100,000 records annually which do not appear in the printed journals. Coverage includes an extensive look at the drug and pharmaceutical literature; environmental, health, pollution control, health economics, hospital management, forensic science and public health.

Applications: For use by physicians, researchers, medical libraries, hospitals, medical schools, chemical and pharmaceutical companies for research.

Subject cross reference: 6.3 and 9.7.

Geographic coverage: International

Time coverage: 1968 to present.

Online vendor(s): DIALOG Information Services, Inc.
DIMDI (EMBASE).

EXSHARE

Producer: Extel Computing, Ltd.
Lowndes House
1-9 City Road
London, England EC1Y 1AA
01/638-5544

Class: Statistical.

Data source: Stock exchanges.

Size: 50,000 securities.

Maintenance: Daily.

Primary subject: Banking, Economics, and Finance.

Secondary subject: N/A

Profile: Contains data for equities, preferred stocks, corporate and government debt instruments, Eurobonds, convertible bonds, insurance and property bonds, offshore and overseas funds, warrants, and unit trusts for most major countries outside of North America. Also contains various *Financial Times* (London) indices as well as daily spot rates for over sixty currencies.

Applications: Securities analysis; currency exchange rate tracking.

Subject cross reference: 1.7 and 1.16.

Geographic coverage: International.

Time coverage: 1972 to present.

Online vendor(s): Business Information Services (Control Data)
Chase Econometrics/Interactive Data Corp.

EXSTAT

Producer: Extel Statistical Services, Ltd.
37-45 Paul Street
London, England EC2A 4PB
(01) 253-3400

Class: Statistical.

Data source: International financial statements, company reports, returns, and accounts.

Size: 2,000+ records.

Maintenance: Weekly.

Primary subject: Banking, Economics, and Finance.

Secondary subject: N/A

Profile: The international equivalent of the Disclosure Database. Exstat provides both a historical and a current financial profile of over 2,000 Japanese, Continental European, United Kingdom, and Australian companies. Information consists of balance sheet and profit & loss data items.

Applications: International company profiles; ratio analysis—international.

Subject cross reference: 1.1, 1.11, 2.1, 2.6, 9.12, and 10.7.

Geographic coverage: International.

Time coverage: 1971 to present.

Online vendor(s): ADP Network Services, Inc.
Business Information Services (Control Data)
Chase Econometrics/Interactive Data Corp.
I.P. Sharp Associates.

FARM AND INDUSTRIAL EQUIPMENT INSTITUTE (FIEI)

Producer: Farm and Industrial Equipment Institute
410 N. Michigan Avenue
Chicago, Illinois 60611
(312) 321-1470

Class: Statistical.

Data source: FIEI.

Size: N/A

Maintenance: Monthly and Annually.

Primary subject: General Management (agriculture).

Secondary subject: N/A

Profile: FIEI contains retail sales, inventories, and some export data for industrial, construction and farm equipment. Data are available from the following product categories: balers, backhoes, combines, corheads, forage harvesters, forklifts, hay stackers, loaders, manure spreaders, moldboard plows, mower conditioners, planters, scrapers, skidders, stack movers, tractors and windrowers.

Applications: Development of regional marketing strategies; examination of inventory patterns; sales potential analysis.

Subject cross reference: 9.1 and 9.17.

Geographic coverage: United States and Canada.

Time coverage: N/A

Online vendor(s): Data Resources, Inc.

FASTOCK II

Producer: ADP Network Services, Inc.
175 Jackson Plaza
Ann Arbor, Michigan 48106
(313) 769-6800

Class: Statistical.

Data source: U.S. and Canadian stock exchanges.

Size: 49,000+ issues.

Maintenance: Daily.

Primary subject: Banking, Economics and Finance (securities).

Secondary subject: N/A

Profile: Covers equity and debt issues as well as options. Contains historical and current trading data and market statistics. Also provides complete dividend and stock distribution statistics for equity issues and bond interest payment data for debt issues.

Applications: Special market analysis and modeling; portfolio analysis.

Subject cross reference: 1.16.

Geographic coverage: United States and Canada.

Time coverage: Five to twelve years of history, depending upon specific issue.

Online vendor(s): ADP Network Services, Inc.

FAST PERMIT REPORTS (FPR)

Producer: Petroleum Information Corporation
4100 Dry Creek Road
Littleton, Colorado 80122
(303) 740-7100

Class: Reference and Statistical.

Data source: Oil well drilling permits.

Size: N/A

Maintenance: Daily.

Primary subject: Long-Range Strategic Planning (energy).

Secondary subject: N/A

Profile: Maintains information on oil well drilling permits issued by the many regional governmental agencies. Data items on each permit include operator name, address, well identification information, location, initial classification, control number, date, and projected depth.

Applications: Gas and oil lease management; lottery administration.

Subject cross reference: 6.3, and 10.5.

Geographic coverage: Domestic.

Time coverage: Most current seven days only.

Online vendor(s): General Electric Information Services Co.

FDIC REPORT OF CONDITION
AND INCOME SYSTEM

Producer: U.S. Federal Deposit Insurance Corporation (FDIC)
550 17th Street, N.W.
Washington, D.C. 20429
(202) 389-4701

Class: Statistical.

Data source: Consolidated Report of Condition and Consolidated Report of Income from member banks.

Size: 14,000 banks.

Maintenance: Quarterly.

Primary subject: Banking, Economics, and Finance.

Secondary subject: N/A

Profile: Comprised of financial information taken from all FDIC-insured commercial and mutual savings banks. Quarterly and annual statements are itemized and available for retrieval. Coverage includes such items as operating income and expenses, assets, changes in equity capital, and net profit.

Applications: Users retrieve data by state, county, SMSA, FDIC number, charter class, assets or deposits.

Subject cross reference: 1.2, 1.11, and 2.1.

Geographic coverage: Domestic.

Time coverage: Current data.

Online vendor(s): ADP Network Services, Inc. (BANCALL®)
Chase Econometrics/Interactive Data Corporation (FDIC)
CompuServe, Inc. (FDIC)
Warner Computer Systems, Inc. (FDIC).

FEDERAL ASSISTANCE PROGRAMS
RETRIEVAL SYSTEM (FAPRS)

Producer: U.S. Office of Management and Budget
New Executive Office Building
Room 6001
Washington, D.C. 20503
(202) 395-3112

Class: Reference.

Data source: *Catalog of Federal Domestic Assistance*, via 57 federal departments, independent agencies, and various commissions.

Size: 1,000 + records.

Maintenance: Monthly.

Primary subject: Multidisciplinary.

Secondary subject: N/A

Profile: Provides information on where to find over 1,050 federal assistance loan and grant programs. Each program is profiled by eligibility requirements, application and award processes, types of assistance, responsible agency and contacts.

Applications: User must specify certain eligibility criteria to extract the appropriate assistance programs.

Subject cross reference: 9.5 and 9.20.

Geographic coverage: Domestic.

Time coverage: Current data only.

Online vendor(s): Business Information Services (Control Data)
General Electric Information Service.

FEDERAL ENERGY DATA INDEX (FEDEX)

Producer: U.S. Department of Energy
Energy Information Administration (EIA)
1726 M Street, N.W.
Washington, D.C. 20461
(202) 633-5602

Class: Reference.

Data source: *Energy Information Administration Publication Directory, Energy Information Administration Data Index,* and various government agencies.

Size: 2,500 citations.

Maintenance: Quarterly.

Primary subject: Long-Range Strategic Planning (energy).

Secondary subject: N/A

Profile: Maintains citations and abstracts on literature produced by the Energy Information Administration of the U.S. Department of Energy. Coverage consists of statistical data relating to energy, prices, reserve, production, consumption, supply and demand. Also deals with the energy crisis and solutions as well as energy programs.

Applications: User may extract several energy related tables and graphs which are separately indexed and abstracted.

Subject cross reference: 6.3 and 10.5.

Geographic coverage: Domestic.

Time coverage: 1977 to present.

Online vendor(s): BRS, Inc.

FEDERAL INDEX (FEDEX)

Producer: Capitol Services, Inc. (CSI)
415 Second Street, N.E.
Washington, D.C. 20002
(202) 546-5600

Class: Reference.

Data source: *The Federal Register, the Congressional Record, Commerce Business Daily,* and Presidential documents are indexed.

Size: 233,550 citations.

Maintenance: Approximately 5,000 citations monthly.

Primary subject: Legal and Legislative Affairs.

Secondary subject: Multidisciplinary.

Profile: Provides coverage of such federal actions as proposed rules, regulations, hearings, roll calls, bill introductions and activities, speeches, reports, vetoes, executive orders, court decisions and contract awards.

Applications: Political analysis; legislative news tracking.

Subject cross reference: 1.9, 2.16, 3.6, 4.6, 5.1, 5.6, 5.8, 5.9, 6.8, 7.12, 8.9, 9.20, and 10.4.

Geographic coverage: Domestic.

Time coverage: 1976 to present.

Online vendor(s): DIALOG Information Services, Inc.
SDC Search Service.

FEDERAL REGISTER ABSTRACTS
(FEDREG)

Producer: Capitol Services, Inc. (CSI)
415 Second Street, N.E.
Washington, D.C. 20002
(202) 546-5600

Class: Reference.

Data source: Abstracts prepared from citations in the *Federal Register*.

Size: 105,000 records.

Maintenance: Approximately 600 records weekly.

Primary subject: Legal and Legislative Affairs.

Secondary subject: Multidisciplinary.

Profile: Provides coverage of federal regulatory agency actions as published in the *Federal Register*, the official U.S. government publication of regulations, proposed rules and legal notices issued by federal agencies. Included are references to meeting and hearing notices, Presidential proclamations, Executive orders, public laws and rules taking effect each day.

Applications: Government rules and regulation decisions; rule status and analysis.

Subject cross reference: 1.19, 2.16, 3.6, 4.6, 5.4, 5.6, 5.8, 6.8, 7.12, 8.9, 9.20, and 10.8.

Geographic coverage: Domestic.

Time coverage: 1976 to present.

Online vendor(s): DIALOG Information Services, Inc.
SDC Search Service.

FEDWIR

Producer: Money Market Services, Inc.
490 El Camino Real
Belmont, California 94002
(415) 595-0610

Class: Statistical and Reference.

Data source: Government statistics and publications.

Size: 2,000+ time series.

Maintenance: Based upon government issue.

Primary subject: Banking, Economics, and Finance.

Secondary subject: N/A

Profile: Provides data on weekly M1 forecasts, M1 growth matrixes, and historical analyses of M1.

Applications: Econometric modeling.

Subject cross reference: 1.8 and 1.9.

Geographic coverage: Domestic and Europe.

Time coverage: Varies by series; most from 1970's.

Online vendor(s): Control Data Corporation.

FERTILIZER FORECAST

Producer: Chase Econometrics/Interactive Data Corp.
486 Totten Pond Road
Waltham, Massachusetts 02154
(617) 890-1234

Class: Statistical.

Data source: U.S. Department of Agriculture and other government agencies.

Size: 350+ time series.

Maintenance: Bimonthly.

Primary subject: General Management.

Secondary subject: N/A

Profile: Provides quarterly (for eight quarters) and yearly (for eight years) forecasts for nitrogen, phosphate, potash, and the derivative fertilizer products of each. Component data items include demand, production, stocks, and prices.

Applications: Agricultural budgeting and forecast analysis.

Subject cross reference: 9.1.

Geographic coverage: Domestic.

Time coverage: 1955 through projected time periods.

Online vendor(s): Chase Econometrics/Interactive Data Corp.

FINANCIAL

Producer: Chase Econometrics/Interactive Data Corporation
486 Totten Pond Road
Waltham, Massachusetts 02154
(617) 890-1234

Class: Statistical.

Data source: Federal Home Loan Bank Board, the Federal Reserve and the U.S. Department of the Treasury.

Size: 3,400 time series.

Maintenance: Continuous.

Primary subject: Banking, Economics, and Finance.

Secondary subject: N/A

Profile: Provides weekly time series on over 5,000 key variables for money supply, commercial loans, assets, and liabilities.

Applications: Economic/industry modeling (using key government statistics in conjunction with your organization's data).

Subject cross reference: 1.2, 1.6, 1.7, 1.8, and 1.14.

Geographic coverage: Domestic.

Time coverage: Varies by series; most from 1945 to present.

Online vendor(s): Chase Econometrics/Interactive Data Corp.

FINANCIAL INSTITUTION DATA BASE

Producer: Cates Consulting Analysts, Inc.
74 Trinity Place
New York, New York 10006
(212) 964-7002

Class: Statistical.

Data source: Commercial bank filings with the FDIC (Federal Deposit Insurance Corporation), and FSLIC (Federal Savings and Loan Insurance Company).

Size: 35,000 + financial institutions.

Maintenance: Quarterly.

Primary subject: Banking, Economics, and Finance.

Secondary subject: N/A

Profile: Maintains financial profile data for over 14,000 commercial banks insured by the FDIC. Also profiled are over 4,500 savings & loan institutions and 16,500 credit unions.

Applications: Competitive profiles; banking activity by geographical segmentation.

Subject cross reference: 1.2, 1.11, 1.12, and 2.1.

Geographic coverage: Domestic.

Time coverage: Current five years of historical data.

Online vendor(s): Business Information Services (Control Data).

FINANCIAL FORECAST

Producer: Chase Econometrics/Interactive Data Corporation
486 Totten Pond Road
Waltham, Massachusetts 02154
(617) 890-1234

Class: Statistical.

Data source: Government agencies, the Chase Econometric Financial Model Service and public and private companies.

Size: 150 time series.

Maintenance: Monthly.

Primary subject: Banking, Economics, and Finance.

Secondary subject: N/A

Profile: Provides 24-month forecasts for interest rates, reserve measures, U.S. Treasury activity, money, stock, credit, bonds, and mortgages.

Applications: Corporate development decisions; econometric modeling.

Subject cross reference: 1.3, 1.6, 1.7, 1.8, and 1.14.

Geographic coverage: Domestic.

Time coverage: 1961 to present with forecasts.

Online vendor(s): Chase Econometrics/Interactive Data Corp.

FINANCIAL POST INVESTMENT DATA BANK

Producer: Maclean-Hunter, Ltd.
481 University Avenue
Toronto, Ontario, Canada M5W 1A7
(416) 596-5693

Class: Statistical.

Data source: U.S. and Canadian stock exchanges and corporate reports.

Size: 300 + Canadian corporations.

Maintenance: Continuous.

Primary subject: Banking, Economics and Finance.

Secondary subject: N/A

Profile: Contains balance sheet and income data taken from the annual reports of over 300 major Canadian corporations. There are approximately 81 annual data items per company. Also, there are 18 data items taken from the quarterly reports of approximately 110 Canadian companies.

Applications: Corporate financial comparisons and analyses (profiles); corporate/marketing opportunity analysis.

Subject cross reference: 1.10, 1.11, 1.12, and 2.1.

Geographic coverage: Canada.

Time coverage: 1959 to present.

Online vendor(s): Dialcom, Inc.
FRI Information Services Limited
I.P. Sharp Associates.

FINTEL COMPANY NEWSBASE

Producer: Fintel Ltd.
102-108 Clerkenwell Road
London, England EC1M 5SA
(01) 251 9321

Class: Reference.

Data source: *Financial Times*—London and Frankfurt editions; *Investor's Chronicle, Money Management,* and *The Banker.*

Size: 30,000 + companies and their worldwide subsidiaries.

Maintenance: Weekly.

Primary subject: Multidisciplinary.

Secondary subject: N/A

Profile: Provides overall corporate, financial, economic, commercial, and business information. Coverage includes market share, senior management, exports, current research, company performance, acquisitions and mergers, industrial relations and investments. The articles are indexed by company name, organization, industry sector, geographical location, people, products, and subject descriptors. References to chart and graphs accompanying any article are also included.

Applications: Competitive profiles, comparisons and opportunity analysis.

Subject cross reference: 1.11, 2.1, 2.6, 2.8, 2.10, 4.4, 8.1, 8.3, 8.4, 9.12, and 9.13.

Geographic coverage: International.

Time coverage: 1981 to present.

Online vendor(s): BRS, Inc.
Data-Star.

FLOW OF FUNDS ACCOUNTS

Producer: U.S. Federal Reserve Board (FRB)
20th and Constitution Avenue, N.W.
Washington, D.C. 20551
(202) 452-3000

Class: Statistical.

Data source: Government agencies, banks, savings and loans, real estate boards, and various associations.

Size: 3,000 + data series.

Maintenance: Quarterly.

Primary subject: Banking, Economics, and Finance.

Secondary subject: N/A

Profile: Maintains statistics covering the source, stock, flow and adjusted flows of funds in the United States economy. Segment coverage includes the federal, state and local governments, commercial banks, savings & loans, life insurance, investment organizations and other financial groups. Specific coverage includes consumer credit, bank deposits, insurance claims, household expenditures, disposable income, interest paid, tax, corporate profits and tax, capital expenditures, mortgages, households, charge accounts and other related fund statistics. Nonfinancial activities of the various sectors are also included.

Applications: Market segment analysis; econometric modeling; market potential and segmentation.

Subject cross reference: 1.19.

Geographic coverage: Domestic.

Time coverage: Annual since 1945; quarterly since 1952.

Online vendor(s): ADP Network Services, Inc. (FLOW OF FUNDS)
Chase Econometrics/Interactive Data Corporation (FLOW OF FUNDS)
National CSS, Inc. (FLOW OF FUNDS)
Time Sharing Resources, Inc. (FRB)
Uni-Coll, Inc. (FLOW OF FUNDS)

FOODS ADLIBRA

Producer: Komp Information Services, Inc.
811 Fountain Avenue
Louisville, Kentucky 40222
(502) 426-7754

Class: Reference.

Data source: Trade periodicals, research journals, and patents.

Size: 52,810 citations.

Maintenance: Approximately 2,000 citations monthly.

Primary subject: Research and Development (miscellaneous).

Secondary subject: N/A

Profile: Information on the latest developments in food technology and packaging. All food products introduced since 1974 are covered as well as nutritional and toxicology information. Coverage includes information on every sector of the food industry including retailers, brokers, processors, equipment suppliers, importers. General coverage includes research and technology advances in processing methods, packaging and company and food association news.

Applications: Food management and planning.

Subject cross reference: 2.7, 7.2, and 8.9.

Geographic coverage: Domestic.

Time coverage: 1974 to present.

Online vendor(s): DIALOG Information Services, Inc.

FOOD SCIENCE AND TECHNOLOGY ABSTRACTS (FSTA)

Producer: International Food Information Service
Lane End House
Shinfield, Reading, England RG2 9BB
(0734) 883895

Class: Reference.

Data source: 1,400 journals from 75 countries and patents from 20 countries.

Size: 200,189 citations.

Maintenance: Approximately 1,500 citations monthly.

Primary subject: General Management (agriculture).

Secondary subject: N/A

Profile: Access to research and new development literatures in the areas related to food science and technology. The disciplines covered include agriculture, chemistry, biochemistry and physics. Related disciplines such as engineering and home economics are covered only when relating to food science.

Applications: Scientific and technological research; food science marketing (promotions, new products and product differentiation).

Subject cross reference: 8.9 and 9.1.

Geographic coverage: International.

Time coverage: 1969 to present.

Online vendor(s): DIALOG Information Services, Inc.
ESA/QUEST
SDC Search Service.

FOREIGN EXCHANGE RATE FORECAST

Producer: Chase Econometrics/Interactive Data Corporation
486 Totten Pond Road
Waltham, Massachusetts 02154
(617) 890-1234

Class: Statistical.

Data source: N/A

Size: 165 + time series.

Maintenance: Monthly.

Primary subject: Banking, Economics, and Finance.

Secondary subject: N/A

Profile: Provides monthly forecasted exchange rates and related explanatory variables for nine quarters for those currencies of the countries listed in geographical coverage.

Applications: International capitalization requirements; international sales and financial management.

Subject cross reference: 1.4, 1.7, and 1.8.

Geographic coverage: U.S., Canada, Great Britain, France, Italy, Germany, Belgium, The Netherlands, Japan, and Brazil.

Time coverage: 1954 through forecasted period.

Online vendor(s): Chase Econometrics/Interactive Data Corp.

FOREIGN TRADERS INDEX (FTI)

Producer: U.S. Department of Commerce
Bureau of Export Development
Commerce ITA/1033/FTI
Washington, D.C. 20230
(202) 377-2988

Class: Reference.

Data source: Collected by the Department of State (Foreign Service).

Size: 155,000 + records.

Maintenance: Quarterly.

Primary subject: General Management (foreign trade).

Secondary subject: N/A

Profile: Directory of manufacturers, service organizations, agent representatives, retailers, wholesalers, distributors and cooperatives in 130 countries outside the United States. Designed to provide information to U.S. companies by listing those firms which either import goods from the United States or stating they are interested in representing United States' exporters. Data coverage includes nature of business (e.g., retailing manufacturing, etc.) as well as the product or service it handles. Also covered are the executive officers, number of employees, relative size and date of establishment.

Applications: International sales prospecting and lead analysis.

Subject cross reference: 2.6, 3.2, 9.6, and 9.9

Geographic coverage: International.

Time coverage: Past five years of data.

Online vendor(s): DIALOG Information Services, Inc.

FOREST PRODUCTS: ABSTRACT INFORMATION DIGEST SERVICE (AIDS)

Producer: Forest Products Research Society
2801 Marshall Court
Madison, Wisconsin 53705
(608) 231-1361

Class: Reference.

Data source: Technical journals, government publications, patents, trade journals, abstract bulletins and monographs.

Size: 14,000 + citations.

Maintenance: Approximately 200 citations bimonthly.

Primary subject: Environmental, Social and Political Affairs.

Secondary subject: N/A

Profile: Covers worldwide literature relative to the entire wood products industry, from harvesting of the standing tree through marketing of the final product. The two areas not covered are chemical pulping and forest practices (unless they impact directly on product quality).

Applications: Forestry educational and organizational research and applications reference.

Subject cross reference: 6.3 and 9.1.

Geographic coverage: Domestic.

Time coverage: 1947 to present.

Online vendor(s): SDC Search Service.

FORESTRY DATA BANKS

Producer: Data Resources, Inc.
29 Hartwell Avenue
Lexington, Massachusetts 02173
(617) 861-0165

Class: Statistical.

Data source: American Plywood Association, National Forest Products Association, Southern Forest Products Association, U.S. Department of Commerce, U.S. Department of Labor—Bureau of Labor Statistics, and the Western Wood Products Association.

Size: N/A

Maintenance: Weekly, monthly, quarterly and annually.

Primary subject: Environmental, Social, & Political Affairs.

Secondary subject: N/A

Profile: Called Forsim by DRI, this data base maintains data on the U.S. and Canadian lumber and plywood industries, the U.S. particleboard and hardboard industries and the Canadian softwood plywood industry. Coverage includes prices, production, imports and exports, capacity, transportation rates, stump growth and cost, shipments, inventories, orders, end-use consumption, production costs and demand indicators.

Applications: Product line forecasting; long-term stumpage price analysis; development of investment, purchasing and marketing strategies.

Subject cross reference: 6.3 and 9.1.

Geographic coverage: U.S. and Canada.

Time coverage: N/A

Online vendor(s): Data Resources, Inc.

FOUNDATION DIRECTORY

Producer: The Foundation Center
888 7th Avenue
New York, New York 10019
(212) 975-1120

Class: Reference and Statistical.

Data source: Voluntary reports of foundations by foundations and IRS foundation filings.

Size: 3,595 listings.

Maintenance: Semiannually.

Primary subject: Multidisciplinary.

Secondary subject: N/A

Profile: Provides descriptions of over 3,500 foundations which have assets of $1 million or more, or which make grants equaling or exceeding $100,000 annually. Each foundation conforms to the general description of a "nongovernmental, nonprofit organization," with funds and programs managed by its own trustees and/or directors, and established to maintain or aid social, charitable, religious, educational, or other activities serving the common welfare. The foundations which qualify for inclusion account for nearly 90% of the assets of all foundations in the United States and 80% of all foundation giving. Grants are given primarily in the fields of education, health, welfare, the sciences and religion.

Applications: Private institution fund raising prospecting; lead generation reference.

Subject cross reference: 3.2, 4.5, 6.7, 9.5, and 9.7.

Geographic coverage: Domestic.

Time coverage: Current data.

Online vendor(s): DIALOG Information Services, Inc.

FTCDATA

Producer: General Electric Information Services Company (GEISCO)
401 N. Washington Street
Rockville, Maryland 20850
(301) 340-4000

Class: Statistical.

Data source: U.S. Corporate Income Tax Form 1120 Filings.

Size: 496 time series.

Maintenance: Quarterly.

Primary subject: Banking, Economics, and Finance.

Secondary subject: N/A

Profile: Using tax form 1120, GEISCO maintains 496 time series of manufacturing organizations' data extrapolations. These data are in aggregate form and expressed in U.S. dollars.

Applications: Corporate financial statement data comparisons and analysis.

Subject cross reference: 1.8, 1.12, 2.8, 10.2, and 10.4.

Geographic coverage: Domestic.

Time coverage: 1947 to present.

Online vendor(s): General Electric Information Services Co.

GEOARCHIVE

Producer: Geosystems
Post Office Box 1024
Westminster, London, England SW1P 2JL
(01) 222-7305

Class: Reference.

Data source: 5,000 serials, books, conferences, doctoral dissertations and technical reports.

Size: 500,000 + citations.

Maintenance: Approximately 10,000 citations monthly.

Primary subject: Environmental, Social and Political Affairs.

Secondary subject: General Management (mining).

Profile: Indexes more than 100,000 references each year. Coverage includes mineral and petroleum production and resources, names of new taxa, new minerals, and new stratigraphic names. Disciplines covered include geophysics, geochemistry, geology, paleontology, and mathematical geology.

Applications: Geological engineering research and analysis.

Subject cross reference: 6.3, 8.9, and 9.1.

Geographic coverage: International.

Time coverage: 1969 to present (some citations' data available to the 1800's, however).

Online vendor(s): DIALOG Information Services, Inc.

GEOLOGICAL REFERENCE FILE (GEOREF)

Producer: American Geological Institute
5205 Leesburg Pike
Falls Church, Virginia 22041
(703) 379-2480
(800) 336-4764

Class: Reference.

Data source: 3,000 + international journals, books, dissertations, theses, and geological maps.

Size: 653,500 records.

Maintenance: Approximately 5,000 records monthly.

Primary subject: Environmental, Social, and Political Affairs.

Secondary subject: General Management (mining).

Profile: Provides access to references related to all aspects of geology, geochemistry, geophysics, minerology, paleontology, petrology and seismology.

Applications: Geological research and analysis reference.

Subject cross reference: 6.3, 8.9, and 9.1.

Geographic coverage: International

Time coverage: 1961 to present, although some references date back to 1875.

Online vendor(s): DIALOG Information Services, Inc.
SDC Search Service.

GPO MONTHLY CATALOG DATA BASE

Producer: U.S. Government Printing Office
Library Division
5236 Eisenhower Avenue
Alexandria, Virginia 22304
(703) 557-2135

Class: Reference.

Data source: Report records, studies, fact sheets, maps, handbooks, conference proceedings, and other government documents.

Size: 101,401 records.

Maintenance: Approximately 2,000 records monthly.

Primary subject: Multidisciplinary.

Secondary subject: N/A

Profile: Data base equivalent of the printed *Monthly Catalog of U.S. Government Publications*. Records of all the Senate and House hearings on private and public bills and laws are included. Maintains a wide range of topics which include: agriculture, economics, energy research, public policy, tax reform, business, law, health, etc. Specific information available includes legislative reports, standards, safety studies, production and distribution statistics, industry reports and projections, labor standards requirements and state of the art summaries on most major issues and technology.

Applications: Multidisciplinary research and reference; political activity guide.

Subject cross reference: 1.19, 2.16, 3.6, 4.6, 5.9, 6.8, 7.12, 8.9, 9.20, and 10.8.

Geographic coverage: Domestic.

Time coverage: 1976 to present.

Online vendor(s): BRS, Inc.
DIALOG Information Services, Inc.
SDC Search Service.

GRANT INFORMATION SYSTEM

Producer: The Oryx Press
2214 N. Central at Encanto
Phoenix, Arizona 85004
(602) 254-6156

Class: Reference.

Data source: Government reports and documents.

Size: 2,200 records.

Maintenance: Revised monthly.

Primary subject: Multidisciplinary.

Secondary subject: N/A

Profile: The source to grant programs available through government (federal, state and local); commercial organizations, associations, and private foundations. The academic discipline(s) for which grants are available are given with each program.

Applications: Educational and research assistance identification.

Subject cross reference: 9.5.

Geographic coverage: Domestic.

Time coverage: Currently "open" grants.

Online vendor(s): DIALOG Information Services, Inc.
SDC Search Service.

GTE FINANCIAL SYSTEM ONE QUOTATION SERVICE

Producer: GTE Information Systems, Inc.
East Park Drive
Mount Laurel, New Jersey 08054
(609) 235-7300

Class: Statistical.

Data source: U.S. and Canadian securities and commodities exchanges.

Size: N/A

Maintenance: Daily.

Primary subject: Banking, Economics, and Finance.

Secondary subject: N/A

Profile: Provides a constantly updated service with separate formats for securities, options, bonds, commodities, and other market data. Data items include the security symbol, exchange identifier, tick, last price, net change, bid, ask, daily high, daily low, yearly high, yearly low, trading denomination, open, close, volume, earnings, price-to-earnings ratio, yield, dividend, time of last trade, and time of latest news release.

Applications: Portfolio analysis.

Subject cross reference: 1.16.

Geographic coverage: United States and Canada.

Time coverage: Current data.

Online vendor(s): GTE Information Systems, Inc.

GUIDANCE INFORMATION SYSTEM (GIS)®

Producer: Time Share Corporation
630 Oakwood Avenue
West Hartford, Connecticut 06110
(203) 522-0136

Class: Reference.

Data source: U.S. Department of Labor; Bureau of Labor Statistics; data from local and state offices.

Size: See profile.

Maintenance: Semiannually.

Primary subject: General Management.

Secondary subject: N/A

Profile: GIS maintains information on 875 primary occupation disciplines and then offers a 2,000 cross reference job referral summary. Educational requirements, salary range, physical demands, aptitudes and personal interests are included. GIS also covers over 100 Armed Services' jobs and training, which includes a cross reference to civilian jobs. College and institutional files maintain information on degrees offered, admission criteria, enrollments, community profile, costs, financial aid and admission deadlines.

Applications: Occupation reference guide; college reference guide.

Subject cross reference: 6.7, 9.5, and 9.20.

Geographic coverage: Domestic.

Time coverage: Most current information.

Online vendor(s): TSC.

HANSARD ORAL QUESTIONS (HOQ)

Producer: House of Commons (Canada)
Computer Systems Branch Post Office Box 1005, South Block
Ottawa, Ontario, Canada K1A 0A6
(613) 593-5224

Class: Reference.

Data source: *House of Commons Debates Official Report.*

Size: 25,700 records.

Maintenance: Biweekly.

Primary subject: Legal and Legislative Affairs.

Secondary subject: N/A

Profile: Maintains full-text recaps of oral questions and responses from the Question Period of each session of the Canadian Parliament's House of Commons. Coverage is broad but includes a variety of topics ranging from business and health to high technology and energy research.

Applications: Political reference (laws and regulations).

Subject cross reference: 5.9.

Geographic coverage: Canada.

Time coverage: 1973 to present.

Online vendor(s): QL Systems Limited.

HARFAX

Producer: Harfax Data Base Publishing
Post Office Box 281
54 Fall Street
Cambridge, Massachusetts 02138
(617) 492-0670

Class: Reference.

Data source: Market research studies, trade journals, monographs, statistical data bases, statistical reports, financial investment analysis, dissertations and industry conference papers.

Size: 25,000 records.

Maintenance: 2,000 records monthly.

Primary subject: Marketing Planning.

Secondary subject: Banking, Economics and Finance.

Profile: Maintains sources of marketing and financial data and information for over 65 industries. References to over 14,000 industry data sources are maintained. Each reference includes such parameters as title, publication date, publisher, pages, price, content summary and coverage.

Applications: Locator of international sources of marketing and financial statistics.

Subject cross reference: 1.19 and 2.16.

Geographic coverage: International.

Time coverage: Current data sources.

Online vendor(s): BRS, Inc.
Data-Star
DIALOG Information Services, Inc.

HARVARD BUSINESS REVIEW

Producer: Harvard Business Review (HBR) with John Wiley & Sons
Soldiers' Field
Boston, Massachusetts 02163
(617) 495-6185
605 Third Avenue
New York, New York 10158

Class: Reference.

Data source: *Harvard Business Review* articles.

Size: All HBR articles.

Maintenance: Monthly.

Primary subject: Multidisciplinary.

Secondary subject: N/A

Profile: Maintains citations and abstracts of the *Harvard Business Review* dating back to 1971. Also, selected older articles appearing before 1971 are available. The user may search by subject and management terms, company names, geographic locations, industry categories, products and services, corporate functions, and types of exhibit data.

Applications: Business research and reference (e.g., forecasting, modeling, portfolio theory, management practices, etc.)

Subject cross reference: 1.19, 2.16, 3.6, 4.6, 5.9, 6.8, 7.12, 8.9, 9.20, and 10.8.

Geographic coverage: Domestic.

Time coverage: 1971 to present.

Online vendor(s): BRS, Inc.

HEALTH PLANNING AND ADMINISTRATION

Producer: U.S. National Library of Medicine
8600 Rockville Pike
Bethesda, Maryland 20209
(301) 496-6217

Class: Reference.

Data source: Health related journals.

Size: 130,000 records.

Maintenance: Approximately 2,000 monthly.

Primary subject: General Management (health care, hospitals, and medicine).

Secondary subject: N/A

Profile: Maintains literature relative to the health-care delivery services. Such areas as budgeting, organization, administration, finance and fund raising are covered.

Applications: Hospital administration guidelines and reference; hospital fund-raising topics reference.

Subject cross reference: 4.5 and 9.7.

Geographic coverage: International.

Time coverage: 1975 to present.

Online vendor(s): BLAISE
BRS, Inc.
DIALOG Information Services, Inc.

HIGHWAY SAFETY LITERATURE (HSL)

Producer: U.S. National Highway Traffic Safety
Administration
400 Seventh Street, S.W.
Room 5108
Washington, D.C. 20590
(202) 426-2768

Class: Reference.

Data source: Reports, monographs and journals.

Size: 30,000 records.

Maintenance: Monthly.

Primary subject: General Management (transportation).

Secondary subject: N/A

Profile: Maintains citations and abstracts of literature relating to highway traffic and motor vehicle safety. Coverage includes traffic safety, pedestrian safety, motor vehicle safety, automotive fuel economy, insurance, laws and codes, traffic accidents, alcohol and traffic accidents.

Applications: Driver training reference and class development.

Subject cross reference: 6.8, 9.3, and 9.18.

Geographic coverage: Domestic.

Time coverage: 1967 to present.

Online vendor(s): Informatics, Inc.

HORSE DATA BANK

Producer: Bloodstock Research Information Services, Inc.
801 Corporate Drive, 3rd Floor
Post Office Box 4097
Lexington, Kentucky 40544
(606) 223-4444

Class: Statistical.

Data source: Racing forms, racing calendars, and various industry publications.

Size: N/A

Maintenance: Daily.

Primary subject: Marketing Planning.

Secondary subject: N/A

Profile: Maintains data on thoroughbred horses breeding and racing in North America. Coverage includes race information, race results (current and historical), earnings, breeding records, pedigrees and actual race records. Pedigree information is available from one to five generations for each thoroughbred.

Applications: A special index is available which designates a class and consistency rating for each horse.

Subject cross reference: 2.1.

Geographic coverage: Domestic.

Time coverage: 1930 to present.

Online vendor(s): Bloodstock Research Information Services, Inc.

ICAO (INTERNATIONAL CIVIL AVIATION ORGANIZATION) TRAFFIC STATISTICS

Producer: International Civil Aviation Organization
Post Office Box 400
1000 Sherbrooke Street, West
Montreal, PQ, Canada H3A 2R2
(514) 285-8064

Class: Statistical.

Data source: International Civil Aviation Organization (reports filed by airlines and airports).

Size: 600+ airlines and 300+ airports.

Maintenance: Annual (every October).

Primary subject: General Management (transportation and shipping).

Secondary subject: N/A

Profile: Maintains international airline traffic statistics for approximately 600 airlines and 300 airports. The airport and airline data consists of yearly and monthly time series. Data coverage includes passengers embarked, disembarked and direct transit; aircraft movements; freight and mail statistics. Airline data coverage includes aircraft kilometers, departures, hours; passengers and freight carried; passenger-kilometers performed; passenger, freight, and mail tonne-kilometers performed; and passenger and weight load factors.

Applications: Airline industry analysis.

Subject cross reference: 2.1, 2.10, 9.18 and 10.3.

Geographic coverage: International.

Time coverage: 1968 to present.

Online vendor(s): I.P. Sharp Associates.

IMF BALANCE OF PAYMENTS

Producer: International Monetary Fund (IMF)
19th and H Streets, N.W.
Washington, D.C. 20431
(202) 393-6362

Class: Statistical.

Data source: Compilation on international economic activity—*Balance of Payments Yearbook*.

Size: Balance of payments data for 114 IMF countries.

Maintenance: Quarterly and annually.

Primary subject: Banking, Economics, and Finance.

Secondary subject: General Management (foreign trade).

Profile: Maintains statistical analysis of economic transactions for over 100 countries. Two methods of presenting the balance of payments are available for each country: the aggregate and the detailed. The analytic presentation is designed to provide statistics unique to a country within a constant framework; the standard presentation contains comparable series for all countries.

Applications: Cross sectional analysis; trade negotiations; foreign trade analyses; analysis of a country's international position.

Subject cross reference: 1.8 and 9.6.

Geographic coverage: International.

Time coverage: Most data are from 1960's to present.

Online vendor(s): Chase Econometrics/Interactive Data Corp.
Data Resources, Inc.
Rapidata, Inc.

IMF DIRECTION OF TRADE STATISTICS (DOTS)

Producer: International Monetary Fund (IMF)
Bureau of Statistics
700 19th Street, N.W.
Washington, D.C. 20431
(202) 477-3206

Class: Statistical.

Data source: IMF data (from reports of contributing countries).

Size: 55,000 time series

Maintenance: Monthly, quarterly, and annually.

Primary subject: General Management (foreign trade).

Secondary subject: N/A

Profile: DOTS data comprise the direction of imports and exports time series by partner countries and areas for about 130 countries. All exports are valued F.O.B. and all important C.I.F. Data are expressed in U.S. dollars.

Applications: Import/export analysis; trade statistics.

Subject cross reference: 1.6, 9.9, and 10.7.

Geographic coverage: International.

Time coverage: Depends upon series.

Online vendor(s): Chase Econometrics/Interactive Data Corp.
Data Resources, Inc.

IMPORTS; OIL IMPORTS

Producer: U.S. Department of Energy
Office of Oil Imports
Post Office Box 19267
Washington, D.C. 20036
(202) 653-3445

Class: Statistical.

Data source: American Petroleum Institute.

Size: 2,000 shipments per month.

Maintenance: Monthly.

Primary subject: Long-Range Strategic Planning (energy).

Secondary subject: N/A

Profile: Tracks imports into the United States of crude oil and petroleum products. Data coverage includes country of origin, port of entry, quantity data, import/export companies involved and ultimate destination of shipment.

Applications: Oil imports analysis.

Subject cross reference: 9.6 and 10.5.

Geographic coverage: Domestic.

Time coverage: 1977 to present.

Online vendor(s): The Computer Company (Oil Imports).
I.P. Sharp Associates (Imports).

INDEX TO API ABSTRACTS/LITERATURE (APILIT)

Producer: American Petroleum Institute (API), Central Abstracting and Indexing Service
156 William Street
New York, New York 10038
(212) 587-9660

Class: Reference.

Data source: Trade journals, technical journals, meeting papers, and government reports.

Size: 250,000 citations.

Maintenance: 1,500 records monthly.

Primary subject: Long-Range Strategic Planning (energy).

Secondary subject: Environmental Affairs.

Profile: Maintains citations and abstracts to literature relative to petroleum refining, petrochemicals, air and water conservation, transportation and storage, and petroleum substitutes. Areas of coverage include alternate energy sources, environmental effects and current technical developments, field chemicals; economic news and general news; petroleum refining, petro-chemicals; transportation and storage.

Applications: New market(s) analysis; industry profiling/opportunities.

Subject cross reference: 6.4, 6.6, and 10.5.

Geographic coverage: International.

Time coverage: 1964 to present.

Online vendor(s): SDC Search Service.

INDEX TO API ABSTRACTS/PATENTS
(APIPAT)

Producer: American Petroleum Institute (API)
Central Abstracting and Indexing Service
156 William Street
New York, New York 10038
(212) 587-9660

Class: Reference.

Data source: Patents.

Size: 100,000 records.

Maintenance: Approximately 500 records monthly.

Primary subject: Long-Range Strategic Planning (energy).

Secondary subject: Research and Development.

Profile: Contains citations to petroleum refining patents from the U.S. and eight other countries. Patents issued on oil field chemicals are also covered. Available on a limited basis to non-subscribing organizations in those countries in which at least one subscriber is located.

Applications: Product research and development.

Subject cross reference: 6.4, 6.6, 8.7, and 10.5.

Geographic coverage: U.S., Great Britain, Belgium, France Japan, The Netherlands, South Africa, and West Germany.

Time coverage: 1964 to present.

Online vendor(s): SDC Search Service.

INDUSTRIAL BANK OF JAPAN

Producer: Industrial Bank of Japan, Ltd.
1-1 Yaesu
5-Chrome
Chuo-Ku, Tokyo 104, Japan
(03) 216-0251

Class: Statistical.

Data source: Company financial statements.

Size: 100+ companies.

Maintenance: Annually.

Primary subject: Banking, Economics, and Finance.

Secondary subject: N/A

Profile: Maintains financial profile data (from income statements and balance sheets) on approximately 100 major internationally- oriented industrial companies in Japan. Provides yearly data for an individual company or for several companies which may designate a specific year's data. Up to six financial statements are provided.

Applications: Japanese international trade; company profile analysis.

Subject cross reference: 1.11 and 2.1.

Geographic coverage: Japan.

Time coverage: N/A

Online vendor(s): General Electric Information Services Co.

INFLATION PLANNER FORECAST

Producer: Chase Econometrics/Interactive Data Corporation
486 Totten Pond Road
Waltham, Massachusetts 02154
(617) 890-1234

Class: Statistical.

Data source: Bureau of Labor Statistics, Chase Econometrics Inflation Planner Model.

Size: 200+ materials.

Maintenance: Monthly.

Primary subject: Banking, Economics, and Finance.

Secondary subject: Multidisciplinary.

Profile: Provides quarterly (for eight months) and yearly (for ten years) forecasts for materials' prices from very specific cents per pound and eight-digit SIC producer prices to aggregate price indices and wage rates. Some of the materials included are aluminum, brass, copper, electrical machinery, furniture, transportation equipment, and textile products.

Applications: Pricing programs and analysis; product introductions; materials management (purchasing).

Subject cross reference: 1.5, 2.14, and 7.10.

Geographic coverage: Domestic.

Time coverage: 1947 through forecasted period.

Online vendor(s): Chase Econometrics/Interactive Data Corp.

THE INFORMATION BANK®

Producer: The New York Times Information Service, Inc.
Mt. Pleasant Office Park
1719A Route 10
Parsippany, New Jersey 07054
(201) 539-5850

Class: Reference.

Data source: Newspapers, business publications, science publications, international publications and periodicals.

Size: Nearly 2 million references.

Maintenance: Approximately 400 records daily.

Primary subject: Multidisciplinary.

Secondary subject: N/A

Profile: A comprehensive current-affairs data base consisting of informative abstracts from many major English-language publications. Coverage includes general news articles, editorials, features, analyses, forecasts, diagrams, charts and surveys.

Applications: New product development input; banking—potential loan customers; economic forecasting issues; and news tracking.

Subject cross reference: 1.19, 2.16, 3.6, 4.6, 5.9, 6.4, 6.8, 7.12, 8.9, 9.20, and 10.8.

Geographic coverage: International.

Time coverage: 1969 to pesent.

Online vendor(s): The New York Times Information Service, Inc.

INFORMATION SERVICE IN MECHANICAL
ENGINEERING (ISMEC)®

Producer: Cambridge Scientific Abstracts
    5161 River Road
    Bethesda, Maryland 20816
    (301) 951-1400
    (800) 638-8076

Class: Reference.

Data source: 250 international journals.

Size: 124,300 citations.

Maintenance: Approximately 1,300 citations monthly.

Primary subject: Industrial and Manufacturing Planning
(engineering).

Secondary subject: N/A

Profile: Maintains an index to significant articles in all aspects
of mechanical engineering, production engineering and
engineering management. The primary engineering areas
covered include mechanical, nuclear, electrical, electronics,
civil, optical, medical and industrial.

Applications: Engineering processes management; engineering
applications analyses.

Subject cross reference: 7.3 and 8.3.

Geographic coverage: International.

Time coverage: 1973 to present.

Online vendor(s): DIALOG Information Services, Inc.
    ESA/QUEST
    SDC Search Service.

INPADOC (IDB)

Producer: International Patent Documentation Center
    INPADOC, Sales Department
    Mollwaldplatz 4
    A-1040 Vienna, Austria
    (0222) 658784

Class: Reference.

Data source: Patents, certificates, and patent applications.

Size: 7 million records.

Maintenance: Bi-weekly.

Primary subject: Research and Development (patents).

Secondary subject: N/A

Profile: Provides references to approximately 16,000 patents
per week from 45 different countries. Covers all types of
patents and contains the standardized bibliographic data in
each record, including patent equivalents in one or more
countries. The classification of patents is according to the
International Patent Classification (IPC) System.

Applications: International patent equivalent comparisons and
analyses; new product research.

Subject cross reference: 2.12, 5.9, and 8.7.

Geographic coverage: International.

Time coverage: 1973 to present.

Online vendor(s): DIALOG Information Services, Inc.

INSTRUCTIONAL RESOURCES
INFORMATION SYSTEM (IRIS)

Producer: U.S. Environmental Protection Agency
    Information Project
    The Ohio State University
    1200 Chambers Road, Room 310
    Columbus, Ohio 43212
    (614) 422-6717

Class: Reference.

Data source: Journals, books, brochures, pamphlets, films,
videotapes, slides and filmstrips from government and
private sources.

Size: 4,000 records.

Maintenance: Semiannually.

Primary subject: Environmental, Social and Political Affairs.

Secondary subject: N/A

Profile: Specialized file of abstracts of educational and
instructional materials on water quality and water
resources. Subject areas covered include water resources
and quality, water treatment, waste disposal, water
pollution and control, safety, standards, toxic substances
and career and occupation information.

Applications: Water resources management.

Subject cross reference: 6.3 and 6.6.

Geographic coverage: Domestic.

Time coverage: 1979 to present.

Online vendor(s): BRS
    DIALOG Information Services, Inc.

INS-U.S. INTERNATIONAL AIR TRAVEL
STATISTICS

Producer: U.S. Department of Transportation
    400 Seventh Street, S.W.
    Washington, D.C. 20590
    (202) 426-4000

Class: Statistical.

Data source: U.S. Department of Transportation and U.S.
Department of Justice, Immigration and Naturalization
Service.

Size: 1 million time series.

Maintenance: Monthly.

Primary subject: General Management (transportation).

Secondary subject: N/A

Profile: Maintains monthly time series showing the number of
passengers flying between the U.S. and other ports. Data
broken down according to passenger citizenship, flight type,
and the nationality of the carrier.

Applications: Analysis of traffic patterns and flows between
geographic areas.

Subject cross reference: 9.18.

Geographic coverage: International.

Time coverage: 1975 to present.

Online vendor(s): The Computer Company
    I.P. Sharp Associates.

INSURANCE FORECAST

Producer: Chase Econometric/Interactive Data Corporation
486 Totten Pond Road
Waltham, Massachusetts 02154
(617) 890-1234

Class: Statistical.

Data source: Institute of Life Insurance, A.M. Best, and Chase Econometrics Insurance Model.

Size: 300 + variables.

Maintenance: Quarterly.

Primary subject: Banking, Economics, and Finance (insurance).

Secondary subject: N/A

Profile: Provides quarterly (for ten quarters) and yearly (for ten years) forecasts for those key variables which affect the life and property-liability insurance industries. Financial variables include consumption, investment, trade, monetary indicators, and consumer indices. Industry variables include premium receipts, operating expenses, reserves, and surplus funds.

Applications: Insurance premium adjustments; pricing policies; insurance industry analyses.

Subject cross reference: 1.8 and 1.13.

Geographic coverage: Domestic.

Time coverage: 1955 through projected time periods.

Online vendor(s): Chase Econometrics/Interactive Data Corp.

INSURANCE INDUSTRY DATA BASE (IIDB)

Producer: National Association of Insurance Commissioners (NAIC)
350 Bishops Way
Brookfield, Wisconsin 53005
(414) 784-9540

Class: Statistical.

Data source: Annual report filings to the NAIC.

Size: 1.6 million records.

Maintenance: Annually.

Primary subject: Banking, Economics, and Finance.

Secondary subject: N/A

Profile: Maintains 1.6 million financial records of over 5,000 U.S. insurance companies. Basic financial statement data are maintained for each company.

Applications: Insurance company financial comparisons and analysis.

Subject cross reference: 1.8, 1.11, and 1.13.

Geographic coverage: Domestic.

Time coverage: 1976 to date.

Online vendor(s): Business Information Services (Control Data).

INTERNATIONAL BUSINESS INTELLIGENCE PROGRAM (B-I-P) INDEX

Producer: SRI International
333 Ravenswood Avenue
Menlo Park, California 94025
(415) 859-6300

Class: Reference.

Data source: B-I-P publications.

Size: 1,000 records.

Maintenance: Semiannually.

Primary subject: Multidisciplinary.

Secondary subject: N/A

Profile: Provides abstracts from four B-I-P publications. Research Reports analyzes key changes which will affect business and industry during the next ten years. Guidelines focuses on short-term business trends. Datalog includes coverage of industry trends, countries and regions, technical developments, and general interest subjects. Scan reviews insights generated by SRI's business environment scanning system.

Applications: Market and industry studies; indentification of emerging technologies; country studies.

Subject cross reference: 2.16, 6.8, 9.12, 10.6, and 10.7.

Geographic coverage: International.

Time coverage: January, 1979, to present.

Online vendor(s): DIALOG Information Services, Inc.

INTERNATIONAL ENERGY DATA BANKS

Producer: U.S. Department of Energy
International Analysis Division
Technical Information Center
Post Office Box 62
Oak Ridge, Tennessee 37830
(615) 596-1155

Class: Statistical.

Data source: Organization for Economic Cooperation and Development (OECD); International Energy Agency.

Size: N/A

Maintenance: Annual.

Primary subject: Long-Range Strategic Planning (energy).

Secondary subject: N/A

Profile: Detail energy sources and uses for all major fuels. Comprised of energy data for many nations of the world. Data are also maintained for member countries of the Organization for Economic Cooperation and Development. Coverage includes fuel types, production, imports, exports, bunkers, capacity and stock additions. OECD country coverage includes production by sector, consumption by sector, imports, exports, supply and distribution.

Applications: Energy production comparisons by country; energy trade comparisons; industrial energy consumption analysis.

Subject cross reference: 9.6 and 10.5.

Geographic coverage: International.

Time coverage: N/A

Online vendor(s): Data Resources, Inc.

INTERNATIONAL FINANCIAL STATISTICS (IFS)

Producer: International Monetary Fund (IMF)
19th and H Street, N.W.
Washington, D.C. 20431
(202) 477-7000

Class: Statistical.

Data source: IMF from statistics supplied by United Nations member countries.

Size: 17,000 time series.

Maintenance: Monthly.

Primary subject: Banking, Economics, and Finance.

Secondary subject: N/A

Profile: Collection of economic and financial statistics for the 150 member nations of the International Monetary Fund. Data are, in many examples, standardized to permit compatibility across countries. Coverage includes exchange rates, international reserves and components; money and banking statistics; interest rates, prices and production; international trade, including imports, exports, and balance of payments data; government finance, revenue, expenditures and financing; select national income accounts and population statistics.

Applications: Analyses of a country's general economic and financial profile.

Subject cross reference: 1.3, 1.4, 1.5, 1.7, 1.8, 1.9, 1.14, 2.5, and 9.12.

Geographic coverage: International.

Time coverage: 1948 to present.

Online vendor(s): ADP Network Services, Inc.
Business Information Services (Control Data)
Chase Econometrics/Interactive Data Corp.
COMSHARE, Inc.
Data Resources, Inc.
FRI Information Services
I.P. Sharp Associates
Rapidata, Inc.

INTERNATIONAL PHARMACEUTICAL ABSTRACTS (IPA)

Producer: American Society of Hospital Pharmacists (ASHP)
4630 Montgomery Avenue
Washington, D.C. 20014
(301) 657-3000

Class: Reference.

Data source: 600 pharmaceutical, medical and related journals.

Size: 71,513 citations.

Maintenance: Bimonthly.

Primary subject: General Management (health care, hospitals, and medicine).

Secondary subject: Research and Development

Profile: Contains information on all phases of the development and use of drugs and on professional pharmaceutical practice. Coverage ranges from clinical, practical and theoretical to economic and scientific aspects of the literature.

Applications: Tracking new drug developments.

Subject cross reference: 2.12, 5.7, 5.8, 7.7, 8.1, 8.2, 8.6, 8.7, and 8.8.

Geographic coverage: International.

Time coverage: 1970 to present.

Online vendor(s): BRS, Inc.
DIALOG Information Services, Inc.

INTERNATIONAL SOFTWARE DIRECTORY

Producer: Imprint Editions
1520 South College
Fort Collins, Colorado 80520
(303) 482-5574

Class: Reference.

Data source: *International Microcomputer Software Directory*.

Size: 5,000 records.

Maintenance: Monthly.

Primary subject: General Management (information processing technology).

Secondary subject: N/A

Profile: Maintains a list of all commercially available software for any type of microcomputer. Records consist of a short two or three line description of each software item with indexing by broad applications categories such as medical, dental, educational, scientific and systems. Items are coded by names of compatible microcomputers such as Apple, Atari, TRS-80, etc. Purchase prices and supplier names and addresses are included.

Applications: Designed to keep the microcomputer owner informed of the wide range of available software.

Subject cross reference: 9.11.

Geographic coverage: International.

Time coverage: Currently available sources.

Online vendor(s): DIALOG Information Services, Inc.

IRON AND STEEL FORECAST

Producer: Chase Econometrics/Interactive Data Corporation
486 Totten Pond Road
Waltham, Massachusetts 02154
(617) 890-1234

Class: Statistical.

Data source: Government agencies and the Chase Econometric Iron and Steel Model.

Size: Several time series.

Maintenance: Quarterly.

Primary subject: Industrial and Manufacturing Planning.

Secondary subject: N/A

Profile: Provides import data for all 7-digit U.S. tariff schedule (TSUSA) codes for iron and steel which are classified on two value bases and quantity, by country of origin, district, and region of entry.

Applications: Industrial forecasts; materials management.

Subject cross reference: 7.5, 7.6, 7.10, 9.1, and 10.5.

Geographic coverage: U.S., Japan and Europe.

Time coverage: 1960 through forecasted time period.

Online vendor(s): Chase Econometrics/Interactive Data Corp.

KEY ISSUES TRACKING (KIT)^{SM}

Producer: The New York Times Information Service, Inc.
Mt. Pleasant Office Park
1719-A Route 10
Parsippany, New Jersey 07054
(201) 539-5850
(800) 631-8056

Class: Reference.

Data source: Over 40 leading publications.

Size: N/A

Maintenance: Daily.

Primary subject: Multidisciplinary.

Secondary subject: N/A

Profile: KIT originated as a concept developed jointly by the New York Times Information Service and the White House to track the important social, political and economic issues that affect our society. KIT maintains information on key political (law, labor, etc.) figures, organizations and issues.

Applications: Special news issue tracking.

Subject cross reference: 1.19, 2.16, 3.6, 4.6, 5.9, 6.8, 7.12, 8.9, 9.20, and 10.8.

Geographic coverage: International.

Time coverage: 1978 to present.

Online vendor(s): The New York Times Information Service, Inc.

LABORDOC

Producer: International Labour Office (ILO)
CH-1211
Geneva 22, Switzerland
(22) 998684

Class: Reference.

Data source: Monthly bulletins, periodicals, and books.

Size: 4,800 citations.

Maintenance: Approximately 500 items monthly.

Primary subject: General Management (union/labor activity).

Secondary subject: N/A

Profile: Covers worldwide journal and monographic literature in the fields of labor and labor-related areas, including industrial relations, economic and social development, education, management, demography, law and the environment.

Applications: Labor relations administration and analyses.

Subject cross reference: 9.8, 9.14, and 9.19.

Geographic coverage: International.

Time coverage: 1965 to present.

Online vendor(s): SDC Search Service.

LATIN AMERICA DATA BANK

Producer: Data Resources, Inc.
29 Hartwell Avenue
Lexington, Massachusetts 02173
(617) 861-0165

Class: Statistical.

Data source: Official (government backed) national agencies.

Size: Time series on seven countries.

Maintenance: Monthly, quarterly and annually.

Primary subject: Business (economics).

Secondary subject: N/A

Profile: Maintains a variety of economic and financial information designed to provide an in-depth current profile of Latin America. The main concepts covered include balance of payments, employment and labor force, finance, foreign trade, national income accounts, prices and production.

Applications: Latin American economic monitoring and forecasting.

Subject cross reference: 1.8, 1.9, and 9.12.

Geographic coverage: Argentina, Brazil, Chile, Colombia, Jamaica, Mexico, and Venezuela.

Time coverage: Varies by series.

Online vendor(s): Data Resources, Inc.

LEGAL RESOURCE INDEX (LRI)®

Producer: Information Access Corporation (IAC)
885 N. San Antonio Road
Los Altos, California 94022
(415) 941-1100

Class: Reference.

Data source: 660 key law journals, 5 law newspapers and government publications from the Library of Congress MARC data base.

Size: 53,000 records.

Maintenance: Approximately 3,000 records monthly.

Primary subject: Legal and Legislative Affairs.

Secondary subject: N/A

Profile: Indexes articles, book reviews, case notes, president's pages, columns, letters to the editor, obituaries, transcripts, biographical pieces and editorials.

Applications: Secondary information sources for the legal profession and others.

Subject cross reference: 5.4.

Geographic coverage: International.

Time coverage: 1980 to present.

Online vendor(s): DIALOG Information Services, Inc.

LEXIS

Producer: Mead Data Central
200 Park Avenue
New York, New York 10017
(212) 883-8560

Class: Reference.

Data source: Newspapers, magazines and wire services.

Size: 1.25 million records.

Maintenance: Approximately 10,000 records monthly, but varies by file.

Primary subject: Legal and Legislative Affairs.

Secondary subject: N/A

Profile: A collection of files (libraries) which contain full text reference to court decisions, regulations, news, government affairs and statutes. Includes both federal and state activities.

Applications: Legislation tracking; quotations from recent court decisions; court reporter information access.

Subject cross reference: 5.1, 5.2, 5.3, 5.4, 5.5, 5.6, 5.7, and 5.8.

Geographic coverage: U.S., France and the United Kingdom.

Time coverage: Depends upon the specific file, some go back to 1890's.

Online vendor(s): Mead Data Central

LIBRARY AND INFORMATION SCIENCE ABSTRACTS (LISA)

Producer: The Library Association
7 Ridgemount Street
London, England WC1E 7AE
(01) 636 7543

Class: Reference.

Data source: The British Library and the Association of Special Libraries and Information Bureaux.

Size: 42,800 records.

Maintenance: Approximately 900 records bimonthly.

Primary subject: General Management (information processing technology).

Secondary subject: N/A

Profile: Provides coverage of all phases of librarianship and library services as well as micrographics, word processing, electronic publishing, viewdata, and teletext. A special feature for business is the secondary index service of data base producers and the information industry.

Applications: Data base directory; information management (source directory).

Subject cross reference: 2.9 and 9.11.

Geographic coverage: International.

Time coverage: 1969 to date.

Online vendor(s): DIALOG Information Services, Inc.
SDC Search Service.

MAGAZINE INDEX®

Producer: Information Access Corporation
404 Sixth Avenue
Menlo Park, California 94025
(415) 367-7171
(800) 227-8431

Class: Reference.

Data source: 370 U.S. and foreign journals and magazines.

Size: 588,500 citations.

Maintenance: Approximately 10,000 records monthly.

Primary subject: Multidisciplinary.

Secondary subject: N/A

Profile: Magazine Index was the first online data base to offer an index to a broad coverage of general magazines. Topics covered include: current affairs, leisure time activities, sports, recreation, travel, business, science and technology, consumer product evaluations and other areas.

Applications: Market research (companies in the news); public relations and government relations; news item tracking.

Subject cross reference: 1.19, 2.16, 3.6, 4.6, 5.9, 6.8, 7.12, 8.9, 9.20 and 10.8.

Geographic coverage: U.S. and Canada.

Time coverage: 1976 to present.

Online vendor(s): DIALOG Information Services, Inc.

MANAGEMENT CONTENTS®

Producer: Management Contents, Inc.
2265 Carlson Drive, Suite 5000
Northbrook, Illinois 60062
(312) 564-1006
(800) 323-5354

Class: Reference.

Data source: 325 U.S. and foreign journals, magazines and proceedings.

Size: 90,100 citations.

Maintenance: Approximately 1,200 citations monthly.

Primary subject: Multidisciplinary.

Secondary subject: N/A

Profile: Maintains current information on a variety of business and management related topics. Business disciplines covered include marketing, management, economics, operations research, organization behavior, public administration, accounting and finance.

Applications: Consulting firms, government agencies, educational institutions and libraries can reference contents to aid decisionmaking, forecasting and planning.

Subject cross reference: 1.19, 2.16, 3.6, 4.6, 5.9, 6.8, 7.12, 8.9, 9.20, and 10.8.

Geographic coverage: International.

Time coverage: 1974 to present.

Online vendor(s): BRS, Inc.
DATA-STAR
DIALOG Information Services, Inc.
SDC Search Service.

MARKETBASE®

Producer: Urban Decision Systems, Inc.
2032 Armacost Avenue
Post Office Box 25953
Los Angeles, California 90025
(213) 820-8931

Class: Statistical.

Data source: U.S. Census Bureau, Bureau of Labor Statistics, Bureau of Economic Analysis and several local and regional planning agencies.

Size: 200+ census parameters.

Maintenance: Estimates annually; zip code data semiannually.

Primary subject: Marketing Planning.

Secondary subject: N/A

Profile: A combined demographics data base and reporting system which allows the user to generate a demographic study of any size or shape within the United States; add data to be used in conjunction with the system's demographic data; design custom output, either printed reports or machinereadable files; and perform various ranking analyses of the data.

Applications: Users may select demographic studies by zip code, county and areas of dominant influence.

Subject cross reference: 2.3 and 2.4.

Geographic coverage: Domestic.

Time coverage: 1970 and 1980 censuses; 1985 projections.

Online vendor(s): National CSS, Inc.

MARKET PROGRAM

Producer: Marshall and Swift Publication Company
1617 Beverly Boulevard
Post Office Box 26307
Los Angeles, California 90026
(213) 624-6451
(800) 421-8042

Class: Statistical.

Data source: Participating mortgage and savings/loan companies in 28 states from the California Market Data Cooperative and the SREA Market Data Center.

Size: 1 million + records.

Maintenance: Biweekly.

Primary subject: General Management (real estate and building trends).

Secondary subject: N/A

Profile: Retrieves current sales information on single-family residences in a specific neighborhood. There are over 50 property characteristics for individual sales. A special program is used to analyze individual neighborhoods and to select comparable sales. Multiple regression analysis can also be used in order to determine the property characteristics' effect on sales price and to predict sales price.

Applications: Comparative housing (price and standards) studies; filing complex housing forms assistance.

Subject cross reference: 9.15.

Geographic coverage: Domestic.

Time coverage: Current 18 months.

Online vendor(s): Marshall and Swift Publication Co.

MEDIA GENERAL DATA BASE

Producer: Media General Financial Services
301 East Grace
Richmond, Virginia
(804) 649-6736

Class: Statistical.

Data source: Domestic stock exchanges.

Size: 3,200+ companies.

Maintenance: Weekly.

Primary subject: Banking, Economics, and Finance.

Secondary subject: N/A

Profile: Maintains financial profile information for over 3,200 companies listed on the New York, American, and Over-the-Counter Exchanges from over 180 industries. Data covers 52 statistical indicators and includes stock price, P/E ratio, earnings and earnings per share, dividends, revenue and volume.

Applications: Company (financial) comparisons; industry analysis.

Subject cross reference: 1.11, 1.16, 2.1, and 9.13.

Geographic coverage: Domestic.

Time coverage: N/A

Online vendor(s): Dow Jones & Company, Inc.

MEDICAL DOCUMENTS (MEDOC)

Producer: University of Utah
Eccles Health Sciences Library, Bldg. 89
Salt Lake City, Utah 84112
(801) 581-5269

Class: Reference.

Data source: Food and Drug Administration and miscellaneous documents.

Size: 7,000 records.

Maintenance: Quarterly.

Primary subject: General Management (health care).

Secondary subject: N/A

Profile: Covers an assortment of government literature in medicine, health services, food, drugs, mental health, and biomedical engineering. Coverage includes medicine, veterinary medicine, Medicare and Medicaid, nutrition, aging, child development, welfare, behavioral science and consumer safety issues.

Applications: Biomedical research and analysis; annual biomedicine reference aid.

Subject cross reference: 9.3, 9.7, and 9.8.

Geographic coverage: Domestic.

Time coverage: 1976 to present.

Online vendor(s): BRS, Inc.

MEDLINE

Producer: U.S. National Library of Medicine
8600 Rockville Pike
Bethesda, Maryland 20209
(301) 496-6217

Class: Reference.

Data source: *Index Medicus, Index to Dental Literature*, and *International Nursing Index*.

Size: 3.4 million records.

Maintenance: Approximately 20,000 records monthly.

Primary subject: General Management (health care, hospitals, and medicine).

Secondary subject: N/A

Profile: A major source for biomedical literature. Medline indexes articles from over 3,000 international journals published in the U.S. and 70 other countries.

Applications: Biomedical research and reference aid.

Subject cross reference: 8.9 and 9.7.

Geographic coverage: International.

Time coverage: 1977 to present.

Online vendor(s): BRS, Inc.
DIALOG Information Services, Inc.
National Library of Medicine.

MERGERS AND ACQUISITIONS®

Producer: Securities Data Company
62 William Street
6th Floor
New York, New York 10005
(212) 668-0940

Class: Statistical.

Data source: Circular Offerings.

Size: 1,200 records.

Maintenance: Daily.

Primary subject: Long-Range Strategic Planning (mergers).

Secondary subject: Banking, Economics, and Finance.

Profile: Provides information on mergers, tender offers, and exchange offers domestically and internationally. Data items include the target and the acquiror's financial status, managers, fees, specifics of all transactions, price tracking, and geographical location of the target and acquiror.

Applications: Market research; new merger analysis.

Subject cross reference: 1.11, 1.18, 5.5, and 10.1.

Geographic coverage: International.

Time coverage: 1981 to present.

Online vendor(s): Securities Data Company.

MERRILL LYNCH ECONOMICS NATIONAL DATA BASE

Producer: Merrill Lynch Economics, Inc.
One Liberty Plaza
165 Broadway
New York, New York 10080
(212) 766-6200

Class: Statistical.

Data source: U.S. Government and private organization statistics.

Size: 12,000+ time series.

Maintenance: Daily.

Primary subject: Banking, Economics, and Finance.

Secondary subject: N/A

Profile: Maintains data on national income, international transactions (federal), plant/equipment expenditures, Federal Reserve Board production indices, survey of manufacturers, consumer/wholesale price indices, retail/wholesale trade, monetary statistics, motor vehicle registration information, and various other national economic and financial data.

Applications: Econometric forecasting.

Subject cross reference: 1.8, 1.9, and 9.13.

Geographic coverage: Primarily domestic.

Time coverage: Varies by series, many from 1940's.

Online vendor(s): National CSS, Inc.

MERRILL LYNCH ECONOMICS REGIONAL DATA BASE

Producer: Merrill Lynch Economics, Inc.
One Liberty Plaza
165 Broadway
New York, New York 10080
(212) 766-6200

Class: Statistical.

Data source: U.S. government and private organization statistics.

Size: 50,000 + time series.

Maintenance: Daily.

Primary subject: Banking, Economics, and Finance.

Secondary subject: Marketing Planning.

Profile: Maintains demographic and economic data for individual states and SMSA's on labor force trends, population, tax payments, industrial profiles, retail sales, construction, income, and housing starts.

Applications: Econometric forecasting; trend analysis of any of the above factors.

Subject cross reference: 1.8, 1.9, 2.4, 2.5, 7.5, and 9.15.

Geographic coverage: Domestic.

Time coverage: Varies by series.

Online vendor(s): National CSS, Inc.

METALS WEEK

Producer: McGraw-Hill, Inc.
1221 Avenue of the Americas
New York, New York 10020
(212) 997-1221

Class: Statistical.

Data source: *Metals Week* quotations.

Size: 42 nonferrous metals series.

Maintenance: Weekly.

Primary subject: Banking, Economics, and Finance.

Secondary subject: N/A

Profile: Includes historical time series for all metal prices quoted by *Metals Week* and four exchange rates (British, German, Japanese and Malaysian). Metal prices are listed in the following frequencies: daily; weekly averages of dailies; monthly averages of dailies; weekly; monthly averages of weeklies; annual averages of monthly averages.

Applications: Contract pricing of metals and ores; determining freight rates.

Subject cross reference: 1.16, 2.8, 2.10, 2.14, and 7.10.

Geographic coverage: International.

Time coverage: 1972 to present.

Online vendor(s): Chase Econometrics/Interactive Data Corp.

METEOROLOGICAL AND GEOASTROPHYSICAL ABSTRACTS (MGA)

Producer: American Meteorological Society
45 Beacon Street
Boston, Massachusetts 02108
(617) 227-2425

Class: Reference.

Data source: Technical journals, monographs, proceedings and reviews.

Size: 81,900 records.

Maintenance: Approximately 7,200 records yearly.

Primary subject: Environmental, Social and Political Affairs.

Secondary subject: N/A

Profile: Provides current citations in English for the most important meteorological and geoastrophysical research published in worldwide literature sources. Subject coverage includes meteorology, astrophysics, physical oceanography, hydrosphere/hydrology, environmental sciences and glaciology.

Applications: Environmental/meteorological studies and reference aid.

Subject cross reference: 6.3.

Geographic coverage: International.

Time coverage: 1970 to present.

Online vendor(s): DIALOG Information Services, Inc.

MICROCOMPUTER INDEX®

Producer: Microcomputer Information Service
2464 El Camino Real
Suite 247
Santa Clara, California 95051
(408) 984-1097

Class: Reference.

Data source: Journal articles, book reviews, software reviews, and discussions of applications.

Size: 6,000 records.

Maintenance: Quarterly.

Primary subject: General Management.

Secondary subject: N/A

Profile: Subject and abstract guide to magazine articles from over 21 microcomputer journals. Publications include *Byte, Interface Age, InfoWorld, Personal Computing, Softside* and *Dr. Dobb's Journal*.

Applications: Business applications processing alternatives; microcomputer selection reference.

Subject cross reference: 9.11.

Geographic coverage: International.

Time coverage: 1980 to present.

Online vendor(s): DIALOG Information Services, Inc.

MICROQUOTE

Producer: CompuServe
Internation Services Division
5000 Arlington Centre Boulevard
Columbus, Ohio 43220
(614) 457-8600

Class: Statistical.

Data source: Major U.S. stock exchanges and Over-The-Counter stocks.

Size: 40,000 records.

Maintenance: Daily.

Primary subject: Banking, Economics, and Finance (securities).

Secondary subject: N/A

Profile: Provides statistics and descriptive information on stocks, bonds, and options. Data items on stocks include current and historical high, low, and closing prices, volumes, dividends, earnings per share, ratings, and shares outstanding. Data items on bonds include yields, maturity dates, and Moody's ratings. Data items on options include exercise prices, expiration dates, and underlying stock prices.

Applications: Stock portfolio analysis.

Subject cross reference: 1.16.

Geographic coverage: Domestic.

Time coverage: 1973 to present.

Online vendor(s): CompuServe, Inc.

MIDDLE EAST DATA BASE (MEDAB)®

Producer: The New York Times Information Service, Inc. and the Middle East Research Centre (MERC)
Mt. Pleasant Office Park
1719-A Route 10
Parsippany, New Jersey 07054
(201) 539-5850
(800) 631-8056

Class: Reference.

Data source: MERC and the NYTIS (summaries of approximately 20 journals and wire services).

Size: 20,000 records.

Maintenance: Daily.

Primary subject: General Management (international news).

Secondary subject: N/A

Profile: Maintains business and economic articles pertaining to the Middle East. Daily news summaries are telexed directly from the Middle East.

Applications: Users (oil companies and related energy companies) may view current political, economic, agricultural and educational news items from the Middle East.

Subject cross reference: 2.6, 6.2, 6.4, 6.7, 7.5, 9.1, 9.12, 9.13, and 10.5.

Geographic coverage: Middle East.

Time coverage: 1980 to present.

Online vendor(s): The New York Times Information Service, Inc.

MINSYS

Producer: Geosystems
Post Office Bos 1024
Westminster, London
England SW1P 2JL
(01) 222-7305

Class: Reference.

Data source: Journals, serials, books, press releases, shareholder statements, annual reports, and direct data from mining companies and equipment manufacturers.

Size: 9,000 records.

Maintenance: Daily.

Primary subject: General Management (agriculture and mining).

Secondary subject: N/A

Profile: Maintains information on mining resources, minerals, and related mineral topics, organizations, and locations. Coverage includes mineral processing, exploration, production, development, extractive metallurgy, equipment, management, environmental considerations, marketing and governmental relations.

Applications: Location of mining resources; mineral research.

Subject cross reference: 7.10, 8.2, and 9.1.

Geographic coverage: International.

Time coverage: 1980 to present.

Online vendor(s): Geosystems.

MONEY MARKET RATES (MRATE)

Producer: I.P. Sharp Associates
145 King Street West
Toronto, Ontario, Canada M5H 1J8
(416) 364-5361

Class: Statistical.

Data source: *Financial Times of London, Toronto's Globe and Mail, Bond and Money Market Letters.*

Size: 200+ time series.

Maintenance: Daily.

Primary subject: Banking, Economics and Finance.

Secondary subject: N/A

Profile: A growing collection of approximately 200 time series of money market data from around the world. Coverage includes Eurodollar data (interest rates), prime rates, banker acceptance rates, certificates of deposit, dollar swaps, U.S. treasury bill status, mortgage data and trust company paper information.

Applications: Data for international financial transactions.

Subject cross reference: 1.3, 1.4, 1.6, 1.8, 1.14, and 1.15.

Geographic coverage: International.

Time coverage: 1979 to present.

Online vendor(s): I.P. Sharp Associates.

NABSCAN DATA BASE®

Producer: Nabscan
485 Lexington Avenue
New York, New York 10017
(212) 557-1843

Class: Statistical.

Data source: Individual supermarket product movement data.

Size: 500+ stores.

Maintenance: Weekly.

Primary subject: Marketing Planning.

Secondary subject: N/A

Profile: Provides product price and movement data from 500+ stores representing 30+ chains and wholesalers in 80+ SMSA's. The data represent 175,000 Universal Product Codes (UPC) in approximately 800 product categories. Data may be reported by individual store, chains, or geographic area.

Applications: User may generate by location, specific product/brand groupings, time designation, store classification, price and other UPC identifiers.

Subject cross reference: 2.1, 2.2, 2.3, 2.14, 9.16, and 9.17.

Geographic coverage: Domestic.

Time coverage: Current data; some data from 1980.

Online vendor(s): Management Science Associates, Inc.

NATIONAL AUTOMATED ACCOUNTING RESEARCH SYSTEM (NAARS)

Producer: American Institute of Certified Public Accountants (AICPA)
1211 Avenue of the Americas
New York, New York 10017
(212) 575-6393

Class: Reference.

Data source: Financial staements, auditor's reports, selected annual reports, proxy statements, and various accounting literature.

Size: 4,000+ companies and various accounting promulgations.

Maintenance: Weekly.

Primary subject: Banking, Economics, and Finance.

Secondary subject: N/A

Profile: A full-text data base consisting of several files, each pertaining to the accounting discipline. The general information accounting literature file contains references to proxy and opinion statements and full-text reviews of related auditing promulgations. The annual reports file contains financial reports with footnotes and auditor's reports from the annual statements of 4,000+ companies.

Applications: Company profiles and comparisons; accounting reference aid.

Subject cross reference: 1.1, 1.11, and 2.1.

Geographic coverage: Domestic.

Time coverage: Most current references.

Online vendor(s): Mead Data Central.

NATIONAL COAL RESOURCES DATA SYSTEM (NCRDS)

Producer: U.S. Geological Survey
Office of Energy Resources
115 National Center
Reston, Virginia 22092
(703) 860-6086

Class: Statistical.

Data source: U.S. Geological Survey Laboratories, Department of Energy, U.S. Bureau of Mines, and other government agencies.

Size: 100,000+ records.

Maintenance: As new data become available.

Primary subject: General Management (mining).

Secondary subject: Research and Development.

Profile: Maintains published coal resource quality and quantity data for selected coal producing states. Coal analyses data are available through the departments above. Data in the system are available through four separate data bases: (1) ECOAL—Coal resource estimates for states east of the Mississippi; (2) WCOAL—Same for states west; (3) BMALYT—Coal sample chemical analyses; and (4) USCHEM—Element analysis of coal.

Applications: Coal production analyses; composition analyses.

Subject cross reference: 8.4, 8.6, and 9.1.

Geographic coverage: Domestic.

Time coverage: 1974 to present.

Online vendor(s): Computer Sciences Corporation.

NATIONAL ELECTRICAL MANUFACTURERS ASSOCIATION DATA BASE (NEMA)

Producer: National Electrical Manufacturers Association (NEMA)
2101 L Street N.W.
Suite 300
Washington, D.C. 20037
(202) 457-8400

Class: Statistical.

Data source: NEMA Quarterly—*Survey of Business Trends in the Electrical Manufacturing Industry*.

Size: Several time series.

Maintenance: Quarterly.

Primary subject: Industrial and Manufacturing Planning.

Secondary subject: N/A

Profile: Maintains time series on orders (unfilled and filled) and shipments for seven major segments of the electrical manufacturing industry. Equipment categories include power, industry, building, insulation, lighting, wire and cable. User must be a NEMA member to access this data base.

Applications: Supply and demand analysis; forecasting; market planning reference.

Subject cross reference: 2.8, 7.10, and 7.12.

Geographic coverage: Domestic.

Time coverage: Current order status.

Online vendor(s): General Electric Information Services Co.

NATIONAL NEWSPAPER INDEX (NNI)®

Producer: Information Access Corporation
404 Sixth Avenue
Menlo Park, California 94025
(415) 367-7171
(800) 227-8431

Class: Reference.

Data source: *New York Times, Wall Street Journal,* and the *Christian Science Monitor.*

Size: 391,400 records.

Maintenance: Monthly.

Primary subject: Multidisciplinary (news).

Secondary subject: N/A

Profile: Provides front to back page indexing of the *Christian Science Monitor*, the *New York Times* and the *Wall Street Journal*. Items not appearing in this data base include weather charts, stock market tables, crossword puzzles and horoscopes.

Applications: Answers to general reference questions; acts as a valuable adjunct in such areas as market research, journalism, social sciences, food and nutrition and public relations.

Subject cross reference: 1.19, 2.16, 3.6, 4.6, 5.9, 6.4, 6.8, 7.12, 8.9, 9.20, and 10.8.

Geographic coverage: International.

Time coverage: 1979 to present.

Online vendor(s): DIALOG Information Services, Inc.

NATIONAL PLANNING ASSOCIATION ECONOMIC DATA (NPA/ECONOMIC)

Producer: National Planning Association (NPA)
1606 New Hampshire Avenue, N.W.
Washington, D.C. 20009
(202) 265-7685

Class: Statistical.

Data source: The NPA

Size: 200,000 time series.

Maintenance: Daily.

Primary subject: Banking, Economics, and Finance.

Secondary subject: Marketing Planning.

Profile: The NPA data base contains over 200,000 annual time series of economic data for the United States. These data are segmented by county, state, region, BEA (Bureau of Economic Analysis) economic area, and SMSA (Standard Metropolitan Statistical Area). Each area maintains 56 items (or accounts) covering employment, income, earnings and population.

Applications: U.S. economic projections and analysis.

Subject cross reference: 1.8, 2.4, 2.5, 2.10, and 2.13.

Geographic coverage: Domestic.

Time coverage: 1967 to present.

Online vendor(s): I.P. Sharp Associates.

NATIONAL TECHNICAL INFORMATION SERVICE (NTIS)®

Producer: U.S. National Technical Information Service
Office of Data Base Services, 5285 Port Royal Road
Springfield, Virginia 22161
(703) 487-4600

Class: Reference.

Data source: Department of Commerce, NASA, HUD, HEW, DOE and the DDC.

Size: 863,500 citations.

Maintenance: Approximately 2,500 citations biweekly.

Primary subject: Research and Development.

Secondary subject: N/A

Profile: Consists of government sponsored research, development and engineering. Special analyses are also provided by federal agencies, their contractors and grantees. Unclassified, publicly available, unlimited reports are made available from such agencies as NASA, HUD and DOT. NTIS includes material from both the hard and soft sciences, including substantial data on technological applications, business procedures and regulatory matters.

Applications: Environmental, energy and technological analysis and planning reference.

Subject cross reference: 5.8, 6.3, 6.6, 7.3, 8.2, 8.3, 8.9, and 10.5.

Geographic coverage: Domestic.

Time coverage: 1964 to present.

Online vendor(s): BRS, Inc.
DIALOG Information Services, Inc.
SDC Search Service.

NEW ISSUES OF CORPORATE SECURITIES

Producer: Security Data Company
62 William Street, 6th Floor
New York, New York 10005
(212) 668-0940

Class: Statistical.

Data source: Securities and Exchange Commission.

Size: 13,000 records.

Maintenance: Daily.

Primary subject: Banking, Economics, and Finance.

Secondary subject: N/A

Profile: Provides information on taxable debt, common stock, and preferred stock offered publicly and underwritten in the United States. Data items include number of shares, offering price, and pricing history for common stock; coupon, offering price, maturity, call/sinking fund provisions, and dividend, offering price, and redemption/sinking fund provisions for secured stock.

Applications: Pricing decisions for underwriters; various stock portfolio analyses.

Subject cross reference: 1.11 and 1.16.

Geographic coverage: Domestic.

Time coverage: 1970 to present.

Online vendor(s): Securities Data Company.

NEW ISSUES OF MUNICIPAL DEBT

Producer: Securities Data Company
62 William Street, Sixth Floor
New York, New York 10005
(212) 668-0940

Class: Statistical.

Data source: Securities and Exchange Commission.

Size: 2,300 records.

Maintenance: Daily.

Primary subject: Banking, Economics, and Finance.

Secondary subject: N/A

Profile: Provides data on new issues of publicly offered and privately placed tax-exempt negotiated debt offerings. Data items include descriptive information on each issue, such as coupon, offering price, maturity, call and sinking fund provisions, underwriters and fees, trustee, and issuer's location.

Applications: Pricing decisions for underwriters; market research.

Subject cross reference: 1.16.

Geographic coverage: Domestic.

Time coverage: 1980 to present.

Online vendor(s): Securities Data Company.

NEWSBEAT

Producer: GTE Information Systems, Inc.
East Park Drive
Mount Laurel, New Jersey 08054
(609) 235-7300

Class: Reference.

Data source: Dow Jones newswire, *Wall Street Journal*, and *Barron's*.

Size: N/A

Maintenance: Daily.

Primary subject: Banking, Economics, and Finance.

Secondary subject: N/A

Profile: Provides real-time access to news stories which have appeared in the above sources. Options include headline scanning (by date or company), complete story retrieval, and subjection classification scanning. A separate "Hot News" feature allows the user to search headlines of important and timely topics.

Applications: Users can track news stories from a "headline list" and select by security or subject code.

Subject cross reference: 1.9, 1.12, 1.15, 1.16, 9.13, and 9.20.

Geographic coverage: International.

Time coverage: Latest 90 days.

Online vendor(s): GTE Information Systems, Inc.

NEWSEARCH®

Producer: Information Access Corporation
404 Sixth Avenue
Menlo Park, California 94025
(415) 367-7171
(800) 227-8431

Class: Reference.

Data source: Newspapers, magazines and periodicals.

Size: Varies depending upon day of month (files begin fresh each month).

Maintenance: Daily.

Primary subject: Multidisciplinary.

Secondary subject: N/A

Profile: A daily index of more than 2,000 news stories, information articles and book reviews from over 1,400 important newspapers, magazines and periodicals. Current articles are index every day, including items such as corporate news, executive news, theatre reviews, books, records, etc., are indexed. At the end of each month, the magazine article data is transferred to the Magazine Index data base (DIALOG Information Services, Inc.).

Applications: News reference aids; marketing research (names, corporations, products, etc.).

Subject cross reference: 1.19, 2.16, 3.6, 4.6, 5.9, 6.4, 6.8, 7.12, 8.9, 9.20, and 10.8.

Geographic coverage: International.

Time coverage: Current month only.

Online vendor(s): DIALOG Information Services, Inc.

NEWSPAPER INDEX (NDEX)

Producer: Bell & Howell
Micro Photo Division
Old Mansfield Road
Wooster, Ohio 44691
(216) 264-6666
(800) 321-9881

Class: Reference.

Data source: *Chicago Sun-Times, Chicago Tribune, Denver Post, Detroit News, Houston Post, L.A. Times, New Orleans Times Picayune, San Francisco Chronicle,* the *Washington Post* and the *St. Louis Post Dispatch.* Also, the *Index to Black Newspapers, Amsterdam New York News, Atlanta Daily World, Baltimore Afro-American, Bilalian News, Chicago Defender, Cleveland Call and Post, Norfolk Journal and Guide, Los Angeles Sentinel, Michigan Chronicle, New Pittsburgh Courier* and the *St. Louis Argus.*

Size: 1 million +

Maintenance: Monthly.

Primary subject: Multidisciplinary.

Secondary subject: N/A

Profile: Maintains citations to local, state, national and international news on all business related topics.

Applications: General news reference aid; market research.

Subject cross reference: 1.19, 2.16, 3.6, 4.6, 5.9, 6.4, 6.8, 7.12, 8.9, 9.20, and 10.8.

Geographic coverage: Primarily domestic.

Time coverage: 1976 to present.

Online vendor(s): SDC Search Service.

NEW YORK CITY MODEL DATA BANK

Producer: Data Resources, Inc.
29 Hartwell Avenue
Lexington, Massachusetts 02173
(617) 861-0165

Class: Statistical.

Data source: Federal Reserve Bank of New York, New York State Department of Labor, New York State Division of Housing and Community Renewal, U. S. Department of Commerce, Bureau of Economic Analysis, U. S. Department of Labor, Bureau of Labor Statistics.

Size: N/A

Maintenance: Monthly and quarterly.

Primary subject: Banking, Economics, and Finance.

Secondary subject: N/A

Profile: Maintains a detailed economic data base for the New York Metropolitan area. Data is at the macroeconomic level and includes employment, hours and earnings, personal income by major source, population, housing, prices, financial indicators and retail sales.

Applications: Measuring business activity by specific location; simulating the impact of new/lost business; assessing the impact of changes in public transit fares.

Subject cross reference: 1.8, 2.3, 2.5, and 2.13.

Geographic coverage: New York City and 13 counties surrounding the city.

Time coverage: N/A

Online vendor(s): Data Resources, Inc.

NEXIS®

Producer: Mead Data Central
200 Park Avenue
New York, New York 10017
(212) 883-8560

Class: Reference.

Data source: Newspapers, magazines, wire services and newsletters.

Size: 4.5 billion source characters.

Maintenance: Depending on source, daily to weekly.

Primary subject: Multidisciplinary.

Secondary subject: N/A

Profile: Maintains full-text general and business news. Coverage includes business, management, technology, chemicals, engineering, finance, metals, banking, aerospace, science, politics, religion, media, and mining.

Applications: Marketing reference (markets, industries, corporations, executives, products, promotions, etc.).

Subject cross reference: 1.19, 2.16, 3.6, 4.6, 5.9, 6.4, 6.8, 7.12, 8.9, 9.20, and 10.8.

Geographic coverage: International.

Time coverage: 1977 to present.

Online vendor(s): Mead Data Central.

NIELSEN RETAIL INDEX

Producer: A. C. Nielsen Company
Nielsen Plaza
Northbrook, Illinois 60062
(312) 498-6300

Class: Statistical.

Data source: Neilsen field surveys and audits of selected sample stores.

Size: 85,000 audits in 11,000+ retail stores.

Maintenance: Monthly.

Primary subject: Marketing Planning.

Secondary subject: N/A

Profile: Measures consumer buying patterns by store type, sales area or region, by brand/product, and price. Data are indexed by major media advertising expenditures, in-house advertising support, retailer's gross profits and retail inventory profiles. Product coverage includes food, drug, beauty, health, beer, wine and liquors.

Applications: Promotional effectiveness studies; market share analysis; competitive performance ratings.

Subject cross reference: 2.2, 2.3, 2.5, 2.14, 4.1, 4.4, and 9.16.

Geographic coverage: Domestic.

Time coverage: Current audit data.

Online vendor(s): A. C. Nielsen Company.
ADP Network Services, Inc.
Interactive Market Systems, Inc.
Management Science Associates, Inc.

NIELSEN STATION INDEX

Producer: A.C. Nielsen Company
Nielsen Plaza
Northbrook, Illinois 60062
(312) 498-6300

Class: Statistical.

Data source: Selected households.

Size: 220 television markets.

Maintenance: Monthly.

Primary subject: Marketing and Sales Promotion.

Secondary subject: Marketing Planning.

Profile: Keeps track of family viewing habits by tracking the results of each family's diary. The results are used by advertisers in buying time and by stations for program evaluation.

Applications: Promotional (media) selection; promotional budgeting.

Subject cross reference: 2.2, 2.5, 2.11, 4.1, and 4.4.

Geographic coverage: Domestic.

Time coverage: Varies by market; some for last 8 years.

Online vendor(s): Interactive Market Systems, Inc.
Management Science Associates, Inc.
Market Science Associates, Inc.
Telmar Media Systems, Inc.

NIELSEN TELEVISION INDEX

Producer: A.C. Nielsen Company
Nielsen Plaza
Northbrook, Illinois 60062
(312) 498-6300

Class: Statistical.

Data source: Selected television viewers.

Size: 1,200 television households.

Maintenance: Weekly to monthly.

Primary subject: Marketing and Sales Promotion.

Secondary subject: Marketing Planning.

Profile: Provides national television audience estimates by recording minute-by-minute tuning records of selected viewers. These records are identifiable by geographic location, income, education, and presence of children.

Applications: Audience response analysis; media selection studies.

Subject cross reference: 2.2, 2.5, 2.11, 4.1, and 4.4.

Geographic coverage: Domestic.

Time coverage: 1970 to present.

Online vendor(s): Interactive Market Systems, Inc.
Management Science Associates, Inc.
Market Science Associates, Inc.
Telmar Media Systems, Inc.

NIKKEI ECONOMIC STATISTICS

Producer: Nikkei (Nihon Keizai Shimbun)
Databank Bureau
1-9-5 Okmachi Chiyoda-Ku
Tokyo, Japan 100
(03) 2700251

Class: Statistical.

Data source: Government and private agencies and individual companies.

Size: 130 time series.

Maintenance: Monthly.

Primary subject: Banking, Economics, and Finance.

Secondary subject: N/A

Profile: Also known as the Japanese Data Bank, Nikkei provides macroeconomic data on the Japanese economy. Maintains approximately 130 time series covering national income accounts, products, business activity, finance, household income and expenditures, balance of payments, labor, prices and trade.

Applications: Japanese macroeconomic forecasting; Japanese investment analysis; assessing Japan's impact on specific U.S. industries.

Subject cross reference: 1.4, 1.5, 1.6, 1.7, 1.8, 2.6, and 9.12.

Geographic coverage: Japan.

Time coverage: 1955 to present.

Online vendor(s): Data Resources, Inc.

NIKKEI ENERGY DATA BANK

Producer: Data Resources, Inc.
29 Hartwell Avenue
Lexington, Massachusetts 02173
(617) 861-0165

Class: Statistical.

Data source: Japanese government and energy industrial organizations.

Size: 2,400 time series.

Maintenance: Monthly.

Primary subject: Long-Range Strategic Planning (energy).

Secondary subject: General Management.

Profile: Comprised of 2,400 time series covering energy demand, supply and prices, in addition to essential international and domestic data series for a variety of applications. Data coverage includes general macroeconomic data on the Japanese economy, related industrial statistics, domestic supply and demand data, imported petroleum data, coal and coal sector data, gas data, electricity and nuclear power data and other energy data.

Applications: Examination of current and historical analysis of energy consumption, supply, production and pricing in Japan.

Subject cross reference: 2.6, 7.5, 9.6, and 10.5.

Geographic coverage: Japan.

Time coverage: Depends upon specific series.

Online vendor(s): Data Resources, Inc.

NON-FERROUS METALS FORECAST

Producer: Chase Econometrics/Interactive Data Corporation
486 Totten Pond Road
Waltham, Massachusetts 02154
(617) 890-1234

Class: Statistical.

Data source: Various government agencies and departments.

Size: Multiple time series.

Maintenance: Quarterly.

Primary subject: Industrial and Manufacturing Planning.

Secondary subject: N/A

Profile: Provides quarterly (for eight quarters) and yearly (for ten years) forecasts for lead, zinc, copper, aluminum, tin, silver, magnesium, and nickel. Supply, demand, production, inventory, and market price data are included for each metal.

Applications: Industry forecasts and planning.

Subject cross reference: 7.10 and 9.1.

Geographic coverage: U.S., Japan, and Europe.

Time coverage: 1950's through forecasted time periods.

Online vendor(s): Chase Econometrics/Interactive Data Corp.

OCEANIC ABSTRACTS®

Producer: Cambridge Scientific Abstracts
5161 River Road
Bethesda, Maryland 20816
(301) 951-1400
(800) 638-8076

Class: Reference.

Data source: *Oceanic Abstracts* (OA) from books, journals, technical reports and government publications.

Size: 131,200 records.

Maintenance: Approximately 1,500 records bimonthly.

Primary subject: Environment.

Secondary subject: Research and Development.

Profile: Organizes and indexes technical literature published worldwide on marine-related subjects. Major subject headings include oceanography, marine biology, marine pollution, ships and shipping, geology and geophysics, meteorology and legal aspects of marine resources.

Applications: Oceanographic reference and analysis.

Subject cross reference: 6.6 and 8.9.

Geographic coverage: International.

Time coverage: 1964 to present.

Online vendor(s): DIALOG Information Services, Inc.
ESA/QUEST
SDC Search Service.

OECD DATA BASE

Producer: Organization for Economic Cooperation and Development
Development Center
94 rue Chardon-Lagache
F-75016 Paris, France
(01) 524-8200

Class: Statistical.

Data source: Various regional associations of third world countries.

Size: 10,000 time series.

Maintenance: Monthly.

Primary subject: Banking, Economics, and Finance.

Secondary subject: N/A

Profile: Maintains international economic data on 29 countries and country groups. The data are divided into three categories: primary economic indicators, quarterly national accounts and annual national accounts. Contains over 10,000 time series consisting of information on industrial production, internal trade, wages and prices, consumption, production and capital formation. Focus is primarily on the developing countries.

Applications: International economic analysis and forecasting.

Subject cross reference: 1.8, 2.5, 2.6 and 9.12.

Geographic coverage: International.

Time coverage: 1950 to present.

Online vendor(s): I. P. Sharp Associates.

OECD QUARTERLY OIL STATISTICS

Producer: Organization for Economic Cooperation and
Development
International Development Energy Agency (IEA)
2 rue Andre Pascal
F 75775 Paris Cedex 16, France
(01) 524-8200

Class: Statistical.

Data source: Importing oil companies.

Size: 1,000 time series.

Maintenance: Quarterly.

Primary subject: Long-Range Strategic Planning (energy).

Secondary subject: N/A

Profile: Data originating in the Quarterly Oil Statistics report
of the OECD is available for the 24 member countries of the
organization. Data coverage includes balances of
production, trade, refinery intake/output, consumption,
stock levels, import and export origin and destination.

Applications: International energy analysis, forecasts and
budgeting.

Subject cross reference: 7.10 and 10.5.

Geographic coverage: Australia, Austria, Belgium, Canada,
Denmark, Finland, France, Germany, Greece, Iceland,
Ireland, Italy, Japan, Luxembourg, The Netherlands, New
Zealand, Norway, Portugal, Spain, Sweden, Switzerland,
Turkey, The United Kingdom and the United States.

Time coverage: 1974 to present.

Online vendor(s): I. P. Sharp Associates.

OFFICIAL AIRLINE GUIDE (OAG)

Producer: Official Airlines Guides, Inc.
200 Clearwater Drive
Oak Brook, Illinois 60521
(312) 654-6000

Class: Statistical.

Data source: Airline schedules.

Size: 2 million + records.

Maintenance: Monthly.

Primary subject: General Management (transportation).

Secondary subject: N/A

Profile: Covers scheduled activities of approximately 600
international and North American airlines. Information is
separated by cargo and passenger flights. Every flight
(150,000 each month) maintains over 20 items of
information including origin, destination, service,
frequency, departure and arrival and equipment used.

Applications: Passenger and freight flight information and
planning guide.

Subject cross reference: 9.18.

Geographic coverage: International.

Time coverage: Most current only.

Online vendor(s): I. P. Sharp Associates.

ONLINE CHRONICLE

Producer: Online, Inc.
11 Tannery Lane
Weston, Connecticut 06883
(203) 227-8466

Class: Reference.

Data source: *Online* and *Database* magazines and other related
data base service news.

Size: New.

Maintenance: Biweekly.

Primary subject: General Management (Information
Processing Technology).

Secondary subject: N/A

Profile: An up-to-date full text source for the latest news in the
online industry. Coverage includes online industry news,
events, new data bases, computer equipment, search aids
and people in the online world.

Applications: Data base news reference.

Subject cross reference: 9.11.

Geographic coverage: Primarily domestic.

Time coverage: Current six months.

Online vendor(s): DIALOG Information Services, Inc.

ONLINE SITE EVALUATION SYSTEM (ONSITE)®

Producer: Urban Decision Systems, Inc.
Post Office Box 25953
Los Angeles, California 90025
(213) 820-8931

Class: Statistical.

Data source: U.S. Census Bureau and various local, county and
regional sources.

Size: 600 + data items.

Maintenance: Annually.

Primary subject: Marketing Planning.

Secondary subject: N/A

Profile: Provides trade area demographic data of more than
600 aggregate data items. Coverage includes such
demographics as consumer expenditures, updated income,
population and household equipment and figures.

Applications: User may examine almost any geographical area
for demographical analysis.

Subject cross reference: 2.4 and 2.5.

Geographic coverage: Domestic.

Time coverage: Latest census data.

Online vendor(s): National CSS, Inc.

OPTDAT

Producer: National Computer Network of Chicago, Inc. (NCN)
1929 N. Harlem Avenue
Chicago, Illinois 60635
(312) 622-6666

Class: Statistical.

Data source: The Chicago, American, Pacific, Midwest and Philadelphia Stock Exchanges from the Monchik-Weber Corporation.

Size: 60 + data items per option.

Maintenance: Daily.

Primary subject: Banking, Economics, and Finance.

Secondary subject: N/A

Profile: Maintains current and historical data on the above exchanges options underlying stocks, call and put options. Data includes high, low, bid, open and close. Data are also available for commodities (COMEX) and bonds (FISCAL).

Applications: Portfolio management and analysis.

Subject cross reference: 1.16.

Geographic coverage: U.S., Canada and Europe.

Time coverage: Latest 54-month period.

Online vendor(s): National Computer Network of Chicago, Inc.

ORR SYSTEM OF CONSTRUCTION COST MANAGEMENT®

Producer: Cost System Engineers, Inc.
131 E. Exchange Avenue, Suite 222
Fort Worth, Texas 76106
(817) 625-1177
(800) 433-2153

Class: Statistical.

Data source: N/A

Size: 50,000 cost items.

Maintenance: Quarterly.

Primary subject: General Management (real estate and building trends).

Secondary subject: N/A

Profile: Provides a flexible system integrating the user's experience and judgment with the computers' resources to perform cost estimating at all levels of planning and development. Maintains a data base of over 50,000 separate cost construction items. The user can develop an accurate estimate of costs for over 100 metropolitan areas. Preliminary estimates of cost are developed using references from 2,000 + actual projects. Eight levels of cost data are maintained. The most basic level calculates costs based on comparative historical costs at low, medium, or high project specifications. The project is then adjusted for time and location. The final level will produce a detailed quantity survey or buying list.

Applications: Project cost control (man-hour requirements, chart of accounts, value engineering and life cycle costs).

Subject cross reference: 9.15.

Geographic coverage: Over 100 metropolitan areas.

Time coverage: Current data.

Online vendor(s): Business Information Services (Control Data)
General Electric Information Services Co.

PAPER AND PULP DATA BANK

Producer: Data Resources, Inc.
29 Hartwell Avenue
Lexington, Massachusetts 02173
(617) 861-0165

Class: Statistical.

Data source: The American Paper Institute, The Organization for Economic Cooperation and Development, and the Canadian Pulp and Paper Association.

Size: 5,000 time series.

Maintenance: Continuous.

Primary subject: Industrial and Manufacturing Planning.

Secondary subject: N/A

Profile: Contains indicators directly related to the U.S. and International pulp and paper industry and its end markets. Coverage includes production, capacity, imports/exports, inventories, costs, prices, and shipments. The pulp banks contain international data covering printing and writing paper, wrapping, packaging, newsprint, bleached/unbleached and sulphate pulp. The paper banks contain raw material boxboard, paperboard, printing and writing papers, container board and fiber-box data.

Applications: Paper/pulp forecast of demand, price and availability by paper type; raw materials consumption analysis.

Subject cross reference: 7.2 and 7.10.

Geographic coverage: United States, United Kingdom, Germany, France, Japan, Sweden, Canada, Norway, Italy, Brazil, Denmark, Belgium, and the Netherlands.

Time coverage: Varies by specific series.

Online vendor(s): Data Resources, Inc.

PASSENGER CAR

Producer: Chase Econometrics/Interactive Data Corporation
486 Totten Pond Road
Waltham, Massachusetts 02154
(617) 890-1234

Class: Statistical.

Data source: Motor Vehicle Manufacturers Association, *Automotive News* and The U.S. Department of Commerce.

Size: 1,000 time series.

Maintenance: Continuous.

Primary subject: Marketing Planning.

Secondary subject: Multidisciplinary.

Profile: Provides time series data on the automobile industry. Monthly data include passenger car sales, performance with industry, market segment, corporate, and product line detail. Quarterly sales data are on an industry and segment basis with selected price and performance data.

Applications: Market segmentation analysis; new car development; price analysis.

Subject cross reference: 2.1, 2.2, 2.3, 2.8, 2.10, 2.12, 2.14, 4.3, 4.4, and 8.4.

Geographic coverage: Domestic.

Time coverage: 1963 to present.

Online vendor(s): Chase Econometrics/Interactive Data Corp.

PCS/ENERGY DATA BASE: API MONTHLY AND QUARTERLY DRILLING REPORTS

Producer: American Petroleum Institute (API)
2101 L Street, N.W.
Washington, D.C. 20037
(202) 457-7141

Class: Statistical.

Data source: Individual well drillers input.

Size: 2,500 time series.

Maintenance: Monthly and quarterly.

Primary subject: Long-Range Strategic Planning (energy).

Secondary subject: N/A

Profile: Provides statistics on well depths. Data items include total wells drilled and well depth by type of well (oil, gas or dry hole) and by state, district or region; and total new-field wildcat wells, number and depth, by type of well and geographic location.

Applications: Oil well depth analysis.

Subject cross reference: 10.5.

Geographic coverage: Domestic.

Time coverage: 1978 to present.

Online vendor(s): Proprietary Computer Systems, Inc.

PCS/ENERGY DATA BASE: API WEEKLY STATISTICAL BULLETIN

Producer: American Petroleum Institute (API)
2101 L Street, N.W.
Washington, D.C. 20037
(202) 457-7141

Class: Statistical.

Data source: U.S. oil company reports to API.

Size: 500 time series.

Maintenance: Weekly.

Primary subject: Long-Range Strategic Planning (energy).

Secondary subject: N/A

Profile: Provides data on refinery operations, refinery output of seven petroleum products, stocks of eight petroleum products; production, imports and stocks of crude oil, locations of crude oil stocks, and imports of fourteen petroleum products.

Applications: Analysis of stock-level patterns; forecasting.

Subject cross reference: 10.5.

Geographic coverage: Domestic.

Time coverage: Current week, year-ago week, and last three weeks.

Online vendor(s): Proprietary Computer Systems, Inc.

PCS/ENERGY DATA BASE: DOE ENERGY DATA REPORTS

Producer: U.S. Department of Energy (DOE)
12th Street and Pennsylvania Avenue, N.W.
Washington, D.C. 20461
(202) 556-6061

Class: Statistical.

Data source: DOE.

Size: 2,000 time series.

Maintenance: Monthly.

Primary subject: Long-Range Strategic Planning (energy).

Secondary subject: N/A

Profile: Provides two separate reports, The Petroleum Statement and The P.A.D. District Supply/Disposition Report. These reports are similar to, but more comprehensive than, the DOE Monthly Petroleum Statistics Report and the API Weekly Statistical Bulletin. For refinery operations, provides data on domestic and foreign crude runs, total input to distillation units, operable capacity and utilization percent by P.A.D. district and sub-P.A.D. district. For crude oil, provides data on production, demand, and stocks by stock and P.A.D. district.

Applications: Analysis of stock level patterns; forecasting.

Subject cross reference: 10.5.

Geographic coverage: Primarily domestic.

Time coverage: 1976 to present.

Online vendor(s): Proprietary Computer Systems, Inc.

PCS/ENERGY DATA BASE: DOE MONTHLY PETROLEUM STATISTICS REPORT

Producer: U.S. Department of Energy (DOE)
12th Street and Pennsylvania Avenue, N.W.
Washington, D.C. 20461
(202) 556-6061

Class: Statistical.

Data source: DOE.

Size: 800 + time series.

Maintenance: Monthly.

Primary subject: Long-Range Strategic Planning (energy).

Secondary subject: N/A

Profile: Provides data on refinery operations, refinery output of eight petroleum products, stocks of crude oil and ten petroleum products, imports by country of origin of crude oil and nine petroleum products, and imports of crude oil by Petroleum Administration for Defense (P.A.D.) districts into the U.S. and Puerto Rico.

Applications: Analysis of stock level patterns; forecasting.

Subject cross reference: 9.9 and 10.5.

Geographic coverage: Primarily domestic.

Time coverage: 1979 to present.

Online vendor(s): Proprietary Computer Systems, Inc.

PCS/ENERGY DATA BASE: ELECTRIC UTILITY INFORMATION

Producer: U.S. Department of Energy (DOE)
12th Street and Pennsylvania Avenue, N.W.
Washington, D.C. 20461
(202) 556-6061

Class: Statistical.

Data source: DOE.

Size: 5,500 electricity generating plants.

Maintenance: Monthly.

Primary subject: Long-Range Strategic Planning (energy).

Secondary subject: N/A

Profile: Provides information on fuel consumption by domestic public and private utility companies. Data include kilowatt hours of electricity generated, amount of fuel consumed, and coal and fuel oil supplies held in stock by the utilities. Plant data are organized by capacity, status, fuel-usage type, prime-mover type, ownership, and geographic location.

Applications: Electric utility industry analysis.

Subject cross reference: 10.3 and 10.5.

Geographic coverage: Domestic.

Time coverage: 1971 to present.

Online vendor(s): Proprietary Computer Systems, Inc.

PCS/ENERGY DATA BASE: FEDERAL ENERGY DATA SYSTEM (FEDS)

Producer: U.S. Department of Energy (DOE)
12th Street and Pennsylvania Avenue, N.W.
Washington, D.C. 20461
(202) 556-6061

Class: Statistical.

Data source: DOE.

Size: Several time series.

Maintenance: No longer being updated.

Primary subject: Long-Range Strategic Planning (energy).

Secondary subject: N/A

Profile: Provides data on energy consumption in physical units and British Thermal Units (BTUs) for various types of energy by state, industry, and economic sector. Sectors measured include residences, commerce, industry, and transportation. Data on energy types include asphalt and road oil, coal, petroleum refinery coke, distillate fuel, electricity gasoline, jet fuel, kerosene, liquid petroleum gas, natural gas, residual fuel, feedstocks, and raw materials. FEDS also provides demographic and economic data for use in correlation to energy consumption.

Applications: Analysis of energy-consumption patterns.

Subject cross reference: 10.5.

Geographic coverage: Domestic.

Time coverage: 1960 to 1977.

Online vendor(s): Proprietary Computer Systems, Inc.

PCS/ENERGY DATA BASE: HUGHES RIG COUNT

Producer: Hughes Tool Company
5425 Polk Avenue
Houston, Texas 77023
(713) 924-2222

Class: Statistical.

Data source: Hughes Tool Company Rotary Rig Count.

Size: Varies weekly.

Maintenance: Weekly.

Primary subject: Long-Range Strategic Planning (energy).

Secondary subject: N/A

Profile: Provides a rig count total, for rigs actively engaged in oil and gas exploration, by state and region. Historical data from 1974 to the present include weekly totals and monthly averages by state and for the entire U.S. The 1949 to 1974 historical data show weekly totals and monthly averages for the U.S. only.

Applications: Drilling activity analysis.

Subject cross reference: 10.5.

Geographic coverage: Domestic.

Time coverage: 1949 to present.

Online vendor(s): Proprietary Computer Systems, Inc.

PCS/ENERGY DATA BASE: JOINT ASSOCIATION SURVEY ON DRILLING COSTS

Producer: American Petroleum Institute (API)
2101 L Street, N.W.
Washington, D.C. 20037
(202) 457-7141

Class: Statistical.

Data source: Survey of the API in conjunction with the Independent Petroleum Association of America and the Mid-Continent Oil and Gas Association.

Size: N/A

Maintenance: Annually.

Primary subject: Long-Range Strategic Planning (energy).

Secondary subject: N/A

Profile: Provides data on the total number, depths, and costs of U.S. wells by well type and geographic location.

Applications: Drilling depth analysis; drilling cost analysis.

Subject cross reference: 10.5.

Geographic coverage: Domestic.

Time coverage: 1975 to present.

Online vendor(s): Proprietary Computer Services, Inc.

PCS/ENERGY DATA BASE: REED ROCK BIT COMPANY RIG CENSUS

Producer: Reed Rock Bit Company
6501 Navigation Boulevard
Houston, Texas 77011
(713) 924-5200

Class: Statistical.

Data source: Reed Rock Bit Company's U.S. rotary rig census.

Size: Varies yearly.

Maintenance: Yearly.

Primary subject: Long-Range Strategic Planning (energy).

Secondary subject: N/A

Profile: Based on each year's August census, provides data on the total number of domestic rotary rigs by active or idle status, by oil company or drilling contract ownership, by land, off-shore or barge drilling base, and by drilling-depth capacity.

Applications: Drilling activity analysis.

Subject cross reference: 10.5.

Geographic coverage: Domestic.

Time coverage: 1955 to present.

Online vendor(s): Proprietary Computer Systems, Inc.

PCS/ENERGY DATA BASE: STATE ENERGY DATA SYSTEM (SEDS)

Producer: U.S. Department of Energy (DOE)
12th Street and Pennsylvania Avenue, N.W.
Washington, D.C. 20461
(202) 556-6061

Class: Statistical.

Data source: DOE.

Size: N/A

Maintenance: Yearly.

Primary subject: Long-Range Strategic Planning (energy).

Secondary subject: N/A

Profile: Provides energy consumption data in British Thermal Units (BTUs) by state and total U.S., type of energy, economic sector, and economic sector correlated with energy types. Economic sectors included are residences, commerce, industry, transportation, and electric utilities. Energy types included are coal, natural gas, nuclear power, hydroelectric power, geothermal power, wood/waste, and petroleum. Petroleum subcategories included are asphalt, aviation gasoline, distillate fuel, jet fuel, kerosene, liquid petroleum gas, lubricants, motor gasoline, residual fuel, road oil, and all other petroleum.

Applications: Correlation studies of energy consumption to economic sector.

Subject cross reference: 10.5.

Geographic coverage: Domestic.

Time coverage: 1960 through 1978; will be updated yearly.

Online vendor(s): Proprietary Computer Systems, Inc.

PCS/SPEC

Producer: Production Systems for Architects and Engineers, Inc. (PSAE), U.S. Naval Facilities Engineering Command and the U.S. Army Corps of Engineers
1735 New York Avenue, N.W.
Washington, D.C. 20006
(202) 626-7550
(800) 424-5080

Class: Reference.

Data source: Master land-based construction specifications. These specifications are recognized industry equivalents, the entire master 16 division Construction Specifications Institute (CSI) specifications, and the Saudi-Oriented Guide Specifications (SOGS).

Size: N/A

Maintenance: Quarterly.

Primary subject: General Management (real estate and building trends).

Secondary subject: N/A

Profile: Maintains three file sets which comprise a master construction specifications data base for architects and engineers. Used to prepare final specifications from a master data base of specifications.

Applications: Construction specifications reference guide.

Subject cross reference: 7.3, 7.4, and 9.15.

Geographic coverage: U.S. and Saudi Arabia.

Time coverage: N/A

Online vendor(s): Proprietary Computer Systems, Inc.

PEST CONTROL LITERATURE DOCUMENTATION (PESTDOC)

Producer: Derwent Publications Ltd.
Rochdale House
128 Theobalds Road
London, England WCIX 8RP
(01) 242-5823

Class: Reference.

Data source: 230 scientific journals.

Size: 100,000 records.

Maintenance: Approximately 2,000 records quarterly.

Primary subject: General Management (Agriculture).

Secondary subject: N/A

Profile: Maintains a collection of journal, reports and conference proceedings on pesticides, herbicides and plant fertilizers.

Applications: Extensive analysis of insecticides, herbicides, fungicides, molluscicides and rodenticides.

Subject cross reference: 8.6 and 9.1.

Geographic coverage: International.

Time coverage: 1968 to present.

Online vendor(s): SDC Search Service.

PETROLEUM ABSTRACTS DATA BASE (TULSA)®

Producer: University of Tulsa
Information Services Division
Jersey Hall, Room 128-1133 North Lewis Ave.
Tulsa, Oklahoma 74110
(918) 939-6351 (X295)

Class: Reference.

Data source: *Petroleum Abstracts*—worldwide literature, and government reports.

Size: 220,000 records.

Maintenance: Approximately 1,200 records monthly.

Primary subject: Long-range Strategic Planning (energy).

Secondary subject: N/A

Profile: Maintains information (citations) of literature relating to oil and gas exploration, development and production. Coverage includes well logging, well drilling; well completion and servicing; petroleum geology; exploration geophysics; geochemistry; oil and gas production; reservoir studies and recovery methodologies; pollution; alternate fuels; and transportation and storage.

Applications: Energy development, drilling, recovery and maintenance.

Subject cross reference: 10.5.

Geographic coverage: International.

Time coverage: 1965 to present.

Online vendor(s): SDC Search Service.

PETROLEUM ARGUS®

Producer: Europ-Oil Prices
Star House
104-108 Grafton Road
London, England NW5 4BD
(01) 485-8792

Class: Statistical.

Data source: *Petroleum Argus*—a daily petroleum publication.

Size: Several time series.

Maintenance: Daily.

Primary subject: General Management (energy).

Secondary subject: N/A

Profile: Covers spot prices in Northwest Europe and West Mediterranean. Product coverage includes gas, oil, naptha, kerosene and heavy fuel oils.

Applications: Petroleum Price Analysis—Europe.

Subject cross reference: 2.6, 2.14 and 10.5.

Geographic coverage: Europe.

Time coverage: 1979 to present.

Online vendor(s): General Electric Information Services Co.
I. P. Sharp Associates.

PETROLEUM/ENERGY BUSINESS NEWS INDEX (P/E NEWS)

Producer: American Petroleum Institute
2101 L Street, N.W.
Washington, D.C. 20037
(202) 457-7141

Class: Reference.

Data source: *Oil and Gas Journal, Oil Daily, Middle East Economic Survey, The Petroleum Economist, Platt's Oilgram News, Oil and Gas Journal, Oil and Energy Trends, Petroleum News SE Asia, The Lundberg Letter, Petroleum Intelligence Weekly* and *Bulletin de l'Industrie Petroliere.*

Size: 183,939 records.

Maintenance: Approximately 700 records weekly.

Primary subject: Long-Range Strategic Planning (energy).

Secondary subject: N/A

Profile: Maintains information relative to the petroleum and energy industries; general news categories such as governmental influence, price, distribution, resources, change and trends are covered.

Applications: Energy reference aid for forecasts; production decisions; price adjustments; planning.

Subject cross reference: 5.8, 7.10, and 10.5.

Geographic coverage: International.

Time coverage: 1975 to present.

Online vendor(s): SDC Search Service.

PETROSERIES

Producer: American Petroleum Institute (API) and the U.S. Department of Energy (DOE)
2101 L Street, N.W.
Washington, D.C. 20037
(202) 457-7141

Class: Statistical.

Data source: *API Weekly Statistical Bulletin*, DOE *Monthly Petroleum Statement*, DOE *International Petroleum Annual*, DOE *Monthly Energy Review*, and API *Liquified Petroleum Gas Report.*

Size: 30,000 time series.

Maintenance: Monthly.

Primary subject: Long-Range Strategic Planning (energy).

Secondary subject: N/A

Profile: A collection of petroleum time series covering production, supply, demand, stocks, imports and refinery input and output.

Applications: Review monthly energy statistics by geographical region.

Subject cross reference: 10.5.

Geographic coverage: International.

Time coverage: Varies depending upon individual time series; many are 1960 to present.

Online vendor(s): I. P. Sharp Associates.

PHARMACEUTICAL LITERATURE DOCUMENTATION (RINGDOC)

Producer: Derwent Publications Ltd.
Rochdale House
128 Theobalds Road
London, England WC1X 8RP
(01) 242-5823

Class: Reference.

Data source: Scientific journal articles.

Size: 600,000 citations.

Maintenance: Approximately 3,500 citations monthly.

Primary subject: Research and Development.

Secondary subject: N/A

Profile: Maintains worldwide pharmaceutical literature which is specifically designed to cover all aspects of drugs, including analysis, biochemistry, chemistry, endocrinology, microbiology, nutrition, pharmacology, side-effects and therapeutics.

Applications: Pharmaceutical manufacturer's desk reference; research in pharmacology.

Subject cross reference: 8.3, 8.6, and 9.7.

Geographic coverage: International.

Time coverage: 1964 to present.

Online vendor(s): SDC Search Service.

PHARMACEUTICAL NEWS INDEX (PNI)®

Producer: Data Courier, Inc.
620 South Fifth Street
Louisville, Kentucky 40202
(502) 582-4111
(800) 626-2823

Class: Reference.

Data source: SCRIP *World Pharmaceutical News*; FDC Reports (The Pink Sheet); Drug Research Reports (The Blue Sheet); Medical Devices, Diagnostics and Instrumentation Reports (The Gray Sheet); Weekly Pharmacy Reports (The Green Sheet); Quality Control Reports (The Gold Sheet).

Size: 65,000 citations.

Maintenance: Approximately 1,000 citations monthly.

Primary subject: General Management (Health Care, Hospitals and Medicine).

Secondary subject: N/A

Profile: PNI cites and indexes all articles from the above publications on drugs, corporate and industrial sales, mergers, acquisitions and government legislation, regulations and litigations; and requests for proposals, research grant applications, industry speeches, press releases and other news items.

Applications: Drug industry news and analysis; market information reference; product planning and forecasting.

Subject cross reference: 2.1, 2.12, 5.6, 5.7, 5.8, 7.7, 8.2, 8.6, 9.7, 10.3, and 10.6.

Geographic coverage: International.

Time coverage: 1974 to present.

Online vendor(s): BRS, Inc.
DIALOG Information Services, Inc.
ESA/IRS.

PHARMACEUTICAL PROSPECTS®

Producer: The Futures Group and IMS America Ltd.
124 Hebron Avenue
Glastonburg, Connecticut 06033
(203) 633-3501

Class: Statistical.

Data source: Corresponds to printed *Pharmaceutical Prospects.*

Size: 120 indicators.

Maintenance: Bimonthly and/or annually.

Primary subject: General Management (health care, hospitals, and medicine).

Secondary subject: N/A

Profile: Maintains a collection of forecasts for over 120 pharmaceutical industrial indicators. Coverage includes pharmaceutical sales, distribution, retailing, industry characteristics, demographics, economics and personal health information. All forecasts include econometric variables.

Applications: Pharmaceutical forecasts and associated trend information indicators.

Subject cross reference: 9.7 and 10.6.

Geographic coverage: Domestic.

Time coverage: Current and projected data.

Online vendor(s): General Electric Information Services Co.

PIRA

Producer: The Research Association for the Paper and Board, Printing and Packaging Industries
Randalls Road
Leatherhead Surrey, England KT22 7RU
929810

Class: Reference.

Data source: Paper and Board Abstracts, Printing Abstracts, Packaging Abstracts, Management and Marketing Abstracts which comprise over 700 periodicals, reports and other materials.

Size: 61,300 citations.

Maintenance: Approximately 1,000 citations monthly.

Primary subject: Industrial and Manufacturing Planning.

Secondary subject: N/A

Profile: Produced from literature from around the world including over 600 periodicals, books, pamphlets, standards, specifications, legislation, translations, conference papers, research reports and trade literature. Coverage includes manufacturing, printing, photography, book-binding, packaging materials, shipping containers, production management, advertising, retailing, public relations, personnel and industrial relations.

Applications: Pulp and paper management, analysis, forecasting, modeling and budgeting reference.

Subject cross reference: 7.2 and 7.10.

Geographic coverage: International.

Time coverage: 1975 to present.

Online vendor(s): DIALOG Information Services, Inc.

PLATT'S DATA BANK

Producer: McGraw-Hill, Inc.
1221 Avenue of the Americas
New York, New York 10020
(212) 997-1221

Class: Statistical.

Data source: Platt's "Oil Price Handbook and Oilmanac" and "Oilgram Price Report" for data obtained via the U.S. Bureau of Labor Statistics, the Independent Petroleum Association of America, and various other printed statistical sources.

Size: 3,000 + time series.

Maintenance: Daily, weekly, monthly and annually.

Primary subject: Long-Range Strategic Planning (energy).

Secondary subject: N/A

Profile: Maintains time series for both domestic and foreign oil prices. Refinery and terminal prices by city are available for such fuels as motor gasoline, liquified petroleum gas, distillate and fuel oils and lubes.

Applications: Analysis of government regulations on price and demand of oil products; forecasting state and regional gasoline prices.

Subject cross reference: 7.10 and 10.5.

Geographic coverage: International.

Time coverage: Depends upon specific time series.

Online vendor(s): Data Resources, Inc.

POLLUTION ABSTRACTS®

Producer: Cambridge Scientific Abstracts
5161 River Road
Bethesda, Maryland 20816
(800) 638-8076
(301) 951-1400

Class: Reference.

Data source: Journal articles, government reports/documents, and special studies.

Size: 83,216 citations.

Maintenance: Approximately 1,500 records bimonthly.

Primary subject: Environmental, Social & Political Affairs.

Secondary subject: N/A

Profile: A leading resource for references to environmentally-related literature on pollution, its sources, and its control. Subjects covered include air pollution, environmental quality, noise pollution, pesticides, radiation, solid wastes and water pollution.

Applications: Environmental analysis and decisions.

Subject cross reference: 6.6.

Geographic coverage: International.

Time coverage: 1970 to present.

Online vendor(s): BRS, Inc.
DIALOG Information Services, Inc.

POPULATION BIBLIOGRAPHY

Producer: University of North Carolina
Carolina Population Center
University Square—East 300A
Chapel Hill, North Carolina 27514
(919) 933-3081

Class: Reference.

Data source: Journals, monographs, technical reports, government documents, conference proceedings, dissertations and many unpublished reports on population.

Size: 53,500 records.

Maintenance: Approximately 1,000 records bimonthly.

Primary subject: Marketing Planning.

Secondary subject: N/A

Profile: Information on abortion, demography, migration, family planning, fertility studies, and all general areas of population research. Areas such as population policy, law, education and research methodology are covered.

Applications: Developing country population analysis; socioeconomic implications of population.

Subject cross reference: 2.4, 2.5, 2.13, and 6.7.

Geographic coverage: Primarily domestic.

Time coverage: 1967 to present.

Online vendor(s): DIALOG Information Services, Inc.

POPULATION INFORMATION ONLINE (POPLINE)

Producer: U.S. National Library of Medicine
8600 Rockville Pike
Bethesda, Maryland 20209
(301) 496-6217

Class: Reference.

Data source: Journal articles, monographs, conference proceedings, and various government agencies.

Size: 80,000 records.

Maintenance: Approximately 1,000 records monthly.

Primary subject: Marketing Planning.

Secondary subject: General Management (health care).

Profile: Maintains citations and abstracts to journal articles and technical reports pertaining to population, demographics, biology, fertility control, contraception technology, family planning, law, and related policy issues.

Applications: Family planning research reference; demographic studies.

Subject cross reference: 2.4, 9.7, and 9.20.

Geographic coverage: International.

Time coverage: Generally 1970 to present; some earlier.

Online vendor(s): National Library of Medicine (MEDLARS).

PRE-MED

Producer: BRS, Inc.
1200 Route 7
Latham, New York 12110
(518) 374-5011
(800) 833-4707

Class: Reference.

Data source: *Abridged Index Medicus* from major medical journals.

Size: 5,000 records.

Maintenance: Weekly.

Primary subject: Research and Development.

Secondary subject: General Management (health care).

Profile: Maintains citations to articles which have appeared in 125 medical journals. Coverage includes such topics as hospital management, nursing, medical techniques and news. Records appear here prior to insertion into Medline.

Applications: Biomedical research reference; medical research.

Subject cross reference: 8.9 and 9.7.

Geographic coverage: U.S., United Kingdom and Canada.

Time coverage: Most current information only.

Online vendor(s): BRS, Inc.
DATA-STAR.

PRIVATE PLACEMENTS

Producer: Securities Data Company
62 William Street
Sixth Floor
New York, New York 10005
(212) 668-0940

Class: Statistical.

Data source: Securities and Exchange Commission.

Size: 900 records.

Maintenance: Daily.

Primary subject: Banking, Economics and Finance.

Secondary subject: N/A

Profile: Provides data on private placements of taxable debt and common and preferred stock. The data items include coupon, maturity, and type of security for debt; total dollar amount offered, number of shares, and price for common; total dollar amount offered, number of shares, dividend, and par value for preferred.

Applications: Private placement historical research.

Subject cross reference: 1.11 and 1.16.

Geographic coverage: Domestic.

Time coverage: 1981 to present.

Online vendor(s): Securities Data Company.

PROSPECTS®

Producer: The Futures Group
76 Eastern Avenue
Glastonbury, Connecticut 06033
(203) 633-3501

Class: Statistical.

Data source: Private and governmental information as well as the Futures Group client data.

Size: 100+ time series.

Maintenance: Twenty indicators are updated monthly while all are updated at least annually.

Primary subject: Marketing Planning.

Secondary subject: N/A

Profile: A data base for consumer forecasting. Sample data coverage includes households, families, marriage, divorce, education, labor force, population and lifestyle indicators. Forecasts are accompanied by a list of projected events based upon historical trends and related events. Forecasts may contain over 100 indicators used to describe the American Consumer and his/her behavior. Also used for forecasting the hospital supply and pharmaceutical industries.

Applications: Consumer Demand Forecasts (from Futures Group); econometric model forecasting.

Subject cross reference: 1.8, 2.2, 2.3, 2.4, 2.8, 2.10, 2.13, 2.15 and 9.7.

Geographic coverage: Domestic.

Time coverage: Varies by series.

Online vendor(s): General Electric Information Services Co.

PTS INDEXES

Producer: Predicasts, Inc.
200 University Circle Research Center
11001 Cedar Avenue
Cleveland, Ohio 44106
(216) 795-3000
(800) 321-6388

Class: Reference.

Data source: Predicasts' *Index United States, Index International* and *Index Europe* comprising material selected from over 2,500 printed sources.

Size: 1,750,000 citations.

Maintenance: Approximately 12,000 citations monthly.

Primary subject: Marketing Planning.

Secondary subject: General Management.

Profile: Covers both domestic and international company, product and industry information. Information coverage includes corporate acquisitions and mergers, new products, technological news, and sociopolitical factors. It summarizes analyses of companies by securities firms, contains forecasts of company sales and profits by company officers and reports on factors influencing future sales and earnings (such as price changes, government actions, sales and licensing agreements and joint ventures).

Applications: Analysis of environmental, political, sociological and other external market variables on a company's financial position.

Subject cross reference: 2.1, 2.8, 2.10, 2.11, 3.4, 4.3, 4.4, 6.4, 9.10, 9.13, 10.1, 10.3, and 10.6.

Geographic coverage: International.

Time coverage: 1972 to present.

Online vendor(s): BRS, Inc.
DATA-STAR
DIALOG Information Services, Inc.

PTS INTERNATIONAL FORECASTS ABSTRACTS

Producer: Predicasts, Inc.
200 University Circle Research Center
11001 Cedar Avenue
Cleveland, Ohio 44106
(216) 795-3000
(800) 321-6388

Class: Statistical and Reference.

Data source: Journals, annual reports, industry reports, special surveys, and related printed matter.

Size: 230,000 citations.

Maintenance: Approximately 12,000 citations quarterly.

Primary subject: Banking, Economics and Finance.

Secondary subject: General Management.

Profile: Maintains abstracts of published forecasts with historical data for all counties of the United States. Coverage includes general economics, all industries, detailed products, and end-use data.

Applications: Forecasting; marketing research; industrial influences.

Subject cross reference: 1.8, 2.6, 2.10, 9.12, and 10.7.

Geographic coverage: International.

Time coverage: 1972 to present.

Online vendor(s): DIALOG Information Services, Inc.

PTS INTERNATIONAL TIME SERIES

Producer: Predicasts, Inc.
200 University Circle Research Center
11001 Cedar Avenue
Cleveland, Ohio 44106
(216) 795-3000
(800) 321-6388

Class: Statistical.

Data source: United Nations, International Monetary Fund, and other international organizations.

Size: 136,285 citations.

Maintenance: Quarterly.

Primary subject: Marketing Planning.

Secondary subject: Banking, Economics and Finance.

Profile: Maintains approximately 2,500 forecast time series consisting of 50 key series for 50 major countries of the world. Time series include historical data and projected consensus of published forecasts through 1990. Coverage includes employment, population, Gross National Product, income, production, products, energy and vehicles and other economic, demographic, industrial and product data.

Applications: Econometric modeling (forecasting) variables assignments.

Subject cross reference: 1.4, 1.5, 1.8, 2.2, 2.4, 2.5, 2.6, 2.8, 2.13, 9.1, 9.12 and 10.7.

Geographic coverage: International.

Time coverage: 1957 to present.

Online vendor(s): DIALOG Information Services, Inc.

PTS PROMPT

Producer: Predicasts, Inc.
200 University Circle Research Center
11001 Cedar Avenue
Cleveland, Ohio 44106
(216) 795-3000
(800) 321-6388

Class: Reference.

Data source: See profile.

Size: 381,500 citations.

Maintenance: Monthly.

Primary subject: Marketing Planning.

Secondary subject: Multidisciplinary.

Profile: PROMPT (Predicasts' Overview of Markets and Technology) abstracts significant information appearing in thousands of newspapers, business magazines, government reports, trade journals, bank letters and international reports. Coverage includes acquisitions, capacities, end uses, environment, foreign trade, market data, new products, production, regulations and technology for the following industries: chemical, communications, computer, electronic, energy, fiber, food, instrumentation and rubber.

Applications: Users may enter search logic and receive regular "key-word" updates on significant data base items categorized in profile.

Subject cross reference: 1.19, 2.16, 3.6, 4.6, 7.12, 8.9, and 9.20.

Geographic coverage: International.

Time coverage: 1972 to present.

Online vendor(s): BRS, Inc.
DATA-STAR
DIALOG Information Services, Inc.
SDC Search Service.

PTS U.S. FORECASTS ABSTRACTS

Producer: Predicasts, Inc.
200 University Circle Research Center
11001 Cedar Avenue
Cleveland, Ohio 44106
(216) 795-3000
(800) 321-6388

Class: Statistical and Reference.

Data source: Journals, annual reports, industry reports, special surveys, and related printed matter.

Size: 200,000+ citations.

Maintenance: Quarterly.

Primary subject: Banking, Economics and Finance.

Secondary subject: General Management.

Profile: Maintains abstracts of published forecasts with historical data for the United States. Coverage includes general economics, all industries, details products, and end-use data.

Applications: Forecasting; marketing research; industrial influences.

Subject cross reference: 1.8, 2.10, 9.13, and 10.7.

Geographic coverage: Domestic.

Time coverage: 1971 to present.

Online vendor(s): DIALOG Information Services, Inc.

QUICK QUOTE

Producer: CompuServe, Inc.
Information Services Division
5000 Arlington Centre Boulevard
Columbus, Ohio 43220
(614) 457-8600

Class: Statistical.

Data source: New York, American, and Over-The-Counter Exchanges.

Size: 9,000+ securities.

Maintenance: Several times daily.

Primary subject: Banking, Economics, and Finance (securities).

Secondary subject: N/A

Profile: Provides high, low, closing, volume, and net change figures on securities of public U.S. corporations.

Applications: Stock portfolio analysis.

Subject cross reference: 1.16.

Geographic coverage: Domestic.

Time coverage: Current day only.

Online vendor(s): CompuServe, Inc.

QUOTRON 800®

Producer: Quotron Systems, Inc.
5454 Beethoven Street
Los Angeles, California 90066
(213) 398-2761

Class: Statistical.

Data source: All major stock exchanges.

Size: N/A

Maintenance: Daily.

Primary subject: Banking, Economics, and Finance (securities).

Secondary subject: N/A

Profile: An up-to-the-minute online financial information service. This service maintains a diverse range of securities information (stocks, bonds, commodities, options) for 26 industrial groupings. Data coverage includes last sale price, open, high, low, bid, ask, and time of last trade.

Applications: Market statistics and indicators analysis and reference guide; portfolio management.

Subject cross reference: 1.16.

Geographic coverage: Domestic.

Time coverage: Current.

Online vendor(s): Quotron Systems, Inc.

RANGE MANAGEMENT

Producer: The Oryx Press
2214 North Central at Encanto
Phoenix, Arizona 85004
(602) 254-6156

Class: Reference.

Data source: *U.S.—Canadian Range Management* from journal articles and monographs.

Size: 25,000 records.

Maintenance: Annually.

Primary subject: General Management (agriculture).

Secondary subject: N/A

Profile: Maintains citations to U.S. and Canadian literature relative to range management, pastures, plants, livestock, ranching, resources, animal wildlife, grazing tips, economics, education and related research.

Applications: Range reference aid for short-cuts, forecasts, budgeting and range planning.

Subject cross reference: 6.3, 6.8, 9.1, and 9.20.

Geographic coverage: U.S. and Canada.

Time coverage: 1935 to present.

Online vendor(s): SDC Search Service.

RAPRA ABSTRACTS

Producer: Rubber and Plastics Research Association of Great Britain (RAPRA)
Shawbury, Shrewsbury, Shropshire
England SY4 4NR
(0939) 250383

Class: Reference.

Data source: Conference proceedings, journals, books, special reports, and dissertations.

Size: 148,600 records.

Maintenance: Approximately 2,000 records monthly.

Primary subject: Research and Development.

Secondary subject: N/A

Profile: Covers the commercial as well as the technical aspects of the rubber and plastics industries. Coverage includes synthesis and polymerization, raw materials, monomers, compounding ingredients, processing technology, machinery and test equipment, properties and testing. For the administrator or analyst, Rapra provides economic and commercial information and both general and industry specific information on industrial organization and management.

Applications: Application analysis of polymers, toxicity, environmental hazards and health hazards. Rubber/plastics industrial management reference.

Subject cross reference: 8.2, 8.3, 8.4, 8.6, and 8.8.

Geographic coverage: International.

Time coverage: 1973 to present.

Online vendor(s): DIALOG Information Services, Inc.
ESA/QUEST.

REGIONAL

Producer: Chase Econometrics/Interactive Data Corporation
486 Totten Pond Road
Waltham, Massachusetts 02154
(617) 890-1234

Class: Statistical.

Data source: Bureau of Economic Analysis, Bureau of Labor Statistics, and the U.S. Census Bureau.

Size: 30,000+ time series (per state).

Maintenance: Continuous.

Primary subject: Banking, Economics, and Finance.

Secondary subject: Multidisciplinary.

Profile: Provides industry, macroeconomic, and employment coverage for each state and for over 260 SMSA's. The time-series data for the states include personal income, employment, housing, manufacturing, financial data, energy statistics, government revenue, population, cash receipts from crops and livestock, and retail sales. The SMSA macro data include personal income, employment, population, housing, retail sales, department store sales and a consumer price index.

Applications: Regional analysis of demographics; sales territory comparisons and potential analysis.

Subject cross reference: 1.5, 1.8, 2.4, 2.5, 3.4, 4.4, 9.15, and 9.16.

Geographic coverage: Domestic.

Time coverage: Varies by series; most from 1955 to present.

Online vendor(s): Chase Econometrics/Interactive Data Corp.

REGIONAL DATA ASSOCIATES (RDA)

Producer: Regional Data Associates (RDA)
194 Nassau Street
Princeton, New Jersey 08540
(609) 924-4611

Class: Statistical.

Data source: Surveys, RDA estimates, government sources and private organizations.

Size: 20,000 time series.

Maintenance: Continuous.

Primary subject: Banking, Economics, and Finance.

Secondary subject: Marketing Planning.

Profile: Supplies housing, demographic, financial/economic, and non-residential construction data for all fifty states, the District of Columbia, and over 200 Standard Metropolitan Statistical Areas (SMSAs). Some of the data items include housing starts by type; existing home sales; sales prices of new and existing homes; population by age group; net migration; elementary school enrollment; employment by SIC code; savings deposits; and, construction permits by category. 4,000 individual series are forecasted for ten years.

Applications: User may analyze housing starts, prices, age statistics, mortgage activities, or employment, as they relate to his organization and region.

Subject cross reference: 1.2, 1.5, 1.8, 1.12, 2.3, 2.4, 2.5, 2.13, 2.14, and 9.15.

Geographic coverage: Domestic.

Time coverage: 1960 to present plus several forecasts.

Online vendor(s): Chase Econometrics/Interactive Data Corp.

REGIONAL EMPLOYMENT

Producer: Chase Econometrics/Interactive Data Corporation
486 Totten Pond Road
Waltham, Massachusetts 02154
(617) 890-1234

Class: Statistical.

Data source: U.S. Department of Labor, Bureau of Labor Statistics.

Size: 18,000 + time series.

Maintenance: Monthly.

Primary subject: Multidisciplinary.

Secondary subject: N/A

Profile: Provides time series for every state and 200 + SMSA's at the 2, 3, and 4-digit SIC code and aggregate levels. Data items include employment figures, hourly earnings, and weekly hours.

Applications: Analysis of hours and earnings employment statistics by SIC (industry), SMSA, or state.

Subject cross reference: 2.4, 2.5, 3.4, 6.7, and 9.14.

Geographic coverage: Domestic.

Time coverage: Varies by series.

Online vendor(s): Chase Econometrics/Interactive Data Corp.

REGIONAL FORECAST

Producer: Chase Econometrics/Interactive Data Corporation
486 Totten Pond Road
Waltham, Massachusetts 02154
(617) 890-1234

Class: Statistical.

Data source: Government agencies data with the Chase Econometrics Regional Model.

Size: 6,000 + time series.

Maintenance: Quarterly.

Primary subject: Marketing Planning.

Secondary subject: Banking, Economics, and Finance.

Profile: Provides state and SMSA quarterly and annual forecasts. State forecast data include personal income, retail sales, housing starts, employment, monetary statistics, value added and employment by 2-digit SIC code, energy demand, and population. SMSA forecast data include employment figures, personal income, prices, and population.

Applications: Sales comparison/potential analysis by sales location; forecasting model inputs.

Subject cross reference: 1.2, 1.5, 1.8, 2.3, 2.4, 2.5, and 9.15.

Geographic coverage: Domestic.

Time coverage: 1960 to present with forecasts.

Online vendor(s): Chase Econometrics/Interactive Data Corp.

REGIONAL INDUSTRY

Producer: Chase Econometrics/Interactive Data Corporation
486 Totten Pond Road
Waltham, Massachusetts 02154
(617) 890-1234

Class: Statistical.

Data source: Annual survey of manufacturers.

Size: 11,000 + time series.

Maintenance: Annually.

Primary subject: Banking, Economics, and Finance.

Secondary subject: N/A

Profile: Provides historical data in the form of ten series per state for each of 21 two-digit SIC codes. Specific data items include employment, wages, payroll, man-hours, cost of materials, value added, value of shipments, capital expenditures, and inventories.

Applications: Industry comparisons and analysis; forecasting.

Subject cross reference: 1.4, 1.8, 7.6, 9.14, and 9.18.

Geographic coverage: Domestic.

Time coverage: 1955 to present.

Online vendor(s): Chase Econometrics/Interactive Data Corp.

REMARC

Producer: Carrollton Press
1911 N. Fort Myer Drive, Suite 905
Arlington, Virginia 22209
(703) 525-5940

Class: Reference.

Data source: Library of Congress Catalog.

Size: 5,200,000 records.

Maintenance: Periodical Updates.

Primary subject: Multidisciplinary.

Secondary subject: N/A

Profile: Maintains records representing the catalogued collections of the U.S. Library of Congress from 1897 to December, 31, 1978. Remarc will provide library acquisitions alternatives for library cataloguing and bibliographic verification. Coverage includes book collections by author, title, subject, series and publication date.

Applications: Library acquisitions analysis and research.

Subject cross reference: 9.5.

Geographic coverage: International.

Time coverage: 1897-1978.

Online vendor(s): DIALOG Information Services, Inc.

SAFETY

Producer: Cambridge Scientific Abstracts
5161 River Road
Bethesda, Maryland 20816
(800) 638-8076
(301) 951-1400

Class: Reference.

Data source: Journal articles, government reports, conference proceedings, books, patents and dissertations.

Size: 75,000 citations.

Maintenance: Approximately 3,500 citations bimonthly.

Primary subject: Industrial and Manufacturing Planning.

Secondary subject: N/A

Profile: Maintains a rather broad interdisciplinary coverage of literature related to the issues of safety. The thrust of this service is to capture information devoted to identifying, evaluating, eliminating and controlling safety hazards. Major subject categories include general safety, aviation, aerospace safety, medical safety, ecological and environmental safety. Topical coverage consists of pollution, fire, waste, disposal, prediction, legislative, urban development, drugs, radiation, criminal acts (child abuse, arson, etc.), epidemics, education, prevention and psychological factors influencing safety.

Applications: Safety research and analysis reference; transportation safety statistics and standards.

Subject cross reference: 5.6, 5.7, 6.3, 7.1, and 7.7.

Geographic coverage: International.

Time coverage: 1975 to present.

Online vendor(s): SDC Search Service.

SAMI

Producer: Selling Areas-Marketing, Inc. (SAMI)
541 N. Fairbanks Court
Chicago, Illinois 60611
(312) 329-6800

Class: Statistical.

Data source: Chain stores, grocery wholesalers and rack operators.

Size: 75 product groups; 39 major markets.

Maintenance: Monthly.

Primary subject: Marketing Planning.

Secondary subject: N/A

Profile: Maintains data on warehouse distribution activity to supermarkets. Data coverage includes consumer prices by dry goods, household supplies, health and beauty supplies. Many specialized reporting functions are available for data analysis.

Applications: Market penetration analysis; brand performance; competitive trends.

Subject cross reference: 2.1, 2.2, 2.3, 2.5, 2.14, and 3.4.

Geographic coverage: Domestic.

Time coverage: Varies by series; most are for last 2 years.

Online vendor(s): Interactive Market Systems, Inc. (SAMI)
Management Science Associates, Inc. (SAMI)
Market Science Associates, Inc. (SAMI)
Telmar Media Systems, Inc. (SAMI)
Tymshare, Inc. (SOLO).

SAVINGS AND LOAN

Producer: Federal Home Loan Bank Board
320 First Street
Washington, D.C. 20552
(202) 377-6000

Class: Statistical.

Data source: Financial statements.

Size: 4,000 + savings and loan institutions.

Maintenance: Semiannually.

Primary subject: Banking, Economics, and Finance.

Secondary subject: N/A

Profile: Data items cover the income statement, balance sheet, and performance measures of the federally chartered savings and loan institutions of the United States.

Applications: Savings and loan comparisons; merger and acquisition analysis; investment decisions.

Subject cross reference: 1.2, 1.11, and 1.15.

Geographic coverage: Domestic.

Time coverage: 1974 to present.

Online vendor(s): ADP Network Services, Inc.
CompuServe, Inc. (FHLB)
Time Sharing Resources, Inc.

SEARCHABLE PHYSICS INFORMATION NOTICES (SPIN)®

Producer: American Institute of Physics (AIP)
335 E. 45th Street
New York, New York 10017
(212) 661-9404

Class: Reference.

Data source: American and Soviet Physics Journals.

Size: 151,700 citations.

Maintenance: Approximately 2,000 citations monthly.

Primary subject: Research and Development.

Secondary subject: N/A

Profile: Current indexing and abstracting of the world's most significant physics journals. Coverage includes all the major areas of physics, mathematical and statistical physics, astronomy, astrophysics and geophysics.

Applications: Product(s) related technology and reference guide; new product research.

Subject cross reference: 8.4, 8.6, and 8.8.

Geographic coverage: U.S. and U.S.S.R.

Time coverage: 1970 to present.

Online vendor(s): DIALOG Information Services, Inc.

SECURITIES

Producer: Financial Post
Investment Databank
481 University Avenue
Toronto, Ontario, Canada M5W 1A7
(416) 596-5692

Class: Statistical.

Data source: All Canadian exchanges and the American Exchange and the New York Stock Exchange.

Size: 9,000 stocks.

Maintenance: Daily.

Primary subject: Banking, Economics, and Finance.

Secondary subject: N/A

Profile: Maintains stock trading information for all Canadian exchanges (Montreal, Toronto, Calgary and Vancouver), the New York Stock Exchange and the American Stock Exchange. Coverage includes daily volume, high, low, and close as well as various composites and indices.

Applications: User may access previous day's trading data on above items.

Subject cross reference: 1.9 and 1.16.

Geographic coverage: U.S. and Canada.

Time coverage: Most current data with some history.

Online vendor(s): Dialcom, Inc.
I. P. Sharp Associates.

SERVICE DIFFICULTY REPORTING SYSTEM (SDR)

Producer: Federal Aviation Administration
Flight Standard National Field Office
800 Independence Avenue, S.W.
Washington, D.C. 20591
(202) 426-4000

Class: Statistical.

Data source: General aviation defect and malfunction reports, air carrier mechanical reliability reports.

Size: 138,000 citations.

Maintenance: Biweekly.

Primary subject: Industrial and Manufacturing Planning.

Secondary subject: N/A

Profile: Maintains data on aircraft and aircraft component failures and malfunctions. Coverage includes malfunction type, degree of severity, aircraft type, part description, engine type, time and location.

Applications: Air industry safety analysis; parts management and obsolescence decisions.

Subject cross reference: 7.3, 7.7, and 9.18.

Geographic coverage: Domestic.

Time coverage: 1975 to present.

Online vendor(s): United Telecom Computer Group.

SHIP ABSTRACTS (SHIP)

Producer: The Ship Research Institute of Norway,
Netherlands Maritime Institute, the
Association of Swedish Shipowners
and Shipbuilders
Post Office Box 6099 Etterstad
Oslo 6, Norway
(02) 689280

Class: Reference.

Data source: Ship abstracts from periodicals, research reports, patents, and standards.

Size: 35,000 records.

Maintenance: Approximately 250 records monthly.

Primary subject: Multidisciplinary.

Secondary subject: N/A

Profile: Covers ship management and technical operations. Maintains information on all aspects of ship technology, operations and offshore technology. Coverage includes engineering, power plant analysis, navigation, performance, stability, descriptions, propulsion devices and systems, oscillations and vibrations, nuclear power plants, fuels, gas turbines, electrical systems, automation, operations, management, materials, maritime laws and regulations, pollution control, safety, cargo handling, machinery plants, industry statistics, ports and waterways, transportation, ship repair and maintenance, shipyards, docks and work environment information.

Applications: User may compare relative ship technologies, products, materials, procedures and management tactics.

Subject cross reference: 6.6, 7.1, 7.3, 7.4, 8.4, and 9.18.

Geographic coverage: International.

Time coverage: 1969 to present.

Online vendor(s): Norwegian Centre for Informatics.

SHORT TERM PROJECTIONS (STP) AND LONG TERM PROJECTIONS (LTP)

Producer: Townsend-Greenspan & Co., Inc.
1 New York Plaza
New York, New York 10004
(212) 943-9515

Class: Statistical.

Data source: U.S. Department of Commerce demographics and statistics.

Size: STP-1,000 time series/LTP-700 time series.

Maintenance: STP-quarterly/LTP-semiannually.

Primary subject: Banking, Economics, and Finance.

Secondary subject: N/A.

Profile: Forecasts major U.S. macroeconomic variables, including autos and trucks, balance of payments, federal budget, flow of funds, gross farm product, housing, industrial production (by 3-digit SIC), interest rates, national income and product accounts, oil supply and demand, plant/equipment expenditures, and producer prices.

Applications: Econometric forecasting.

Subject cross reference: 1.3, 1.4, 1.5, 1.6, 1.8, 1.14, 1.15, and 2.3.

Geographic coverage: Domestic.

Time coverage: STP-8 quarters; LTP-10 years.

Online vendor(s): ADP Network Services, Inc.

SIMMONS MARKET RESEARCH BUREAU (SMRB)

Producer: Simmons Market Research Bureau, Inc.
219 East 42nd Street
New York, New York 10017
(212) 867-1414

Class: Statistical.

Data source: Market survey data (interviews and/or questionnaires).

Size: 500+ product and service categories; 3,000+ individual products.

Maintenance: Annually.

Primary subject: Marketing Planning.

Secondary subject: N/A.

Profile: Consists of detailed descriptions of the characteristics of users of individual products, brands, and services and of audiences of individual media. Descriptions include detailed information regarding age, sex, education, occupation, income, geographic location, household description, lifestyle and psychographic data (including hobbies, recreational and leisure activities), respondent self-concept, buying style, and social position.

Applications: Media effectiveness analysis; direct mail targeting.

Subject cross reference: 2.2, 2.4, 2.5, 2.8, 2.10, 2.15, 3.2, and 4.2.

Geographic coverage: Domestic.

Time coverage: Most current data.

Online vendor(s): IMS/Marketronics
Interactive Market Systems, Inc.
Management Science Associates, Inc.
Marketron
Telmar Media Systems, Inc.

SITE II®

Producer: CACI, Inc.
1815 North Fort Myer Drive
Arlington, Virginia 22209
(703) 841-7800
(800) 336-4752

Class: Statistical.

Data source: U.S. Department of Commerce, 1980 Census (Population and Housing) and CACI, Inc. updates from proprietary information.

Size: Data on 60,000+ census tracts.

Maintenance: Annually.

Primary subject: Marketing Planning.

Secondary subject: N/A.

Profile: A comprehensive demographics and housing data bank. The data bank maintains the following information broken down by 60,000 geographic areas: total population; population by age, sex, and race; median and family income; housing (home) values; rental price indices; mobile homes; occupation; automobiles; achieved educational level of adults over 25; household and family composition and major household appliances.

Applications: User may study demographics and market areas by U.S., state, county, census tracts (minor civil divisions), SMSA's and zip codes.

Subject cross reference: 2.3, 2.4, and 2.13.

Geographic coverage: Domestic.

Time coverage: Most current census with annual updates.

Online vendor(s): ADP Network Services, Inc.
Business Information Services (Control Data)
CompuServe, Inc.
Computer Sciences Corporation
COMSHARE, Inc.
Data Resources, Inc.
General Electric Information Services Co.
Tymshare, Inc.

SITE POTENTIAL®

Producer: Caci, Inc.
1815 North Fort Myer Drive
Arlington, Virginia 22209
(703) 841-7800
(800) 336-4752

Class: Statistical.

Data source: U.S. Department of Commerce—Census of Retail Trade Statistics and U.S. Census Bureau's Consumer Expenditure Survey.

Size: Not relevant.

Maintenance: Annually.

Primary subject: Market Planning.

Secondary subject: N/A.

Profile: Provides estimates of the demand (consumer expenditures) by residents within a defined area for approximately 140 product and service items. This data base generates reports covering 16 different retail stores and 3 financial institutions. Coverage includes apparel stores, appliance stores, auto services stores, department stores, drug stores, footwear stores, grocery stores, hair salons, home improvement stores, ice cream stores, optical centers, photo outlets, restaurants, retail bakeries, shopping centers, commercial banks, finance companies, and savings and loan associations.

Applications: Market share and penetration analysis; market entry planning; site evaluation and selection; sales administration design and analysis; sales projections.

Subject cross reference: 2.2, 2.3, 2.4, 2.5, 2.8, 2.13, 3.4, 4.4, 9.16, and 9.17.

Geographic coverage: Domestic.

Time coverage: Most current year's data.

Online vendor(s): ADP Network Services, Inc.
Business Information Services (Control Data)
CompuServe, Inc.
Computer Sciences Corporation
COMSHARE, Inc.
Data Resources, Inc.
General Electric Information Services Co.
Tymshare, Inc.
United Telecom Computer Group.

SMITHSONIAN SCIENCE INFORMATION EXCHANGE (SSIE)®

Producer: Smithsonian Science Information Exchange
300 Madison National Bank Building
1730 M Street, N.W.
Washington, D.C. 20036
(202) 634-3933

Class: Reference.

Data source: Federal, state, local governments, college and university funding organizations.

Size: 125,000 projects per fiscal year.

Maintenance: Monthly.

Primary subject: Research and Development.

Secondary subject: N/A.

Profile: Covers current research in progress for both basic and applied research from over 1,300 funding organizations. Research coverage includes all areas of life, physical, social, behavioral, and engineering sciences. Data coverage includes research descriptions, name and addresses of the investigators, sponsoring organization, funding amount, period funded and contract numbers.

Applications: Technology and other sciences; reference aid for applied research.

Subject cross reference: 7.3, 8.3, 8.4, 8.5, 8.6, and 8.8.

Geographic coverage: Domestic.

Time coverage: 1974 to present.

Online vendor(s): BRS, Inc.
DIALOG Information Services, Inc.
SDC Search Service.

SOCIAL SCISEARCH (SSCI)®

Producer: Institute for Scientific Information (ISI)
University City Science Center
3501 Market Street
Philadelphia, Pennsylvania 19104
(215) 386-0100
(800) 523-1850

Class: Reference.

Data source: Journal articles from the social sciences as well as the natural, physical, and biomedical sciences.

Size: 1,015,000 records.

Maintenance: Approximately 3,500 records monthly.

Primary subject: Environmental, social, and political affairs.

Secondary subject: Multidisciplinary.

Profile: A multidisciplinary data base indexing significant items from the most important social science journals throughout the world. Coverage includes natural, physical and biomedical sciences; business, finance, economics, community health, history, management, marketing, statistics, psychology, psychiatry, sociology, education and philosophy.

Applications: User may search by way of the author's cited references as well as key word indexing.

Subject cross reference: 1.9, 2.2, 2.4, 2.15, 4.1, 6.5, 6.7, 9.8, and 9.13.

Geographic coverage: International.

Time coverage: 1969 to present.

Online vendor(s): BRS, Inc.
DIALOG Information Services, Inc.
SDC Search Service.

SOCIETY OF AUTOMOTIVE ENGINEERS (SAE) ABSTRACTS

Producer: Society of Automotive Engineers (SAE)
400 Commonwealth Drive
Warrendale, Pennsylvania 15096
(412) 776-4841

Class: Reference.

Data source: Abstracts of technical papers presented at conferences.

Size: 10,000 citations.

Maintenance: Approximately 200 abstracts quarterly.

Primary subject: Research and Development.

Secondary subject: General Management (Transportation).

Profile: SAE provides access to various technical papers, conferences and meetings. Subject coverage includes automobile technology, self-propelled vehicles, space vehicles, missiles, military equipment, trucks, tractors, chain saws and marine equipment. Topic coverage includes instrumentation, structures, materials, testing and safety.

Applications: Transportation machinery news, analysis, research and applications reference; automotive industry news.

Subject cross reference: 2.8, 7.3, 7.5, 7.7, 8.2, 8.5, 8.6, 8.8, and 9.18.

Geographic coverage: International.

Time coverage: 1965 to present.

Online vendor(s): SDC Search Service.

SOCIOLOGICAL ABSTRACTS

Producer: Sociological Abstracts
P.O. Box 22206
San Diego, California 92122
(714) 565-6603

Class: Reference.

Data source: Journal articles.

Size: 107,000 citations.

Maintenance: Approximately 2,000 records quarterly.

Primary subject: Environmental, social, and political affairs.

Secondary subject: N/A.

Profile: Covers the world's literature in sociology and related disciplines in the social and behavioral sciences. Over 1,200 journals and other serial publications are scanned each year to provide original research coverage, reviews, discussions, conference reports, panel discussions and case studies.

Applications: Consumer analysis; social trends.

Subject cross reference: 2.2, 2.15, 6.7, and 9.8.

Geographic coverage: International.

Time coverage: 1963 to present.

Online vendor(s): DIALOG Information Services, Inc.

SOLAR ENERGY INFORMATION DATA BANK (SEIDB)

Producer: Solar Energy Research Institute (SERI)
1617 Cole Boulevard
Golden, Colorado 80401
(303) 231-1000

Class: Reference and Statistical.

Data source: Network participants, Department of Energy, and primary research.

Size: 30,000 records.

Maintenance: N/A.

Primary subject: Long-Range Strategic Planning.

Secondary subject: N/A.

Profile: Provides five separate data bases which cover: (1) Solar Manufacturers—lists over 2,000 sources; (2) Solar Biblio—references in solar literature; (3) Solar Education—lists programs and courses; (4) Solar Installations—lists previous solar installations; (5) Solar Legislation—lists current/previous bills.

Applications: Solar energy research reference.

Subject cross reference: 2.12, 5.6, 7.11, and 10.5.

Geographic coverage: Domestic.

Time coverage: 1977 to present.

Online vendor(s): Solar Energy Research Institute.

THE SOURCE℠

Producer: Source Telecomputing Corporation (STC)
1515 Anderson Road
McLean, Virginia 22102
(703) 734-7500
(800) 336-3366

Class: Reference and Statistical.

Data source: News agencies (UPI), stock exchanges, The New York Times Consumer Data Base, Dittler's Airline Itineraries, *Mobil Restaurant Guide*, and various publications.

Size: 1,200+ data bases and related services.

Maintenance: Varies according to the specific data base.

Primary subject: Multidisciplinary.

Secondary subject: N/A.

Profile: Maintains several multidisciplined data bases covering business, consumerism and entertainment. Data bases include business services (airline schedules, travel tips and reservations, bartering, employment, research services, and restaurant reviews); news on the communications industry; current business trends in thirty-six categories; stock and commodity market statistics; programs for information management; tax preparation programs; electronic shopping, trading, and bartering; education and financial aid information; employment opportunities and industry news; legal and Supreme Court activities; government and political news and opinions; legislative updates; consumer affairs; health and medicine; science and technology; general news and commentary; travel, dining, and entertainment, and, a variety of personal items.

Applications: Stock analysis; personal business planning; employment searching and selection; "At home" shopping and itinerary guide.

Subject cross reference: 1.19, 2.16, 3.6, 4.6, 5.9, 6.8, 7.12, 8.9, 9.20, and 10.8.

Geographic coverage: Domestic.

Time coverage: Varies by specific data base.

Online vendor(s): Source Telecomputing Corporation.

SPECIALIZED TEXTILE INFORMATION (STI)

Producer: Shirley Institute
Manchester, England M20 8RX
(061) 445-8141

Class: Reference.

Data source: *World Textile Abstracts* which is produced from 500 international journals, reports, conference proceedings, books, and government documents.

Size: 96,500 records.

Maintenance: Approximately 800 records monthly.

Primary subject: Industrial and Manufacturing Planning.

Secondary subject: Research and Development.

Profile: This data base is the on-line version of *World Textile Abstracts* and indexes world literature on the technical aspects of textile and related materials: economics, management and production of the textile industry; and on the consumption of and international trade in textile materials and products.

Applications: Industry standards and technical comparisons.

Subject cross reference: 7.5, 7.10, 8.2, and 8.8.

Geographic coverage: International.

Time coverage: 1970 to date.

Online vendor(s): DIALOG Information Services, Inc.

SPECTRUM

Producer: Computer Directions Advisors, Inc.
11501 Georgia Avenue
Silver Spring, Maryland 20902
(301) 565-9544

Class: Statistical.

Data source: Securities and Exchange Commission filings.

Size: 6,000+ companies.

Maintenance: Daily.

Primary subject: Banking, Economics, and Finance.

Secondary subject: Long-Range Strategic Planning.

Profile: Maintains financial profile information for publicly held companies on The New York and American Exchanges as well as Over-The-Counter companies. Coverage includes investment company stock holdings, investment company portfolios, institutional stock holdings, institutional portfolios, institutional convertible holdings, five percent beneficial ownership holdings, and insider ownership.

Applications: User may retrieve data by security or owner and date. Data are available by company or individual report filings.

Subject cross reference: 1.11, 1.16, 10.1, and 10.7.

Geographic coverage: Domestic.

Time coverage: Varies by specific data series.

Online vendor(s): Computer Directions Advisors, Inc.

SPORT

Producer: Sport Information Resource Centre (SIRC)
Coaching Association of Canada
333 River Road
Ottawa, Ontario, Canada K1L 8B9
(613) 746-5357

Class: Reference.

Data source: *Sport and Recreation Index* from newsletters, journals, theses, monographs, and conference papers.

Size: 70,000 citations.

Maintenance: Approximately 4,000 citations quarterly.

Primary subject: Multidisciplinary.

Secondary subject: N/A.

Profile: Provides an extensive coverage of individual sports, including practice, training and equipment, recreation, sports medicine, physical education, sport facilities and international sports history.

Applications: Recreation facilities management and training reference; playground training.

Subject cross reference: 9.7 and 9.20.

Geographic coverage: International.

Time coverage: 1975 to present.

Online vendor(s): SDC Search Service.

STANDARD & POOR'S GENERAL INFORMATION FILE

Producer: Standard & Poor's Corporation
25 Broadway
New York, New York 10004
(212) 248-2525

Class: Reference and Statistical.

Data source: Standard & Poor's records.

Size: 3,000 records.

Maintenance: Depends upon data type; some daily.

Primary subject: Banking, Economics, and Finance.

Secondary subject: Multidisciplinary.

Profile: For each company maintained, this service provides a Business Summary, Important Business Developments, Product/Service Line Contributions to Revenue/Profits, and various other financial data items. Also includes general information on the company.

Applications: Stock analyses; marketing expansion programs; company profiles (financial and non-financial).

Subject cross reference: 1.11, 1.16, 2.1, 2.10, 10.3, and 10.6.

Geographic coverage: Domestic.

Time coverage: Depends upon series; EPS is for latest three years.

Online vendor(s): CompuServe.

STANDARD & POOR'S INDUSTRY FINANCIAL DATA BANK

Producer: Data Resources, Inc.
29 Hartwell Avenue
Lexington, Massachusetts 02173
(617) 861-0165

Class: Statistical.

Data source: Standard & Poor's Corporation.

Size: 1,500 + time series.

Maintenance: Annually, quarterly and monthly.

Primary subject: Banking, Economics, and Finance.

Secondary subject: Long-Range Strategic Planning.

Profile: Maintains over 1,500 series describing the financial position of approximately 100 industry groups. This data base contains the following data for each industry: sales, earnings per share, federal income taxes, dividends per share, operating profit, book value, working capital, depreciation and stock history.

Applications: Comparisons of major factors bearing upon sales, profits, dividends, etc.

Subject cross reference: 1.8, 1.12, 1.16, 1.17, 10.6, and 10.7.

Geographic coverage: Domestic.

Time coverage: 1946 to present.

Online vendor(s): Data Resources, Inc.

STANDARD & POOR'S NEWS

Producer: Standard & Poor's Corporation
25 Broadway
New York, New York 10004
(212) 248-3995

Class: Reference and Statistical.

Data source: Annual reports, interim earnings reports, and corporate statistical data which corresponds to the equivalent *Standard & Poor's Corporate Records Daily News* and *Cumulative News*.

Size: 156,000 records.

Maintenance: Approximately 1,700 records weekly.

Primary subject: Banking, Economics, and Finance.

Secondary subject: General Management.

Profile: Maintains both general news and financial data on more than 9,000 publicly-owned domestic companies. Coverage includes earnings, management changes, contract awards, mergers, acquisitions, bond descriptions, corporate background, subsidiaries, litigation and officers.

Applications: A major source for corporate or individual investing and competitive analysis; company profiles.

Subject cross reference: 1.11, 1.16, 2.1, 9.13, 9.20, 10.1, 10.3, and 10.7.

Geographic coverage: Domestic.

Time coverage: 1979 to present.

Online vendor(s): DIALOG Information Services, Inc.

STANDARD & POOR'S
STOCK GUIDE RETRIEVAL SERVICE

Producer: Standard & Poor's Corporation (S&P)
25 Broadway
New York, New York 10004
(212) 248-2525

Class: Statistical.

Data source: U.S. Stock Exchanges.

Size: 5,000 + companies.

Maintenance: Daily.

Primary subject: Banking, Economics, and Finance.

Secondary subject: N/A.

Profile: Supplies security description for common and preferred stocks and warrants—name of company, exchange listing(s), ticker symbol, per share earnings and dividends, net sales/income, and principal business; price and dividend history; and financial statement data.

Applications: Corporate intelligence assistance; portfolio management (institutional investing); personal investing.

Subject cross reference: 1.11, 1.16, and 10.1.

Geographic coverage: Domestic.

Time coverage: Most recent four years.

Online vendor(s): GTE Information Systems, Inc.

STANDARDS & SPECIFICATIONS

Producer: National Standards Association, Inc. (NSA)
5161 River Road
Washington, D.C. 20016
(301) 951-1310
(800) 638-8076

Class: Reference.

Data source: Various standards issuing agencies and organizations.

Size: 72,000 records.

Maintenance: Monthly.

Primary subject: Industrial and Manufacturing Planning.

Secondary subject: N/A.

Profile: Provides access to all government and industry standards, specifications and related documents. Coverage of documentation specifies terminology, testing, safety, materials, products or other requirements and characteristics of interest to a particular technology or industry.

Applications: User has access to standards and specifications through the Federal Supply Class Code, issuing organization, whether documents have been cancelled or superceded, if adopted by an agency of the U.S. government, and designated an American National Standard.

Subject cross reference: 7.9.

Geographic coverage: Domestic.

Time coverage: Latest issues.

Online vendor(s): DIALOG Information Services, Inc.

STATE PUBLICATIONS INDEX (SPI)

Producer: Capitol Services International
415 Second Street N.E. Suite 200
Washington, D.C. 20002
(202) 546-5600

Class: Reference.

Data source: State government documents.

Size: 50,000 citations.

Maintenance: Quarterly (suspended in Fall, 1981).

Primary subject: Multidisciplinary.

Secondary subject: N/A

Profile: A comprehensive source of current state documents issued by all 50 states, The Virgin Islands, and Puerto Rico. Coverage includes regulatory information, energy, parks and recreation, education, labor, law, health and medicine, and finance.

Applications: Reference for state legislative and agency activity.

Subject cross reference: 1.19, 2.16, 3.6, 4.6, 5.9, 6.8, 7.12, 8.9, 9.20 and 10.8.

Geographic coverage: Domestic, Puerto Rico, and Virgin Islands.

Time coverage: 1976 to 1981.

Online vendor(s): BRS, Inc.

STEEL DATA BANKS

Producer: Data Resources, Inc.
29 Hartwell Avenue
Lexington, Massachusetts 02173
(617) 861-0165

Class: Statistical.

Data source: Amerian Metal Market, Bureau of Labor Statistics, Bureau of Mines, U.S. Department of Commerce and the American Iron & Steel Institute. International sources include the International Iron & Steel Institute and the Organization for Economic Cooperation and Development.

Size: Several time series.

Maintenance: Weekly, monthly, quarterly and annually.

Primary subject: Industrial and Manufacturing Planning.

Secondary subject: N/A.

Profile: Maintains time series on iron, steel and raw material usage in the steel industry. Coverage includes raw steel production, steel mill shipments with product and market detail, steel product prices and price indices, raw materials quantities and prices, steel imports and exports for products by country of origin and port of entry and steel workers' wages.

Applications: Monitoring and forecasting steel volume; pricing and costing for the short run; market share analysis; materials purchase planning.

Subject cross reference: 7.10, 7.11, and 9.9.

Geographic coverage: International.

Time coverage: Varies by series.

Online vendor(s): Data Resources, Inc.

SURFACE COATINGS ABSTRACTS (WSCA)

Producer: Paint Research Association
Waldegrave Road
Teddington, Middlesex England TW11 8LD
(01) 977-4427

Class: Reference.

Data source: Journal articles, patents, specifications, books and conference proceedings.

Size: 50,200 citations.

Maintenance: Monthly.

Primary subject: Industrial and Manufacturing Planning.

Secondary subject: N/A

Profile: Maintains references to research literature on all aspects of paints and surface coatings. Coverage includes pigments, dyestuffs, resins, solvents, plasticizers, printing inks, insulations, fire retardants, occurrence and prevention of deterioration, testing, industrial hazards, pollution and marketing.

Applications: Paint coverage analysis for different applications.

Subject cross reference: 7.9.

Geographic coverage: International.

Time coverage: 1976 to present.

Online vendor(s): DIALOG Information Services, Inc.

TARGET GROUP INDEX (TGI)

Producer: Simmons Market Research Bureau, Inc.
219 East 42nd Street
New York, New York 10017
(212) 867-1414

Class: Statistical.

Data source: Market Surveys—Interviews and Questionnaires.

Size: Sample size of 30,000.

Maintenance: No longer maintained.

Primary subject: Marketing Planning.

Secondary subject: N/A

Profile: Maintains audience measurements, media usage, demographics, products and services use, ownership data and buying style characteristics from sampled adult and teenage populations. Data are local, regional, and national.

Applications: Media rate decisions; promotions effectiveness.

Subject cross reference: 2.2, 2.3, 2.4, 2.5, 2.15, and 4.1.

Geographic coverage: Domestic.

Time coverage: 1977.

Online vendor(s): Interactive Market Systems, Inc.
Telmar Media Systems, Inc.

TECH-NET®

Producer: Information Handling Services
Inverness Business Park
15 Inverness Way East
Englewood, Colorado 80150
(303) 779-0600
(800) 525-7052 X328

Class: Reference.

Data source: American National Standards Institute, American Society for Testing and Materials, American Society of Civil Engineers, American Petroleum Institute, Underwriters Laboratories, Inc., and The International Organization for Standardization.

Size: 24,000 vendor catalogs.

Maintenance: Continuous.

Primary subject: Industrial and Manufacturing Planning.

Secondary subject: N/A

Profile: Provides references to sources for vendor products, industry standards, and government documents. Data come from 24,000+ vendor catalogs, 91% of the world's most commonly used industry codes and standards, and a collection of military specs and standards. In total, this data base represents over 10 million industrial products.

Applications: Product analysis and comparisons; vendor selection.

Subject cross reference: 7.10, 7.11, and 8.2.

Geographic coverage: International.

Time coverage: Current data only.

Online vendor(s): Information Handling Services.

TECHNOTEC TECHNOLOGY EXCHANGE DATA BASE®

Producer: Control Data Corporation
HQV001
Post Office Box 0
Minneapolis, Minnesota 55440
(612) 853-3575
(800) 328-1870

Class: Reference.

Data source: Corporate and individual information requests.

Size: 15,000 records.

Maintenance: Approximately 250 records biweekly.

Primary subject: Research and Development.

Secondary subject: Sales Planning.

Profile: Maintains over 15,000 records of available technology in more than 30 countries. The purpose is to promote technology transfer on-line. The file consists of Techno-Stock (technology), Techno-Quest (unsolved problems/opportunities), and Techno-Aide (experts/consultants).

Applications: Locating distributors or reps in foreign countries; technology licensing; locating foreign technology; locating expert consultants.

Subject cross reference: 3.3, 8.3, 8.4, 8.5, 8.6, 8.7, 8.8, and 9.2.

Geographic coverage: International.

Time coverage: Current data only.

Online vendor(s): Control Data Corporation.

TELEQUOTE III®

Producer: Bunker Ramo Information Systems
35 Nutmeg Drive
Trumbull, Connecticut 06609
(203) 377-4141

Class: Statistical.

Data source: U.S. stock and commodity exchanges,
Over-The-Counter quotes, and various wire services.

Size: 6,000 companies.

Maintenance: Daily.

Primary subject: Banking, Economics, and Finance.

Secondary subject: N/A.

Profile: A continuous on-line financial information service
covering stocks, options, bonds and commodities. Financial
coverage includes high, low, P/E ratio, dividend,
ex-dividend rate, last trade, annual high/low, previous close,
bid, ask, open; market indicators and statistics and Dow
Jones indices. Commodity coverage includes open, high, bid,
ask, last price, last split and close information. Various trend
data are also available.

Applications: Corporate and individual portfolio management;
commodities trade analysis.

Subject cross reference: 1.16.

Geographic coverage: United States and Canada.

Time coverage: 1978 to present.

Online vendor(s): Bunker Ramo Information Systems.

TELERATE HISTORICAL DATABASES

Producer: Telerate Systems, Inc.
1 World Trade Center
104th Floor
New York, New York 10048

Class: Statistical.

Data source: Telerate statistics.

Size: 10,200 + time series.

Maintenance: Daily.

Primary subject: Banking, Economics, and Finance.

Secondary subject: N/A.

Profile: Two separate data bases, provides both domestic and
international time-series data on financial activities. The
domestic data base covers major money market instruments,
government and agency securities, financial and commodity
futures, and related economic and Federal Reserve
statistics. The international data base covers foreign
exchange rates, Eurocurrency deposit rates, foreign
currency futures, international money market instruments,
and precious metal markets.

Applications: Corporate and personal financial management;
forecasting reference.

Subject cross reference: 1.8, 1.12, 1.14, 1.15, and 1.16.

Geographic coverage: International.

Time coverage: 1976 to present.

Online vendor(s): Rapidata, Inc.

TEXTILE INFORMATION TREATMENT USERS' SERVICE (TITUS)

Producer: Institut Textile De France
35 rue des Abondances
F-92100 Boulogne sur Seine, France
(01) 825-1890

Class: Reference.

Data source: 800 scientific and technical journals, technical
reports, patents, standards, manufacturers' data sheets and
conference papers.

Size: 120,000 citations.

Maintenance: Approximately 1,600 citations monthly.

Primary subject: Multidisciplinary (for textile industry).

Secondary subject: N/A.

Profile: Provides information relating to the textile industry.
Subject coverage includes fibers, finishing, bonding, agents,
analysis, chemical composition, engineering, management
and environmental protection as it relates to the textile
industry.

Applications: Textile managers, engineers and technicians may
stay abreast of current products, management and industry
standards.

Subject cross reference: 2.12, 6.3, 7.9, and 8.9.

Geographic coverage: International.

Time coverage: 1968 to present.

Online vendor(s): SDC Search Service.

TORONTO STOCK EXCHANGE 300 COMPOSITE INDEX (TSEINDEXHIST)

Producer: I.P. Sharp Associates
145 King Street West
Toronto, Ontario, Canada M58 1J8
(416) 364-5361

Class: Statistical.

Data source: Toronto Stock Exchange trade data.

Size: 300 Stocks.

Maintenance: Daily.

Primary subject: Banking, Economics and Finance (securities).

Secondary subject: N/A.

Profile: Contains trading data for the 300 stocks and 62 major
and minor indices that constitute the Toronto Stock
Exchange 300 Composite Index. Twenty-four data items
are available for each stock and index.

Applications: Toronto Stock Exchange analysis of companies
using various index values, P/E ratios and dividend yields.

Subject cross reference: 1.16.

Geographic coverage: Canada.

Time coverage: 1956 to present for monthly data; 1976 to
present for daily data.

Online vendor(s): I.P. Sharp Associates.

TOXICOLOGY DATA BANK (TDB)

Producer: U.S. National Library of Medicine
Toxicology Information Program (TIP)
8600 Rockville Pike
Bethesda, Maryland 20209
(301) 496-1131

Class: Statistical.

Data source: Published text books and handbooks, journals, and research reports.

Size: 3,400 substances.

Maintenance: Quarterly.

Primary subject: Research and Development.

Secondary subject: General Management (health care).

Profile: Maintains information on known or potentially toxic substances which are exposed to populations. Coverage categories include toxicological data (dose thresholds), pharmacological data (antidotes, treatments), chemical (shelf life, melting point), nomenclature information (molecular formula, registry number), manufacturer's information (major uses) and environmental information (pollution potential).

Applications: Poison control centers reference; manufacturer's new product development; physician on-line reference.

Subject cross reference: 6.6, 7.1, 7.7, 8.6, and 9.7.

Geographic coverage: International.

Time coverage: Most current data.

Online vendor(s): National Library of Medicine.

TOXLINE

Producer: U.S. National Library of Medicine
Toxicology Information Program (TIP)
8600 Rockville Pike
Bethesda, Maryland 20209
(301) 496-1131

Class: Reference.

Data source: World literature abstracts and private organization collections.

Size: 650,000.

Maintenance: Monthly.

Primary subject: General Management (health care, hospitals, and medicine).

Secondary subject: N/A.

Profile: Maintains information (citations and/or abstracts) concerning human and animal toxicity reports, studies and analysis. Coverage includes hazardous household products, chemical substances, pharmaceuticals, mutagens, teratology, pesticides, environmental pollutants and epidemiology.

Applications: Biomedical research reference; aid in diagnosing and treating toxicity cases and abuse.

Subject cross reference: 6.6, 7.1, 7.7, 8.6, and 9.7.

Geographic coverage: International.

Time coverage: 1977 to present.

Online vendor(s): BLAISE
DIMDI
National Library of Medicine.

TRADE AND INDUSTRY INDEX®

Producer: Information Access Corporation
404 Sixth Avenue
Menlo Park, California 94025
(415) 367-7171
(800) 227-8431

Class: Reference.

Data source: 240 special business and trade journals, 1,200 business and industry newspapers, books, government documents and periodicals.

Size: 140,000 records.

Maintenance: Monthly.

Primary subject: Multidisciplinary.

Secondary subject: N/A.

Profile: Maintains an index to business journals relating to trade, industry and commerce. This data base is a current and comprehensive source of major trade journals and industry related periodicals representing all SIC's (Standard Industrial Classifications). Subject categories include banking, insurance, securities, agriculture, oil and gas, utilities, taxation, wholesale/retail trade, construction, design and manufacturing, forestry and paper products.

Applications: Each user may survey articles from the significant publications which are specific to his field(s) of interest and/or industry.

Subject cross reference: 1.19, 2.16, 3.6, 4.6, 5.9, 6.8, 7.12, 8.9, 9.20, and 10.8.

Geographic coverage: International.

Time coverage: 1981 to present.

Online vendor(s): DIALOG Information Services, Inc.

TRADENET

Producer: Barter Worldwide, Inc. (BWW)
6575 Green Valley Circle
Suite 112
Culver City, California 90230
(213) 641-1000

Class: Statistical.

Data source: Barter brokers, corporations, and individuals.

Size: N/A.

Maintenance: Daily.

Primary subject: Multidisciplinary.

Secondary subject: N/A.

Profile: This is the first public online data base established for the bartering and trading of worldwide goods and services. The system allows users to list their own trade items and to "key word" search for items they need.

Applications: Tax advantage analysis; discount asset acquisition(s).

Subject cross reference: 7.10, 7.11, and 9.20.

Geographic coverage: International.

Time coverage: Current items.

Online vendor(s): Source Telecomputing Corporation (The Source).

TRADE OPPORTUNITIES WEEKLY

Producer: U.S. Department of Commerce
Trade Facilitation Information & Services
Division—ITA/1033/FTI
Washington, D.C. 20230
(202) 377-2988

Class: Reference.

Data source: Department of Commerce, U.S. Embassies, and U.S. Foreign Service Officers.

Size: 82,189 records.

Maintenance: Quarterly (From trade opportunities file).

Primary subject: General Management.

Secondary subject: Sales Planning.

Profile: Includes information, both current and historical, on export opportunities overseas. Coverage includes country of origin, opportunity description, contact, products of interest and data.

Applications: Sales leads identification and analysis; new market analysis, inventory reduction management.

Subject cross reference: 3.2, 3.3, 3.5, 9.6, and 9.9.

Geographic coverage: International.

Time coverage: 1976 to present.

Online vendor(s): DIALOG Information Services, Inc.

TRADERS

Producer: Control Data Corporation
HQV001
Post Office Box 0
Minneapolis, Minnesota 55440
(612) 853-3575
(800) 328-1870

Class: Reference.

Data source: U.S. Department of Commerce *Trade Opportunities*.

Size: 60,000 + records.

Maintenance: Monthly.

Primary subject: General Management (import/export).

Secondary subject: N/A.

Profile: An extract of the Trade Opportunities Data Base (also CDC), provides a list of potential customers for U.S. exports and exporters.

Applications: Market analysis; export planning.

Subject cross reference: 3.3 and 9.9.

Geographic coverage: International.

Time coverage: Current data only.

Online vendor(s): Control Data.

TRANSPORTATION

Producer: Data Resources, Inc.
29 Hartwell Avenue
Lexington, Massachusetts 02173
(617) 861-0165

Class: Statistical.

Data source: American Trucking Association, Association of American Railroads, ICC, U.S. Department of Commerce and Motor Vehicle Manufacturers' Association of the United States.

Size: N/A.

Maintenance: Weekly, monthly, quarterly and annually.

Primary subject: General Management (transportation and shipping).

Secondary subject: N/A.

Profile: Maintains an extensive coverage of commodity traffic by mode, carrier operations, financial data and complete equipment (locomotive, railcar, truck and trailer) sales and fleet data. Primary concepts covered include Class I and II rail, Class I and II motor carrier, waterborne (inland, coastline, Great Lakes, import, export) and air. This data base also includes up-to-date information on shipment levels of industries using transportation, as well as model rate and cost information by region.

Applications: Evaluation of shifts in model traffic shares; traffic monitoring for operations, scheduling, capacity and facilities planning.

Subject cross reference: 9.18.

Geographic coverage: Domestic.

Time coverage: N/A.

Online vendor(s): Data Resources, Inc.

TRANSPORTATION COST SERVICE (TCS)

Producer: A.T. Kearney, Inc.
222 S. Riverside Plaza
Chicago, Illinois 60606
(312) 648-0111

Class: Statistical.

Data source: Interstate Commerce Commission filings.

Size: N/A.

Maintenance: Quarterly.

Primary subject: General Management (transportation).

Secondary subject: N/A.

Profile: Maintains a modeling system designed to estimate current and future costs for transportation movements by truck, rail and marine.

Applications: Users must specify relevant information (commodity code, weight, origination, destination and carrier(s) involved) and the computer will then calculate costing.

Subject cross reference: 9.18.

Geographic coverage: Domestic.

Time coverage: Most current data.

Online vendor(s): Data Resources, Inc.

TRIS-ON-LINE

Producer: Transportation Research Board
National Research Council
2101 Constitution Avenue, N.W.
Washington, D.C. 20418
(202) 389-6611

Class: Reference.

Data source: Research project data holdings, journal articles, and government reports.

Size: 164,000 records.

Maintenance: Approximately 1,200 records monthly.

Primary subject: General Management (transportation).

Secondary subject: N/A.

Profile: Provides transportation research information in air, rail, maritime, highway, urban mass transit and other transportation modes. Subject coverage includes energy, regulations and legislation, safety, operations, design, construction, maintenance technology, traffic control, and communications.

Applications: Transportation management—budgeting, forecasting and predicting government influences.

Subject cross reference: 9.18.

Geographic coverage: Domestic.

Time coverage: Three to five most current years.

Online vendor(s): DIALOG Information Services, Inc.

TROPICAL AGRICULTURE (TROPAG)

Producer: Royal Tropical Institute
Department of Agricultural Research
Mauritskade 63
NL-1092 AD Amsterdam, The Netherlands
(020) 924949

Class: Reference.

Data source: Journal articles, theses, conference papers, monographs, and miscellaneous documents.

Size: 30,000 citations.

Maintenance: Approximately 500 records monthly.

Primary subject: General Management (agriculture).

Secondary subject: Research and Development.

Profile: Covers international literature on tropical and subtropical agriculture. Coverage includes crop production and protection, fertilizers, soils, plant nutrition, crop processing, agricultural technology, storage, commercial and statistical information, animal husbandry, inland fisheries, forestry, human nutrition, and public health.

Applications: Agriculture and crop management: planting, growth and storage technological reference; new technologies.

Subject cross reference: 8.9 and 9.1.

Geographic coverage: International.

Time coverage: 1975 to present.

Online vendor(s): SDC Search Service.

TSCA CHEMICAL SUBSTANCES INVENTORY

Producer: U.S. Environmental Protection Agency
Office of Toxic Substances
Industry Assistance Office
401 M. Street, SW MS-TS799
Washington, D.C. 20460
(800) 424-9065
(202) 554-1404

Class: Reference.

Data source: Initial inventory of the Toxic Substances Control Act Chemical Substance Inventory.

Size: 43,728 records.

Maintenance: Irregular.

Primary subject: Industrial and Manufacturing Planning.

Secondary subject: Research and Development.

Profile: A non-bibliographic dictionary listing chemical substances in commercial use in the U.S. as of June 1, 1979. This does not represent a listing of toxic chemicals since toxicity is not a criterion for inclusion in the list. For each substance the following are provided: CAS registry number, synonyms, preferred name and molecular formula.

Applications: Chemical substance availability reference.

Subject cross reference: 7.10 and 8.2.

Geographic coverage: Domestic.

Time coverage: 1979.

Online vendor(s): DIALOG Information Services, Inc.
SDC Search Service.

ULRICH'S INTERNATIONAL PERIODICALS DIRECTORY

Producer: R.R. Bowker Company
1180 Avenue of the Americas
New York, New York 10036
(212) 764-5100

Class: Reference.

Data source: Ulrich's *International Periodicals Directory* and *Ulrich's Sources of Serials.*

Size: 102,000 records.

Maintenance: Each four to six weeks.

Primary subject: Multidisciplinary.

Secondary subject: N/A.

Profile: Maintains citations on 65,000 periodicals and approximately 38,500 annuals, serials, conference proceedings and international continuations.

Applications: Periodical source directory.

Subject cross reference: 1.19, 2.16, 3.6, 4.6, 5.9, 6.8, 7.12, 8.9, 9.20, and 10.8.

Geographic coverage: International.

Time coverage: Current publications.

Online vendor(s): BRS, Inc.

U.S. CENSUS OF AGRICULTURE (1978)

Producer: U.S. Census Bureau
Washington, D.C. 20233
(301) 763-7273

Class: Statistical.

Data source: Agricultural surveys.

Size: 1,500 + variables.

Maintenance: When new survey is conducted (1982).

Primary subject: General Management (agriculture).

Secondary subject: Marketing Planning.

Profile: Maintains data on farms, over 65 different crops and livestock. Farm data treat farm size and value, use of land, market value of agricultural products, and organization/occupation of operator. Other data include livestock and poultry inventory and various forms of crop production.

Applications: Farm comparisons and analysis; agribusiness marketing planning; demographic analysis of the agri-market.

Subject cross reference: 2.4, 2.5, and 9.1.

Geographic coverage: Domestic.

Time coverage: 1978 data published in 1981.

Online vendor(s): On-Line Research, Inc.

U.S. CENSUS OF RETAIL TRADE (1977)

Producer: Census Bureau
Washington, D.C. 20233
(301) 763-7273

Class: Statistical.

Data source: Survey results, IRS, and Social Security Administration records.

Size: 2.5 million respondents.

Maintenance: 1982/83.

Primary subject: Banking, Economics, and Finance.

Secondary subject: Marketing Planning.

Profile: Contains data pertaining to sales revenues, corresponding number of establishments, payroll, and legal form of business. Coverage includes 27 product categories and 113 industrial classifications. Data are by SMSA, state and national. Also covered are 150 areas of dominant influence (ADI's).

Applications: Aggregate data for forecasting; production schedule decisions.

Subject cross reference: 1.9, 2.3, and 2.5.

Geographic coverage: Domestic.

Time coverage: 1977/78 data published in 1980.

Online vendor(s): On-Line Research, Inc.

U.S. CENTRAL DATA BANK (DRI CENTRAL)

Producer: Data Resources, Inc.
29 Hartwell Avenue
Lexington, Massachusetts 02173
(617) 861-0165

Class: Statistical.

Data source: Bureau of Economic Analysis, Census Bureau, Bureau of Labor Statistics and the Federal Reserve Board.

Size: 20,000 macroeconomic series.

Maintenance: Continuous.

Primary subject: Banking, Finance, and Economics.

Secondary subject: N/A

Profile: U.S. Central is a collection of financial, economic and demographic time series dealing in aggregate U.S. statistics. Each series is a collection of major indicators and should provide a measurement of economic activity. Coverage includes national income and products accounts series; retail and wholesale sales; manufacturer's shipments, inventories and orders; aggregate consumer and wholesale price indices; labor force, employment, hours and earnings; housing starts and completions; "Quarterly Financial Report" and other industry data; and financial and consumer credit data.

Applications: Cause and effect analysis of change in the economic climate at the national level; analysis of long-term trends and current economic fluctuations.

Subject cross reference: 1.8, 1.9, and 1.12.

Geographic coverage: Domestic.

Time coverage: Depends upon the specific series.

Online vendor(s): Data Resources, Inc.

U.S. COUNTY DATA BANK

Producer: Data Resources, Inc.
29 Hartwell Avenue
Lexington, Massachusetts 02173
(617) 861-0165

Class: Statistical.

Data source: U.S. Department of Commerce, Bureau of Economic Analysis; Bureau of the Census.

Size: 200,000 time series.

Maintenance: Annually.

Primary subject: Banking, Economics and Finance.

Secondary subject: Marketing Planning.

Profile: Maintains a collection of over 200,000 annual time series. Coverage includes employment by major industrial group; personal income and components (includes a detailed breakdown of labor and proprietor's income by major industry) and population by age and sex.

Applications: Market analysis for plant/building site; analysis of demographics, employment and income changes by region.

Subject cross reference: 1.8, 1.9, 1.12, 2.4, and 2.5.

Geographic coverage: U.S. Counties.

Time coverage: 1965 to present.

Online vendor(s): Data Resources, Inc.

U.S. ECONOMIC

Producer: ADP Network Services, Inc.
175 Jackson Plaza
Ann Arbor, Michigan 48106
(313) 769-6800

Class: Statistical.

Data source: U.S. government statistics.

Size: Several time series.

Maintenance: Daily.

Primary subject: Banking, Economics, and Finance.

Secondary subject: N/A

Profile: Provides a heterogeneous collection of time-series data on the U.S. economy. Important aggregates are available within two to three hours after their release by the appropriate government agency. Includes such concepts as agricultural prices, capacity utilization, consumer/producer prices, employment, money stock measures, population, and productivity.

Applications: Econometric forecasting; sales territory management

Subject cross reference: 1.4, 1.5, 1.7, 1.8, 1.14, and 2.4.

Geographic coverage: Domestic.

Time coverage: 1947 to present.

Online vendor(s): ADP Network Services, Inc.

U.S. ECONOMIC/CE

Producer: Chase Econometrics/Interactive Data Corporation
486 Totten Pond Road
Waltham, Massachusetts 02154
(617) 890-1234

Class: Statistical.

Data source: Corporate filings, Federal Reserve Board and various U.S. governmental agencies.

Size: 10,000+ time series.

Maintenance: Continuous.

Primary subject: Banking, Economics, and Finance.

Secondary subject: N/A

Profile: Provides industrial-related macroeconomic time series (weekly to annually) data on the U.S. economy. Data items covered include employment, production, national income accounts, prices, construction, inventories, shipments, orders, monetary statistics, and housing.

Applications: Product line forecasting; economic analysis as it relates to pricing and budgeting.

Subject cross reference: 1.8, 1.14, 2.4, 7.6, and 9.15.

Geographic coverage: Domestic.

Time coverage: Varies by series; most from 1945 to present.

Online vendor(s): Chase Econometrics/Interactive Data Corp.

U.S. EXPORTS

Producer: U.S. Census Bureau
Foreign Trade Division
Washington, D.C. 20233
(301) 763-5140

Class: Statistical.

Data source: U.S. Census Bureau.

Size: 750,000 records.

Maintenance: Monthly.

Primary subject: General Management (foreign trade).

Secondary subject: N/A

Profile: Maintains export statistics for all commodities in dollar value and shipping weight, reflecting both government and non-government exports of domestic and foreign merchandise from the U.S. and territories to foreign countries. The physical movement of merchandise out of the U.S. is inclusive of intracompany shipments, types and purchases made in the U.S. by foreign representatives, firms or governments.

Applications: Analyzing export trends by specific commodity and/or country.

Subject cross reference: 2.6 and 9.6.

Geographic coverage: International.

Time coverage: 1978 to present.

Online vendor(s): DIALOG Information Services, Inc.

U.S. FINANCIAL

Producer: ADP Network Services, Inc.
175 Jackson Plaza
Ann Arbor, Michigan 48106
(313) 769-6800

Class: Statistical.

Data source: The Federal Reserve Board, Standard & Poor's, The U.S. Treasury, Federal Home Loan Bank Board and Moody's.

Size: Multiple time series.

Maintenance: Daily.

Primary subject: Banking, Economics, and Finance.

Secondary subject: N/A

Profile: Complements the U.S. Economic data base also by ADP. Offers a composite view of the U.S. economy and includes such concepts as bank assets, liabilities, and reserves; consumer credit; interest rates; loans and investments; new corporate security issues; and money market certificates.

Applications: U.S. economic forecasting and simulation analysis.

Subject cross reference: 1.7, 1.8, and 1.4.

Geographic coverage: Domestic.

Time coverage: Varies by series.

Online vendor(s): ADP Network Services, Inc.

U.S. GOVERNMENT CONTRACT AWARDS
(USGCA)

Producer: Washington Representative Services, Inc.
4040 N. Fairfax Drive
Suite 110
Arlington, Virginia 22203
(703) 243-8912
Cuadra Associates, Inc.
1523 Sixth Street
Suite 12
Santa Monica, California 90401
(213) 451-0644

Class: Reference.

Data source: *Commerce Business Daily*.

Size: 39,000 awards.

Maintenance: Approximately 1,000 awards monthly.

Primary subject: Legal and Legislative Affairs (contracts).

Secondary subject: N/A

Profile: Maintains U.S. contract awards for more than 39,000 contracts awarded by the federal government and its public and private sector agencies. Award coverage includes descriptive title, subject category, funding, awardee name and location, date of award, granting agency and contract and RFP number.

Applications: Funding source reference; awards (contracts) analysis by competitor, industry or segment.

Subject cross reference: 5.3.

Geographic coverage: Domestic.

Time coverage: 1978 to present.

Online vendor(s): SDC Search Service.

U.S. IRON AND STEEL IMPORTS

Producer: Chase Econometrics/Interactive Data Corp.
486 Totten Pond Road
Waltham, Massachusetts 02154
(617) 890-1234

Class: Statistical.

Data source: U.S. Department of Commerce.

Size: 250,000 time series.

Maintenance: Monthly.

Primary subject: General Management (import/export).

Secondary subject: N/A

Profile: Maintains monthly time series on the U.S. import values of iron and steel. Provides value and volume of U.S. imports by seven digit U.S. tariff schedule codes by country of origin and entry point. Other data include quantity of import, value of imports, commodity code and customs region designation.

Applications: Iron and steel import analysis.

Subject cross reference: 9.9.

Geographic coverage: Domestic.

Time coverage: 1979 to present.

Online vendor(s): Chase Econometrics/Interactive Data Company.

U.S. MODEL DATA BANK

Producer: Data Resources, Inc.
29 Hartwell Avenue
Lexington, Massachusetts 02173
(617) 861-0165

Class: Statistical.

Data source: Other DRI data bases such as U.S. Central, Platts and U.S. Prices.

Size: 1,100 quarterly time series.

Maintenance: Quarterly.

Primary subject: Banking, Economics, and Finance.

Secondary subject: N/A

Profile: Contains historical data used to support DRI's macroeconomic model of the U.S. economy. This data is actually a subset of some 1,000 key indicators, drawn primarily from other DRI banks. Coverage includes consumer spending, employment and labor, government spending, finance, flow of funds, automobiles, foreign trade, energy, industrial production, business fixed investment, construction and housing, mortgages, inventories, investments, and price and wages.

Applications: Forecasting short and long term economic trends.

Subject cross reference: 1.4, 1.5, 1.6, 1.7, 1.8, 1.14, 9.15, and 10.7.

Geographic coverage: Domestic.

Time coverage: Varies depending upon series; most are from late 1940's.

Online vendor(s): Data Resources, Inc.

USPO/USPA
(UNITED STATES PATENT OFFICE)

Producer: Derwent Publications Ltd.
Rochdale House
128 Theobalds Road
London, England WC1X 8RP
(01) 242-5823

Class: Reference.

Data source: U.S. Government Patent Office.

Size: All U.S. patents from 1971.

Maintenance: Weekly.

Primary subject: Research and Development (patents).

Secondary subject: N/A

Profile: The U.S. Patent Office files cover all domestic patents, continuations, divisionals and defense documents. These files provide access to all information listed on the front page of a U.S. patent, plus all claims and additional data. USPA contains all patent documents issued during the current one and one half year period. (All earlier patents are maintained in USPO.)

Applications: Competitive (product) intelligence; technology intelligence; subject research.

Subject cross reference: 8.7.

Geographic coverage: Domestic.

Time coverage: 1971 to present.

Online vendor(s): SDC Search Service.

UNITED STATES POLITICAL SCIENCE DOCUMENTS (USPSD)

Producer: University of Pittsburgh
University Center for International Studies
4G22 Forbes Quadrangle
Pittsburgh, Pennsylvania 15260
(412) 624-1234

Class: Reference.

Data source: 120 major American journals—*United States Political Science Documents*.

Size: 15,750 records.

Maintenance: Approximately 4,000 records annually.

Primary subject: Legal and Legislative Affairs.

Secondary subject: Environment, Social & Political Affairs.

Profile: Covers foreign policy, international relations, behavioral sciences, public administration, and policy economics, law, world politics and related subject areas.

Applications: User may use USPSD as a central source for significant political and social research.

Subject cross reference: 1.9, 2.6, 5.6, 5.8, 5.9, 6.4, 6.5, and 9.12.

Geographic coverage: International.

Time coverage: 1975 to present.

Online vendor(s): DIALOG Information Services, Inc.

U.S. PRICES DATA BANK

Producer: Data Resources, Inc. and The U.S. Department of Labor
29 Hartwell Avenue
Lexington, Massachusetts 02173
(617) 861-0165

Class: Statistical.

Data source: U.S. Department of Labor, Bureau of Labor Statistics.

Size: 8,600 time series.

Maintenance: Monthly and bimonthly.

Primary subject: Banking, Economics, and Finance.

Secondary subject: N/A

Profile: Prices Data Bank represents a massive collection of consumer, producer and industry sector price indices. Covered are the consumer price index and the producer price index. The majority of these indices are not seasonally adjusted. Included in most of the time series are the published "all urban consumer price index" (CPI-U), the "revised wage earner and clerical worker index (CPIW)" and their components for the U.S. city average, four regions, 26 standard metro statistical areas, two standard consolidated areas and five city population class sizes. Actual prices used to compute the CPIU and CPIW are also available for certain energy categories.

Applications: Consumer spending patterns analyses; use of the CPI as an index of pricing decisions or escalating income payments.

Subject cross reference: 1.5, 1.6, 1.8, 1.9, 1.14, and 9.13.

Geographic coverage: National, four regions, 26 SMSA's, and two SCA's.

Time coverage: Most series from 1940 to present.

Online vendor(s): Data Resources, Inc.

U.S. PUBLIC SCHOOLS DIRECTORY

Producer: U.S. Department of Education
National Center for Education Statistics
400 Maryland Avenue, SW, Room 3009
Washington, D.C. 20202
(202) 436-6729

Class: Reference.

Data source: *U.S. Public Schools Directory*.

Size: 80,240 records.

Maintenance: Annually.

Primary subject: General Management (education).

Secondary subject: N/A

Profile: Provides information on a variety of directory-type data on public schools throughout the U.S. The primary focus is to be able to generate and analyze public schools by location. The directory will list all public schools from elementary through secondary levels. Included are special education and vocational/technical schools.

Applications: Monitoring trends in public education; public school analysis of type, location, and size.

Subject cross reference: 9.5.

Geographic coverage: Domestic.

Time coverage: Most current information.

Online vendor(s): DIALOG Information Services, Inc.

U.S. REGIONAL

Producer: Data Resources, Inc.
29 Hartwell Avenue
Lexington, Massachusetts 02173
(617) 861-0165

Class: Statistical.

Data source: U.S. Department of Commerce, Bureau of Economic Analysis, U.S. Department of Labor, Bureau of the Census, Bureau of Labor Statistics, U.S. Department of Treasury, Internal Revenue Service.

Size: 42,000 time series.

Maintenance: Monthly, quarterly and annually (depends upon specific time series).

Primary subject: Banking, Economics and Finance.

Secondary subject: Marketing Planning.

Profile: Maintains indicators of economic activities in various states, regions and metro areas. Coverage includes personal income and its components; labor force, employment, hours, and earnings; consumer price indices; banking and financial indicators; manufacturing and production; retail sales; housing permits and mortgage rates.

Applications: Comparisons of economic indicators across regions and between states; economic market analysis for utilities and manufacturers; economic activity analysis.

Subject cross reference: 1.8, 1.9, 1.14, 2.4, 2.5, and 9.13.

Geographic coverage: Domestic.

Time coverage: Depends upon specific series.

Online vendor(s): Data Resources, Inc.

U.S. REQUESTS FOR PROPOSALS (USRFP)

Producer: Washington Representative Services, Inc.
4040 N. Fairfax Drive
Suite 110
Arlington, Virginia 22203
(703) 243-8912

Class: Reference.

Data source: *Commerce Business Daily* RFP documents and amendments.

Size: Approximately 250 citations/month (winter) and 600 citations per month (summer).

Maintenance: Daily.

Primary subject: Multidisciplinary.

Secondary subject: N/A

Profile: Maintains announcements and summaries of Federal requests for proposals (RFP's) in research and development, consulting, training, computer services, engineering, evaluation and other professional service areas. USRFP is divided into three files which reflect the different points in the contract procurement cycle. The announcement file (USRFP1) contains information derived primarily from sections A, H and U of the *Commerce Business Daily*. This includes the procurement title, RFP number, order data and RFP date. The RFP summary file (USRFP2) contains detailed abstracts for the released RFP's. This includes data on firms that have held similar contracts. The amendment file (USRFP3) provides announcements of agency amendments to the bidding requirements.

Applications: USRFP provides problem solving information for proposal writers.

Subject cross reference: 5.3.

Geographic coverage: Domestic.

Time coverage: All "open" RFP's.

Online vendor(s): SDC Search Service.

U.S. STOCK OPTIONS DATA BASE

Producer: Interactive Data Services, Inc.
22 Cortlandt Street
New York, New York 10007
(212) 285-0700

Class: Statistical.

Data source: U.S. Stock Exchange Indices.

Size: All options in U.S. Exchanges.

Maintenance: Daily.

Primary subject: Banking, Economics, and Finance.

Secondary subject: N/A

Profile: Covers daily trading activity for all put and call options traded on the major U.S. Exchanges. Twenty data items are associated with each option. Additionally, over 175 U.S. financial market indicators are available. Indices covered include Dow Jones, AMEX, NASDAQ, NYSE, S&P, TSE300, Moody's Bond Yield, Kuhn-Loeb Bond and Salomon Bond.

Applications: Investor analysis; market analysis.

Subject cross reference: 1.16.

Geographic coverage: Domestic.

Time coverage: Most recent 200 trading days.

Online vendor(s): I.P. Sharp Associates.

UNIVERSAL SERIALS AND BOOK EXCHANGE (USBE)

Producer: Universal Serials and Book Exchange
3335 V Street N.E.
Washington, D.C. 20018
(202) 529-2555

Class: Reference.

Data source: USBE records.

Size: 10,000 citations.

Maintenance: Annually.

Primary subject: Multidisciplinary.

Secondary subject: N/A

Profile: Maintains a file of 10,000 serial titles USBE has in inventory. USBE also maintains 3.25 million issues of available periodicals. Each bibliographic citations include title, frequency of publication, subject, Library of Congress number and the international standard serial number.

Applications: Periodical source directory.

Subject cross reference: 1.19, 2.16, 3.6, 4.6, 5.9, 6.8, 7.12, 8.9, 9.20, and 10.8.

Geographic coverage: International.

Time coverage: N/A

Online vendor(s): BRS, Inc.

USCLASS

Producer: Derwent Publications Ltd.
Rochdale House
128 Theobalds Road
London, England WC1X 8RP
(01) 242-5823

Class: Reference.

Data source: U.S. Government Patents Office.

Size: All U.S. patents.

Maintenance: Semiannually.

Primary subject: Research and Development (patents).

Secondary subject: N/A

Profile: Maintains all U.S. classifications, cross-reference classifications and unofficial classifications for all patents issued from the start of the U.S. Patent Law in 1860.

Applications: Patent searching and researching.

Subject cross reference: 8.7.

Geographic coverage: Domestic.

Time coverage: 1860 to present.

Online vendor(s): SDC Search Service.

VALUE LINE II

Producer: Arnold Bernhard & Co.
711 Third Avenue
New York, New York 10017
(212) 687-3965

Class: Statistical.

Data source: Quarterly and annual financial statements.

Size: 400,000 annual and quarterly time series.

Maintenance: Quarterly and Annually.

Primary subject: Banking, Economics, and Finance.

Secondary subject: N/A

Profile: Provides access to over 400,000 time series covering financial developments from the Value Line Investment Survey. This data base contains financial histories and projections for each of the 1,630 major industrial, retail, transportation, banks and utility companies. Annual data covers 22 years of historical and quarterly data. Specific coverage includes balance sheet/income data, sources and uses of funds, sales projections, capital and equity, profit margins and capital ratios, E.P.S., and stock market indicators.

Applications: Financial position verification; comparison of individual corporate balance sheets with that of industry aggregates.

Subject cross reference: 1.10, 1.11, 1.12, 2.1, and 9.13.

Geographic coverage: Domestic.

Time coverage: Depends upon specific time series, many go back to early 1960's.

Online vendor(s): ADP Network Services, Inc.
Chase Econometrics/Interactive Data Corp.
CompuServe, Inc.
Data Resources, Inc.

VETERINARY LITERATURE DOCUMENTATION (VETDOC)

Producer: Derwent Publications, Ltd.
Rochdale House
128 Theobalds Road
London, England WC1X 8RP
(01) 242-5823

Class: Reference.

Data source: *VETDOC Abstracts Journal*: Scientific journals in 16 languages.

Size: 50,000 records.

Maintenance: Approximately 1,000 records quarterly.

Primary subject: General Management (health care).

Secondary subject: N/A

Profile: Covers international literature on veterinary applications of drugs, hormones, vaccines, and growth promotants, for use in domestic and farm animals. Area coverage includes biochemistry, chemistry, endocrinology, microbiology, pathology, pharmacology, zoology, and management.

Applications: This file is specifically designed to meet the information requirements of veterinary pharmaceutical manufacturers.

Subject cross reference: 9.7.

Geographic coverage: International.

Time coverage: 1968 to present.

Online vendor(s): SDC Search Service.

VOTES DATA BASE

Producer: Policy Review Associates, Inc.
7315 Wisconsin Avenue
Suite 727E
Bethesda, Maryland 20014
(301) 762-8008

Class: Statistical.

Data source: The U.S. Congress (*Congressional Record*).

Size: 800 legislative histories and 260,000 member profile records.

Maintenance: Bi-monthly (while Congress is in session).

Primary subject: Legal and Legislative Affairs.

Secondary subject: Multidisciplinary.

Profile: Covers the complete record of roll call voting by members of the U.S. Congress. Contains bills, resolutions, joint resolutions, concurrent resolutions, executive treaties, nominations and other legislative action taken to a roll call vote. Votes includes member profiles with specific votes cast by individual senators and congressmen.

Applications: User may retrieve information by bill name, subject, personal name, district, state, political party, congress, session or roll call number.

Subject cross reference: 5.4, 5.6, and 5.8.

Geographic coverage: Domestic.

Time coverage: 1979 to present.

Online vendor(s): SDC Search Service.

WALL STREET JOURNAL HIGHLIGHTS ON-LINE

Producer: Dow Jones & Company, Inc.
Post Office Box 300
Princeton, New Jersey 08540
(609) 452-2000
(800) 257-5114

Class: Reference.

Data source: The *Wall Street Journal.*

Size: N/A

Maintenance: Daily.

Primary subject: Multidisciplinary.

Secondary subject: Banking, Economics, and Finance.

Profile: Maintains daily abstracts of various economic and business news items, stories and articles extracted from the *Wall Street Journal.*

Applications: Business news reference aid.

Subject cross reference: 1.19, 2.16, 3.6, 4.6, 5.9, 6.8, 7.12, 8.9, 9.20, and 10.8.

Geographic coverage: International.

Time coverage: N/A

Online vendor(s): Dow Jones & Company, Inc.

WALL $TREET WEEK

Producer: Dow Jones & Company, Inc.
Post Office Box 300
Princeton, New Jersey 08540
(609) 452-2000
(800) 257-5114

Class: Reference.

Data source: Television transcripts of "Wall $treet Week."

Size: Non-applicable.

Maintenance: Weekly (as programs are broadcast).

Primary subject: Banking, Economics, and Finance.

Secondary subject: N/A

Profile: Contains the full-text transcripts of the "Wall $treet Week" television broadcast. This broadcast recaps a wide range of U.S. financial and economic variables.

Applications: Users may retrieve entire program transcripts or segments.

Subject cross reference: 1.5, 1.6, 1.7, 1.8, 1.9, 1.10, 1.11, 1.12, 1.14, 1.16, and 1.17.

Geographic coverage: Domestic.

Time coverage: Most current month.

Online vendor(s): Dow Jones & Company, Inc.

WEEKLY ECONOMIC SURVEY

Producer: Money Market Services, Inc.
490 El Camino Real
Belmont, California 94002
(415) 595-0610

Class: Statistical.

Data source: Financial economists and money market dealers.

Size: N/A

Maintenance: Weekly.

Primary subject: Banking, Economics, and Finance.

Secondary subject: N/A

Profile: Maintains weekly forecasts of significant economic indicators from the major forty to fifty U.S. financial institutions. Information includes commentary and analysis, median forecasts of monetary and economic indicators. Special bar charts displaying forecast distribution are also available.

Applications: Econometric modeling.

Subject cross reference: 1.8, 1.9, 1.14, and 1.19.

Geographic coverage: Domestic.

Time coverage: Most current data.

Online vendor(s): Dow Jones & Company, Inc.

WEEKLY ECONOMIC UPDATE

Producer: Dow Jones & Company, Inc.
Post Office Box 300
Princeton, New Jersey 08540
(800) 257-5114
(609) 452-1511

Class: Reference.

Data source: *Wall Street Journal, Barrons, The Dow Jones News Service*, and leading economic experts.

Size: N/A

Maintenance: Weekly.

Primary subject: Banking, Economics, and Finance.

Secondary subject: N/A

Profile: Maintains a detailed review of the past week's economic events and news and provides an analysis of the coming month's economic outlook.

Applications: Executive summary encapsulation of economic news and developments.

Subject cross reference: 1.5, 1.6, 1.9, 1.14, and 1.19.

Geographic coverage: Domestic.

Time coverage: Current week's data.

Online vendor(s): Dow Jones & Company, Inc.

WELDASEARCH

Producer: The Welding Institute
Abington Hall
Abington
Cambridge, England CB1 6AL
(0223) 891 162

Class: Reference.

Data source: Journal articles, books, research findings, patents, standards and theses.

Size: 60,400 records.

Maintenance: Approximately 400 records monthly.

Primary subject: Industrial and manufacturing planning.

Secondary subject: N/A

Profile: Provides primary coverage of the international literature on all aspects of the joining of metals, plastics and related areas such as metals spraying and thermal cutting. Coverage includes weld design, fabrication techniques, destructive testing, welding metallurgy, fatigue and fracture mechanics, welding and joining equipment, corrosion and quality control.

Applications: Metallurgy research, analysis and applications reference.

Subject cross reference: 7.2, 7.3, 7.9, and 8.4.

Geographic coverage: International.

Time coverage: 1967 to present.

Online vendor(s): DIALOG Information Services, Inc.

WHARTON ECONOMETRIC FORECASTING DATA BASES

Producer: Wharton Econometric Forecasting Associates, Inc.
3624 Science Center
Philadelphia, Pennsylvania 19104
(215) 386-9000

Class: Statistical.

Data source: Multiple government and private agencies.

Size: Approximately 37,000 time series.

Maintenance: Continuous (but varies by specific data base).

Primary subject: Banking, Economics, and Finance.

Secondary subject: Marketing Planning.

Profile: Provides several data bases which contain monthly, quarterly and annual time series. Some of the topics covered include national income and product accounts; demographic data; Bureau of Labor Statistics' employment, hours, and earnings; IRS income and tax statistics; Bureau of Economic Analysis investment data and census surveys; producer and consumer prices; housing and construction statistics; manufacturing and trade shipments, orders, and inventories; state personal income totals; cost of material input statistics; consumer credit interest rates and other financial indicators; reserve and deposit statistics; foreign trade values; U.S. Balance of Payments items; and *Business Conditions Digest* indicators.

Applications: Econometric forecasting reference; assessing general economic conditions.

Subject cross reference: 1.19, 2.16, 9.20, and 10.8.

Geographic coverage: International.

Time coverage: Varies by series; many back to 1929.

Online vendor(s): Uni-Coll, Inc.

WORLD AGRICULTURE SUPPLY— DISPOSITION

Producer: Chase Econometrics/Interactive Data Corporation
486 Totten Pond Road
Waltham, Massachusetts 02154
(617) 890-1234

Class: Statistical.

Data source: U.S. Department of Agriculture.

Size: 9,000 time series.

Maintenance: Semiannually.

Primary subject: General Management (agriculture).

Secondary subject: N/A

Profile: Provides U.S.D.A. data on crop, livestock, and meat commodities for over 120 countries.

Applications: Agriculture research and statistics reference.

Subject cross reference: 9.1.

Geographic coverage: International.

Time coverage: 1960 to present.

Online vendor(s): Chase Econometrics/Interactive Data Corp.

WORLD ALUMINUM ABSTRACTS (WAA)

Producer: American Society for Metals
American Metals Information
Metals Park, Ohio 44073
(216) 338-5151

Class: Reference.

Data source: Journal articles, conference proceedings, books, dissertations, government reports and patents.

Size: 81,600 citations.

Maintenance: Approximately 600 records monthly.

Primary subject: Industrial and Manufacturing Planning.

Secondary subject: Research and Development.

Profile: Provides coverage of the world's technical literature on aluminum, ranging from ore processing through end uses. All aspects of the aluminum industry, aside from mining, are covered. Subject coverage includes aluminum industry, ores, alumina production and extraction, melting, casting, foundry, metal-working, fabrication, finishing, physical and mechanical metallurgy, engineering properties and tests, quality control and end uses(s) application.

Applications: Aluminum technical reference; industry statistics on production and extraction and applications.

Subject cross reference: 7.2, 7.5, 7.9, and 8.4.

Geographic coverage: International.

Time coverage: 1968 to present.

Online vendor(s): DIALOG Information Services, Inc.
QL Systems Limited.

WORLD BANK DEBT TABLES

Producer: I.P. Sharp Associates
145 King Street West
Toronto, Ontario, Canada M5H 1J8
(416) 364-5361

Class: Statistical.

Data source: The World Bank—*World Debt Tables*.

Size: 100 countries.

Maintenance: Monthly.

Primary subject: General Management (international).

Secondary subject: N/A

Profile: This data base is actually a subset of the World Bank publication, *World Debt Tables*. This data base maintains annual statistical data on the external public and publicly-guaranteed debt of approximately 100 developing countries. Coverage of categories includes total debt service, net disbursements of repayment schedules, actual commitments, actual disbursements, and repayment of principal schedules.

Applications: User may retrieve data by public debt category and type of creditor.

Subject cross reference: 9.12.

Geographic coverage: International.

Time coverage: Depends upon series, most are from early 1970's.

Online vendor(s): Chase Econometrics/Interactive Data Corp.
I.P. Sharp Associates.

WORLD ENERGY INDUSTRY®

Producer: World Energy Industry Information Services
4202 Sorrento Valley Boulevard
Suite J
San Diego, California 92121
(714) 452-7675

Class: Statistical.

Data source: *World Energy Industry Quarterly, World Energy Industry Monthly Bulletin* and *The Energy Decade*.

Size: 5,000 time series.

Maintenance: Weekly.

Primary subject: Long-Range Strategic Planning (energy).

Secondary subject: N/A

Profile: Maintains monthly, quarterly and annual time series pertaining to the international energy industry (oil, gas, electric, coal and nuclear) for over 100 countries and regions. Coverage includes imports, exports, reserves, production, inventories, demand, prices and related macroeconomic indicators (e.g., trade balances, exchange rates, monetary and inflation statistics).

Applications: International energy research and analysis; product line forecast and planning; price management.

Subject cross reference: 1.8 and 10.5.

Geographic coverage: International.

Time coverage: 1970 to present.

Online vendor(s): World Energy Industry Information Service.

WORLD NUCLEAR POWER PLANT (ELECNUC)

Producer: French Atomic Energy Commission (CEA)
Department des Programmes
26, rue de la Federation
75015 Paris, France
73 60 00

Class: Statistical.

Data source: CEA data filings from newspapers, contractors and nuclear operators.

Size: 750 nuclear power stations.

Maintenance: Quarterly.

Primary subject: Research and Development.

Secondary subject: Industrial and Manufacturing Planning.

Profile: Maintains data on worldwide nuclear power plants and nuclear reactors. Coverage consists of present and expected nuclear power stations. Data items include contractor of the initial design, manufacturers of components, certification data, technical and operational data.

Applications: Nuclear power plant management and technical comparisons.

Subject cross reference: 7.3, 7.4, 7.5, 8.3, 8.4, and 8.8.

Geographic coverage: International.

Time coverage: 1955 to present.

Online vendor(s): CISI
SIA Computer Services.

WORLD PATENTS INDEX (WPI)

Producer: Derwent Publications, Ltd.
Patents Documentation Services
Rochdale House—128 Theobalds Road
London, England WC1X 8RP
(01) 242 5823

Class: Reference.

Data source: *World Patents Abstracts, Electrical Patents Index*, and *Central Patents Index*.

Size: 2.2 million patents.

Maintenance: 10,000 patents weekly.

Primary subject: Research and Development.

Secondary subject: N/A

Profile: WPI is a comprehensive data base which maintains patent specifications issued by the patent offices of the major industrial countries, plus EP, PCT patents and research disclosure. Maintains individual records of a patent "family", which consists of the basic or parent (new invention) and related equivalents (i.e., patent numbers issued in other countries).

Applications: User may retrieve complete patent specifications. Patent abstracts are also available.

Subject cross reference: 8.7.

Geographic coverage: International.

Time coverage: 1974 to present.

Online vendor(s): SDC Search Service.

X/MARKET®

Producer: Economic Information Systems, Inc. (EIS)
310 Madison Avenue
New York, New York 10017
(212) 697-6080

Class: Statistical.

Data source: U.S. Census Bureau, state and industrial directories, various publications and primary research.

Size: 225,000 organizations; 450,000 establishments.

Maintenance: Semiannually.

Primary subject: Banking, Economics, and Finance.

Secondary subject: Multidisciplinary.

Profile: A specialized reporting system which maintains business information on firms which account for nearly 95% of manufacturing sales and services in the U.S. Data are defined by SIC code. Specific coverage includes company name, address, product area, geographical area, industry type, annual sales data, number of establishments (subsidiaries), and share of market statistics.

Applications: Competitive comparisons; market share analysis; market potential; and market opportunity analysis.

Subject cross reference: 1.11, 2.1, 2.5, 2.10, 3.4, 7.5, 9.13, 10.1, and 10.3.

Geographic coverage: Domestic.

Time coverage: Most current data.

Online vendor(s): Business Information Services (Control Data).

ZIP CODE DEMOGRAPHIC DATA BASE (ZDDB)

Producer: Demographic Research Company
233 Wilshire Boulevard
Suite 995
Santa Monica, California 90401
(213) 451-8583

Class: Statistical.

Data source: U.S. census.

Size: 35,000 + zip code profiles.

Maintenance: Annually.

Primary subject: Marketing Planning.

Secondary subject: N/A

Profile: Provides a compilation of the latest statistics on population, education, income, and housing by postal zip code.

Applications: Market analysis; demographic/geographic studies.

Subject cross reference: 2.4, 2.5, and 2.13.

Geographic coverage: Domestic.

Time coverage: Current year's data.

Online vendor(s): Rapidata, Inc.

PART III

Indexes

SUBJECT INDEX

1.0 Banking, Economics, and Finance

2.0 Marketing Planning

3.0 Sales Planning

4.0 Marketing and Sales Promotion

5.0 Legal and Legislative Affairs

6.0 Environmental, Social, Political Affairs

7.0 Industrial and Manufacturing Planning

8.0 Research and Development

9.0 General Management
(Domestic and International) Issues

10.0 Long-Range Strategic Planning

1.1 Accounting Procedures

Accountants' Index
Bank of Canada Weekly Financial Statistics
Currency
Currency Exchange Data Base
Disclosure
EXSTAT
National Automated Accounting Research System
(NAARS)

1.2 Banking, Savings and Loan, and Other Financial Institution Activities

American Banker Index (Banker)
Bancompare
Bank Analysis System (Bankanal)
Bank of Canada Weekly Financial Statistics
Citibase
Citibase Weekly
DRI Financial and Credit Statistics (DRI-FACS)
Eurabank
Evans Economics Financial Data Base
Evans Economics Flow of Funds Data Base
Evans Economics IMF International Financial
Statistics
Evans Economics International Data Base
FDIC Report of Condition and Income System
Financial
Financial Institution Data Base
Regional Data Associates (RDA)
Regional Forecast
Savings and Loan

1.3 Capital Markets

Bank Analysis System (Bankanal)
Bank of Canada Weekly Financial Statistics
Compubond
Currency
DRI Financial and Credit Statistics (DRI-FACS)
DRI-SEC (Securities Data Bank)
Eurabank
Europrospects—European Economic Indicators
Evans Economics Financial Data Base
Financial Forecast
International Financial Statistics (IFS)
Money Market Rates (MRATE)
Short Term Projections/Long Term Projections

1.4 Capital Spending Activity

Conference Board (CBDB)
DRI Financial and Credit Statistics (DRI-FACS)
Evans Economics Financial Data Base
Evans Economics Forecast Data Base
Evans Economics International Data Base
Foreign Exchange Rate Forecast
International Financial Statistics (IFS)
Money Market Rates (MRATE)
Nikkei Economic Statistics
PTS International Time Series
Regional Industry
Short Term Projections/Long Term Projections
U.S. Economic
U.S. Model Data Bank

Regional
Regional Data Associates (RDA)
Regional Forecast
Regional Industry
Short Term Projections/Long Term Projections
Standard & Poor's Industry Financial Data Bank
Telerate Historical Data Bases
U.S. Central Data Bank (DRI Central)
U.S. County Data Bank
U.S. Economic
U.S. Economic/CE
U.S. Financial
U.S. Model Data Bank
U.S. Prices Data Bank
U.S. Regional
Wall $treet Week
Weekly Economic Survey
World Energy Industry

1.9 Economies (General Business Climate)

ABI/Inform
Accountants' Index
Agriculture On-Line Access (AGRICOLA)
Asian Data Bank
Business Conditions Digest (BCD)
Citibase
Cost Forecasting Data Banks
Currency
Dow Jones News/Retrieval Service and Stock Quote
    Reporter
DRI Financial and Credit Statistics (DRI-FACS)
DRI Industry Financial Service Data Bank
    (DRIFS)
Economics Abstracts International
Economist's Statistics
European National Source
Fedwir
International Financial Statistics (IFS)
Latin American Data Bank
Merrill Lynch Economics National Data Base
Merrill Lynch Economics Regional Data Base
Newsbeat
Securities
Social Scisearch
U.S. Census of Retail Trade (1977)
U.S. Central Data Bank (DRI Central)
U.S. County Data Bank
U.S. Political Science Documents (USPSD)
U.S. Prices Data Bank
U.S. Regional
Wall Street Week
Weekly Economic Survey
Weekly Economic Update

1.10 Financial Management Ideas and News

ABI/Inform
Canadian Business Periodicals Index (CBPI)
Citibase
Disclosure
Dow Jones News/Retrieval Service and Stock Quote
    Reporter
Financial Post Investment Data Bank
Value Line II
Wall $treet Week

1.11 Financial Profiles—Company

ABI/Inform
Canadian Bond Market
Canadian Business Periodicals Index (CBPI)
Canadian Department of Insurance
Chemical Data Banks
Chemical Industry Notes (CIN)
Compustat
Credit Data
Disclosure
Dow Jones News/Retrieval Service and Stock Quote
    Reporter
DRI Industry Financial Service Data Bank
    (DRIFS)
Duns Financial Profiles
Dunsprint
EIS Industrial Plants
EIS Non-Manufacturing Establishments
Eurabank
EXSTAT
FDIC Report of Condition and Income Statement
Financial Institution Data Base
Financial Post Investment Data Bank
Fintel Company Newsbase
Industrial Bank of Japan
Insurance Industry Data Base
Media General Data Base
Mergers and Acquisitions
National Automated Accounting Research System
    (NAARS)
New Issues of Corporate Securities
Private Placements
Savings and Loan
Spectrum
Standard & Poor's General Information File
Standard & Poor's News
Standard & Poor's Stock Guide Retrieval Service
Value Line II
Wall $treet Week
X/Market

1.12 Financial Studies—General

ABI/Inform
Association of European Airlines Data Base (AEA)
Bank of Canada Weekly Financial Statistics
Boeckh Building Cost System
Compubond
Compustat
Cost Programs
Disclosure
Dow Jones News/Retrieval Service and Stock Quote
    Reporter
DRI Financial and Credit Statistics (DRI-FACS)
DRI-SEC (Securities Data Bank)
Dunsprint
Economics Abstracts International
European National Source
Financial Institution Data Base
FTCDATA
Newsbeat
Regional Data Associates (RDA)
Standard & Poor's Industry Financial Data Bank
Telerate Historical Databases
U.S. Central Data Bank (DRI CENTRAL)
U.S. County Data Bank
Value Line II
Wall $treet Week

1.13 Insurance

Actuarial Data Base
Best Executive Data Service (BEDS)
Canadian Department of Insurance
Insurance Forecast
Insurance Industry Data Base

1.14 Interest Rates

Citibase
Citibase Weekly
Dow Jones News/Retrieval Service and Stock Quote
    Reporter
DRI Financial and Credit Statistics (DRI-FACS)
Europrospects—European Economic Indicators
Evans Economics Financial Database
Evans Economics IMF International Financial
    Statistics
Evans Economics International Database
Financial
Financial Forecast
International Financial Statistics (IFS)
Money Market Rates (MRATE)
Short Term Projections/Long Term Projections
Telerate Historical Databases
U.S. Economic
U.S. Economic/CE
U.S. Financial
U.S. Model Data Bank
U.S. Prices Data Bank
U.S. Regional
Wall $treet Week
Weekly Economic Survey
Weekly Economic Update

1.15 Investments (Non-Securities)

Australian Bureau of Statistics Data Base
    (ABSDATA)
Best Executive Data Service (BEDS)
Economics Abstracts International
Economist's Statistics
Evans Economics Financial Database
Evans Economics Metals Database
Money Market Rates (MRATE)
Newsbeat
Savings and Loan
Telerate Historical Data Bases

1.16 Securities and Commodities

Accountants' Index
Agriculture Commodities Data Base (AGDATA)
Agriculture Data Bank
Agriculture Forecast
Bridge Data Stock & Options Real Time
    Information System
Canadian Bond Market
Canadian Stock Options
Commodities Market Data Bank

Commodity Data Information System (CDIS)
Compubond
Compuserve
Compustat
Consumer Price Index/Producer Price Index
    (CPI/PPI)
CSS/Quotes+
Dow Jones News/Retrieval Service and Stock Quote
    Reporter
DRI-SEC (Securities Data Bank)
Eurocharts Commodities
Evans Economics Agriculture Database
Evans Economics Financial Database
Evans Economics Producer Price Database
EXSHARE
FASTOCK II
GTE Financial System One Quotation Service
Media General Data Base
Metals Week
Microquote
New Issues of Corporate Securities
New Issues of Municipal Debt
Newsbeat
OPTDATA
Private Placements
Quick Quote
Quotron 800
Securities
Spectrum
Standard & Poor's General Information File
Standard & Poor's Industry Financial Data Bank
Standard & Poor's News
Standard & Poor's Stock Guide Retrieval Service
Telequote
Telerate Historical Data Bases
Toronto Stock Exchange 300 Composite Index
U.S. Stock Options Data Base
Wall $treet Week

1.17 Taxation

ABI/Inform
Accountants' Index
Canadian Business Periodicals Index (CBPI)
Standard & Poor's Industry Financial Data Bank
Wall $treet Week

1.18 Venture Capital

Mergers and Acquisitions

1.19 Miscellaneous and General

Britannica 3
Canadian News Index (CNI)
Canadian Press Newstex (CPN)
Chronolog Newsletter
CIS/Index
Congressional Record Abstracts (CRECORD)
Data Base Index (DBI)
Eurofile
Evans Economics Flow of Funds Data Base
Evans Economics Forecast Database
Evans Economics Regional Housing Service
    Database
Federal Index (FEDEX)
Federal Register Abstracts (FEDREG)
Flow of Funds Accounts
GPO Monthly Catalog Data Base
Harfax
Harvard Business Review
Information Bank
Key Issues Tracking (KIT)
Magazine Index
Management Contents
National Newspaper Index (NNI)
Newsearch
Newspaper Index (NDEX)
Nexis
PTS Prompt
The Source
State Publications Index (SPI)
Trade and Industry Index
Ulrich's International Periodicals Directory
Universal Serials and Book Exchange (USBE)
Wall Street Journal Highlights Online
Weekly Economic Survey
Weekly Economic Update
Wharton Econometric Forecasting Databases

2.1 Competitive Analysis

ABI/Inform
Adtrack
Bancompare
Bank Analysis System (BANKANAL)
Best Executive Data Service (BEDS)
Books in Print (BBIP)
Broadcast Advertisers Report (BAR)
Business Credit Services
Canadian Business Periodicals Index (CBPI)
Chemical Data Banks
Chemical Industry News (CIN)
Claims/Citation
Claims/Uniterm
Claims/U.S. Patents
COMP*U*STAR
Compustat
Defense Market Measures System (DM2)
Disclosure
Dow Jones News/Retrieval Service and Stock Quote
    Reporter
Dunsprint
EIS Industrial Plants
EIS Non-Manufacturing Establishments
Eurabank
EXSTAT
FDIC Report of Condition and Income Statement
Financial Institution Data Base
Financial Post Investment Data Bank

Fintel Company Newsbase
Horse Data Bank
ICAO Traffic Statistics
Industrial Bank of Japan
Media General Data Base
Nabscan Data Base
National Automated Accounting Research System
    (NAARS)
Passenger Car
Pharmaceutical News Index (PNI)
PTS Indexes
SAMI
Standard & Poor's General Information File
Standard & Poor's News
Value Line II
X/Market

2.2 Consumer Behavior—Shifts and Trends

Actuarial Data Base
Advertising & Marketing Intelligence (AMI)
Association of European Airlines Data Base (AEA)
Broadcast Advertisers Report
Consumer Economic Service Data
Consumer Price Index/Producer Price Index
    (CPI/PPI)
Nabscan Data Base
Nielson Retail Index
Nielson Station Index
Nielson Television Index
Passenger Car
Prospects
PTS International Time Series
SAMI
Simmons Market Research Bureau (SMRB)
Site Potential
Social Scisearch
Sociological Abstracts
Study of Major Market Newspapers
Target Group Index (TGI)

2.3 Consumer Spending Patterns

Advertising and Marketing Intelligence (AMI)
American Profile
Association of European Airlines Data Base (AEA)
BI/Data
California Data Bank
Conference Board (CBDB)
Consumer Economic Service Data
Consumer Price Index/Producer Price Index
    (CPI/PPI)
Evans Economics Consumer Price Index Database
Evans Economics Regional Forecasting Service
    Database
Marketbase
Nabscan Data Base
New York City Model Data Bank
Nielsen Retail Index
Passenger Car
Prospects
Regional Data Associates (RDA)
Regional Forecast
SAMI
Short Term Projections/Long Term Projections
Site Potential
Target Group Index (TGI)
U.S. Census of Retail Trade (1977)

2.4 Demographics

Actuarial Data Base
American Profile
BI/Data
Canadian Socio-Economic Information
    Management System (CANSIM)
Consumer Economic Service Data
Marketbase
Merrill Lynch Economics Regional Data Base
National Planning Association Economic Data
Online Site Evaluation System (ONSITE)
Population Bibliography
Population Information Online (POPLINE)
Prospects
PTS International Time Series
Regional
Regional Data Associates (RDA)
Regional Employment
Regional Forecast
Simmons Market Research Bureau (SMRB)
Site Potential
Site II
Social Scisearch
Target Group Index (TGI)
U.S. Census of Agriculture (1978)
U.S. County Data Bank
U.S. Economic
U.S. Economic/CE
U.S. Regional
Zip Code Demographic Data Base (ZDDB)

2.5 Geographic Area Profiles

Advertising and Marketing Intelligence (AMI)
American Profile
Astis Online Database
Australian Bureau of Statistics Data Base
    (ABSDATA)
Business Credit Services
California Data Bank
Canadian Socio-Economic Information
    Management System (CANSIM)
Compustat
Consumer Economic Service Data
Consumer Price Index/Producer Price Index
    (CPI/PPI)
Dodge Construction Analysis System
Economics Abstracts International
European National Source
Evans Economics Consumer Price Index Database
Evans Economics Regional Forecasting Service
    Database
International Financial Statistics (IFS)
Merrill Lynch Economics Regional Data Base
National Planning Association Economic Data
Nielsen Retail Index
Nielsen Station Index
Nielsen Television Index
New York City Model Data Bank
OECD Data Base
Online Site Evaluation System
Population Bibliography
PTS International Time Series
Regional
Regional Data Associates (RDA)
Regional Employment
Regional Forecast
SAMI

Simmons Market Research Bureau (SMRB)
Site Potential
Site II
Target Group Index (TGI)
U.S. Census of Agriculture (1978)
U.S. Census of Retail Trade (1977)
U.S. County Data Bank
U.S. Regional
X/Market
Zip Code Demographic Data Base (ZDDB)

2.6 International Marketing

ABI/Inform
Asian Data Bank
Australian Bureau of Statistics Data Base
    (ABSDATA)
BI/Data
Currency
Economics Abstracts International
EXSTAT
Fintel Company Newsbase
Foreign Traders Index (FTI)
Middle East Data Base (MEDAB)
Nikkei Economic Statistics
Nikkei Energy Data Bank
OECD Data Base
Petroleum Argus
PTS International Forecasts Abstracts
PTS International Time Series
U.S. Exports
U.S. Political Science Documents (USPSD)

2.7 Labeling News

Advertising & Marketing Intelligence
Foods Adlibra

2.8 Market Trends and Outlook

ABI/Inform
Adtrack
Advertising and Marketing Intelligence
California Data Bank
Canadian Business Periodicals Index (CBPI)
Canadian Socio-Economic Information
    Management System (CANSIM)
Chemical Industry News (CIN)
Citibase
Citibase Weekly
Consumer Economic Service Data
Defense Market Measures System (DM2)
Evans Economics USA Database
Fintel Company Newsbase
FTCDATA
Metals Week
National Electrical Manufacturers Association Data
    Base
Passenger Car
Prospects
PTS Indexes
PTS International Time Series
Simmons Market Research Bureau (SMRB)
Site Potential
Society of Automotive Engineers (SAE) Abstracts

2.9 Marketing Information Systems

Auerbach Compar
Compustat
Elcom Data Base
Library and Information Science Abstracts (LISA)

2.10 Marketing Research

ABI/Inform
Adtrack
American Profile
Broadcast Advertisers Report (BAR)
California Data Bank
California Union List of Periodicals (CULP)
Canadian Business Periodicals Index (CBPI)
Chemical Industry News (CIN)
Consumer Economic Service Data
Dunsprint
Economics Abstracts International
EIS Industrial Plants
EIS Non-Manufacturing Establishments
Encyclopedia of Associations (EA)
Fintel Company Newsbase
ICAO Traffic Statistics
Metals Week
National Planning Association Economic Data
Passenger Car
Prospects
PTS Indexes
PTS International Forecasts Abstracts
PTS U.S. Forecasts Abstracts
Simmons Market Research Bureau (SMRB)
Standard & Poor's General Information File
X/Market

2.11 Media Developments

Advertising & Marketing Intelligence
Billboard Magazine/Information Network (BIN)
Broadcast Advertisers Report (BAR)
Nielsen Station Index
Nielsen Television Index
PTS Indexes

2.12 New Product Analysis

ABI/Inform
Adtrack
Billboard Magazine/Information Network (BIN)
Books in Print (BBIP)
Chemical Data Banks
Claims/Citation
Claims/Uniterm
Claims/U.S. Patents
Clinical Toxicology of Commercial Products
    (CTCP)
European Patent Register (EPR)
Inpadoc (IDB)
International Pharmaceutical Abstracts (IPA)
Passenger Car
Pharmaceutical News Index (PNI)
Solar Energy Information Data Bank (SEIDB)
Textile Information Treatment Users' Service
    (TITUS)

2.13 Population and Census

American Profile
BI/Data
DRI Capsule
EEI Capsule
Evans Economics IMF International Financial
    Statistics
National Planning Association Economic Data
New York City Model Data Bank
Population Bibliography
Prospects
PTS International Time Series
Regional Data Associates (RDA)
Site Potential
Site II
Zip Code Demographic Data Base (ZDDB)

2.14 Pricing Trends

ABI/Inform
American Profile
Australian Bureau of Statistics Data Base
    (ABSDATA)
COMP*U*STAR
Consumer Economic Service Data
Consumer Price Index/Producer Price Index
    (CPI/PPI)
Evans Economics Consumer Price Database
Evans Economics Forecast Database
Evans Economics International Database
Inflation Planner Forecast
Metals Week
Nabscan Data Base
Nielsen Retail Index
Passenger Car
Petroleum Argus
Regional Data Associates (RDA)
SAMI

2.15 Psychographic Statistics and Studies

Adtrack
Advertising & Marketing Intelligence
American Profile
Broadcast Advertisers Report (BAR)
Prospects
Simmons Market Research Bureau
Social Scisearch
Sociological Abstracts
Target Group Index (TGI)

2.16 Miscellaneous and General

Britannica 3
Canadian News Index (CNI)
Canadian Press Newstex (CPN)
Chronolog Newsletter
CIS/Index
Congressional Record Abstracts (CRECORD)
Data Base Index (DBI)
Eurofile
Federal Index (FEDEX)
Federal Register Abstracts (FEDREG)
GPO Monthly Catalog Data Base
HARFAX
Harvard Business Review
Information Bank
International Business Intelligence Program Index
Key Issues Tracking (KIT)
Magazine Index
Management Contents
National Newspaper Index (NNI)
Newsearch
Newspaper Index (NDEX)
Nexis
PTS Prompt
The Source
State Publications Index (SPI)
Trade and Industry Index
Ulrich's International Periodicals Directory
Universal Serials and Book Exchange (USBE)
Wall Street Journal Highlights Online
Wharton Econometric Forecasting Databases

3.1 Incentive Sales

Refer to 3.4.

3.2 Lead Generation and Analysis

Defense Market Measures System
Foreign Traders Index (FTI)
Foundation Directory
Simmons Market Research Bureau (SMRB)
Trade Opportunities Weekly

3.3 Manufacturing Agents and Representatives

Technotec Technology Exchange Data Base
Trade Opportunities Weekly
Traders

3.4 Sales Administration and Management

ABI/Inform
Dodge Construction Analysis System
Dunsprint
EIS Industrial Plants
EIS Non-Manufacturing Establishments
PTS Indexes
Regional
Regional Employment
SAMI
Site Potential
X/Market

3.5 Sales Prospecting

Adtrack
Defense Market Measures System (DM2)
EIS Industrial Plants
EIS Non-Manufacturing Establishments
Trade Opportunities Weekly

3.6 Miscellaneous and General

Britannica 3
Canadian News Index (CNI)
Canadian Press Newstex (CPN)
Chronolog Newsletter
CIS/Index
Congressional Record Abstracts (CRECORD)
Data Base Index (DBI)
Eurofile
Federal Index (FEDEX)
Federal Register Abstracts (FEDREG)
GPO Monthly Catalog Data Base
Harvard Business Review
Information Bank
Key Issues Tracking (KIT)
Magazine Index
Management Contents
National Newspaper Index (NNI)
Newsearch
Newspaper Index (NDEX)
Nexis
PTS Prompt
The Source
State Publications Index (SPI)
Trade and Industry Index
Ulrich's International Periodicals Directory
Universal Serials and Book Exchange (USBE)
Wall Street Journal Highlights Online

4.1 Advertising Trends

Adtrack
Advertising & Marketing Intelligence
Broadcast Advertisers Report (BAR)
COMP*U*STAR
Nielsen Retail Index
Nielsen Station Index
Nielsen Television Index
Social Scisearch
Target Group Index (TGI)

4.2 Direct Mail

Dunsprint
Simmons Market Research Bureau

4.3 Management Trends in Marketing

ABI/Inform
Chemical Industry News (CIN)
Passenger Car
PTS Indexes

4.4 Marketing Ideas

Adtrack
Advertising & Marketing Intelligence
American Profile
Broadcast Advertisers Report (BAR)
Chemical Industry News (CIN)
COMP*U*STAR
Fintel Company Newsbase
Nielsen Retail Index
Nielsen Station Index
Nielsen Television Index
Passenger Car
PTS Indexes
Regional
Site Potential

4.5 Public Relations

Foundation Directory
Health Planning and Administration

4.6 Miscellaneous and General

Artbibliographies Modern
Britannica 3
Canadian News Index (CNI)
Canadian Press Newstex (CPN)
Chronolog Newsletter
CIS/Index
Congressional Record Abstracts (CRECORD)
Data Base Index (DBI)
Encyclopedia of Associations (EA)
Eurofile
Federal Index (FEDEX)
Federal Record Abstracts (FEDREG)
GPO Monthly Catalog Data Base
Harvard Business Review
Information Bank
Key Issues Tracking (KIT)
Magazine Index
Management Contents
National Newspaper Index (NNI)

Newsearch
Newspaper Index (NDEX)
Nexis
PTS Prompt
The Source
State Publications Index (SPI)
Trade and Industry Index
Ulrich's International Periodicals Directory
Universal Serials and Book Exchange (USBE)
Wall Street Journal Highlights Online

5.1 Antitrust Activity and Laws

Federal Index (FEDEX)
Lexis

5.2 Arbitration

Lexis

5.3 Contracts

Business Conditions Digest
California Data Bank
Defense Market Measures System (DM2)
Lexis
U.S. Government Contract Awards (USGCA)
U.S. Requests for Proposals (USRFP)

5.4 General Legal News and Affairs

ABI/Inform
All-Canada Weekly Summaries (ACWS)
Bioethicsline
Congressional Record Abstracts (CRECORD)
Federal Register Abstracts (FEDREG)
Legal Resource Index (LRI)
Lexis
Votes Data Base

5.5 Legal Services

Lexis
Mergers and Acquisitions

5.6 Legislative News and Evaluation

Congressional Record Abstracts (CRECORD)
EIS Digests of Environmental Impact Statements
Federal Index (FEDEX)
Federal Register Abstracts (FEDREG)
Lexis
Pharmaceutical News Index (PNI)
Safety Science Abstracts
Solar Energy Information Data Bank (SEIDB)
U.S. Political Science Documents (USPSD)
Votes Data Base

5.7 Product Liability

Accident/Incident Data System (AIDS)
Chemlaw
Epilepsyline
International Pharmaceutical Abstracts (IPA)
Lexis
Pharmaceutical News Index (PNI)
Safety Science Abstracts

5.8 Regulation and Government Control

Accident/Incident Data System
Bioethicsline
Chemical Industry News
Chemlaw
Congressional Record Abstracts (CRECORD)
Defense Market Measures System (DM2)
EIS Digests of Environmental Impact Statements
Environdoq
Federal Index (FEDEX)
Federal Register Abstracts (FEDREG)
International Pharmaceutical Abstracts (IPA)
Lexis
National Technical Information Service (NTIS)
Petroleum/Energy Business News Index (P/E NEWS)
Pharmaceutical News Index (PNI)
U.S. Political Science Documents (USPSD)
Votes Data Base

5.9 Miscellaneous and General

Automated Citation Verification Service (AUTO-CITE)
Britannica 3
Canadian News Index (CNI)
Canadian Press Newstex (CPN)
Chemlaw
Chronolog Newsletter
CIS/Index
Data Base Index (DBI)
Developing Countries Data Bank
Eurofile
Federal Index (FEDEX)
GPO Monthly Catalog Data Base
Hansard Oral Questions
Harvard Business Review
Information Bank
Inpadoc (IDB)
Key Issues Tracking (KIT)
Lexis
Magazine Index
Management Contents
National Newspaper Index (NNI)
Newsearch
Newspaper Index (NDEX)
Nexis
The Source
State Publications Index (SPI)
Trade and Industry Index
Ulrich's International Periodicals Directory
Universal Serials and Book Exchange (USBE)
U.S. Political Science Documents (USPSD)
Wall Street Journal Highlights Online

6.1 Crime

Refer to 6.7.

6.2 Defense Issues

Defense Market Measures System (DM2)
Middle East Data Base (MEDAB)

6.3 Environmental Concerns (Non-Pollution)

Agriculture Data Bank
Agriculture On-Line Access (AGRICOLA)
Agricultural Research Projects (AGREP)
Aquatic Sciences and Fisheries Abstracts (ASFA)
Astis Online Data Base
Canadian Environment (CENV)
Coal Data Base
Cold Regions
Current Research Information System (CRIS)
DOE Energy Data Base (EDB)
EIS Environmental Impact Statements
Electric Power Industry Abstracts (EPIA)
Energy Projects (ENG)
Energy Bibliography and Index (EBI)
Enviroline
Environdoq
Environmental Periodicals Bibliography (EPB)
Excerpta Medica (EMBASE)
Fast Permit Reports (FPR)
Federal Energy Data Index (FEDEX)
Forest Products Abstract Information Digest Service (AIDS)
Forestry Data Banks
Geoarchive
Geological Reference File (GEOREF)
Instructional Resources Information System (IRIS)
Meteorological and Geoastrophysical Abstracts (MGA)
National Technical Information Service (NTIS)
Range Management
Safety Science Abstracts
Textile Information Treatment Users' Service (TITUS)

6.4 General and Special News Issues

ABI/Inform
Biography Master Index
Books in Print (BBIP)
Compuserve
Enviroline
Index to API Abstracts/Literature (APILIT)
Index to API Abstracts/Patents (APIPAT)
Information Bank
Middle East Data Base (MEDAB)
National Newspaper Index (NNI)
Newsearch
Newspaper Index (NDEX)
Nexis
PTS Indexes
U.S. Political Science Documents (USPSD)

6.5 Political Activity

Enviroline
Social Scisearch
U.S. Political Science Documents (USPSD)

6.6 Pollution Issues

Air Pollution Technical Information Center
    (APTIC)
Aqualine
Aquatic Sciences and Fisheries Abstracts (ASFA)
Astis Online Database
BIIPAM
Canadian Environment (CENV)
DOE Energy Data Base (EDB)
EIS Environmental Impact Statements
Electric Power Industry Abstracts (EPIA)
Energy Bibliography and Index (EBI)
Envirodoq
Enviroline
Environmental Periodicals Bibliography (EPB)
Index to API Abstracts/Literature (APILIT)
Index to API Abstracts/Patents (APIPAT)
Instructional Resources Information System
National Technical Information Service (NTIS)
Oceanic Abstracts
Pollution Abstracts
Ship Abstracts (SHIP)
Toxicology Data Bank (TDB)
Toxline

6.7 Social Conditions/Issues

AIM/ARM
Alcohol Information Retrieval System (AIRS)
Bioethicsline
Child Abuse and Neglect
Drug Info and Alcohol Use/Abuse
Foundation Directory
Guidance Information System (GIS)
Middle East Data Base (MEDAB)
Population Bibliography
Regional Employment
Social Scisearch
Sociological Abstracts

6.8 Miscellaneous and General

Artbibliographies Modern
Book Review Index (BRI)
Britannica 3
CA Search
California Union List of Periodicals (CULP)
Canadian News Index (CNI)
Canadian Press Newstex (CPN)
CAS Source Index (CASSI)
Chemlaw
Chronolog Newsletter
CIS/Index
Congressional Record Abstracts (CRECORD)
Data Base Index (DBI)
Developing Countries Data Bank
Energy Projects (ENG)
Eurofile
Federal Index (FEDEX)
Federal Register Abstracts (FEDREG)
GPO Monthly Catalog Data Base

Harvard Business Review
Highway Safety Literature (HSL)
Information Bank
International Business Intelligence Program Index
Key Issues Tracking (KIT)
Magazine Index
Management Contents
National Newspaper Index (NNI)
Newsearch
Newspaper Index (NDEX)
Nexis
Range Management
The Source
State Publications Index (SPI)
Trade and Industry Index
Ulrich's International Periodicals Directory
Universal Serials and Book Exchange (USBE)
Wall Street Journal Highlights Online

7.1 Accident and Safety Issues

Chemlaw
Electric Power Industry Abstracts (EPIA)
Safety Science Abstracts
Ship Abstracts (SHIP)
Toxicology Data Bank (TDB)
Toxline

7.2 Containers and Packaging

Foods Adlibra
Paper and Pulp Data Bank
PIRA
Weldasearch
World Aluminum Abstracts (WAA)

7.3 Engineering

American Men and Women of Science
Artbibliographies Modern
BHRA Fluid Engineering
BIIPAM
CA Search
Cold Regions
Compendex
Conference Papers Index (CPI)
Electric Power Industry Abstracts (EPIA)
Information Service in Mechanical Engineering
    (ISMEC)
National Technical Information Service (NTIS)
PCS/SPEC
Service Difficulty Reporting System (SDR)
Ship Abstracts (SHIP)
Smithsonian Science Information Exchange
    (SSIE)
Society of Automotive Engineers (SAE) Abstracts
Weldasearch
World Nuclear Power Plant (ELECNUC)

7.4 Factories, Plants, and Building Sites

California Data Bank
Cost Programs
Dodge Construction Analysis System
EIS Industrial Plants
Electric Power Industry Abstracts (EPIA)
PCS/SPEC
Ship Abstracts (SHIP)
World Nuclear Power Plant (ELECNUC)

7.5 Industrial Development

ABI/Inform
Citibase
Compendex
CRU Mine Smelter and Refinery Databank
Dodge Construction Analysis System
DRI Industry Financial Service Data Bank
  (DRIFS)
Electric Power Industry Abstracts (EPIA)
Iron and Steel Forecast
Merrill Lynch Economics Regional Data Base
Middle East Data Base (MEDAB)
Nikkei Energy Data Bank
Society of Automotive Engineers (SAE)
Specialized Textile Information (STI)
World Aluminum Abstracts (WAA)
World Nuclear Power Plant (ELECNUC)
X/Market

7.6 Inventories

Business Conditions Digest
Evans Economics USA Database
Iron and Steel Forecast
Regional Industry
U.S. Economic/CE

7.7 Product Safety

Chemlaw
International Pharmaceutical Abstracts (IPA)
Pharmaceutical News Index (PNI)
Safety Science Abstracts
Service Difficulty Reporting System (SDR)
Society of Automotive Engineers (SAE) Abstracts
Toxicology Data Bank (TDB)
Toxline

7.8 Purchasing—Agents and Activities

Refer to 7.11.

7.9 Quality Control

Dodge Construction Analysis System
Electric Power Industry Abstracts (EPIA)
Standards & Specifications
Surface Coatings Abstracts
Textile Information Treatment Users' Service
  (TITUS)
Weldasearch
World Aluminum Abstracts

7.10 Raw Materials—Pricing and Sources

Boeckh Building Cost System
Cost Programs
Dodge Construction Analysis System
Electric Power Industry Abstracts (EPIA)
Electronic Materials Information Services (EMIS)
Energy Data Bank
Inflation Planner Forecast
Iron and Steel Forecast
Metals Week
MINSYS
National Electrical Manufacturers Association Data
  Base
Nonferrous Metals Forecast
OECD Quarterly Oil Statistics
Paper and Pulp Data Bank
Petroleum/Energy Business News Index (P/E
  NEWS)
PIRA
Platt's Data Bank
Specialized Textile Information (STI)
Steel Data Banks
Tech-Net
Tradenet
TSCA Chemical Substances Inventory

7.11 Supplier and Vendor Evaluation

Auerbach Compar
Business Credit Services
Dodge Construction Analysis System
EIS Industrial Plants
EIS Non-Manufacturing Plants
Solar Energy Information Data Bank (SEIDB)
Steel Data Banks
Tech-Net
Tradenet

7.12 Miscellaneous and General

Britannica 3
Canadian News Index (CNI)
Canadian Press Newstex (CPN)
Chronolog Newsletter
CIS/Index
Congressional Record Abstracts (CRECORD)
Data Base Index (DBI)
Eurofile
Federal Index (FEDEX)
Federal Register Abstracts (FEDREG)
GPO Monthly Catalog Data Base
Harvard Business Review
Information Bank
Key Issues Tracking (KIT)
Magazine Index
Management Contents
National Electrical Manufacturers Association
National Newspaper Index (NNI)
Newsearch
Newspaper Index (NDEX)
Nexis
PTS Prompt
The Source
State Publications Index (SPI)
Trade and Industry Index
Ulrich's International Periodicals Directory
Universal Serials and Book Exchange (USBE)
Wall Street Journal Highlights Online

8.1 Competition on New Products

ABI/Inform
Auerbach Compar
Canadian Business Periodicals Index (CBPI)
Claims/Chem
Claims/Citation
Claims/Uniterm
Claims/U.S. Patents
Clinical Toxicology of Commercial Products
    (CTCP)
Defense Market Measures System (DM2)
Fintel Company Newsbase
International Pharmaceutical Abstracts (IPA)

8.2 Components and Materials

CA Search
CAS Online
CAS Source Index (CASIS)
Chemlaw
Chemsearch
Chem Singly Indexed Substances (CHEMSIS)
Clinical Toxicology of Commercial Products
    (CTCP)
Elcom Data Base
Electronic Materials Information Service (EMIS)
International Pharmaceutical Abstracts (IPA)
MINSYS
National Technical Information Service (NTIS)
Pharmaceutical News Index
Rapra Abstracts
Society of Automotive Engineers (SAE) Abstracts
Specialized Textile Information (STI)
Tech-Net
TSCA Chemical Substances Inventory

8.3 Future Technologies

Auerbach Compar
BHRA Fluid Engineering
Biosis Previews
Chemsearch
Chemsis Singly Indexed Substances (CHEMSIS)
Compendex
Conference Papers Index (CPI)
Elcom Data Base
Fintel Company Newsbase
National Technical Information Service (NTIS)
Pharmaceutical Literature Documentation
    (RINGDOC)
Rapra Abstracts
Smithsonian Science Information Exchange (SSIE)
Technotec Technology Exchange Data Base
World Nuclear Power Plant (ELECNUC)

8.4 Industrial Technologies

BHRA Fluid Engineering
BIIPAM
Chemical Industry News
Compendex
Dechema Thermophysical Properties
    (DETHERM-SDR)
Elcom Data Base
Fintel Company Newsbase
Information Service in Mechanical Engineering
    (ISMEC)

National Coal Resources Data System (NCRDS)
Passenger Car
Rapra Abstracts
Searchable Physics Information Notices (SPIN)
Ship Abstracts (SHIP)
Smithsonian Science Information Exchange (SSIE)
Technotec Technology Exchange Data Base
Weldasearch
World Aluminum Abstracts
World Nuclear Power Plant (ELECNUC)

8.5 Inventions

Claims/Citation
Claims/Uniterm
Claims/U.S. Patents
Smithsonian Science Information Exchange (SSIE)
Society of Automotive Engineers (SAE) Abstracts
Technotec Technology Exchange Data Base

8.6 Laboratory Research Findings

Bioethicsline
Biosis Previews
CA Search
CAS Online
CAS Source Index (CASSI)
Chemlaw
Chemsearch
Chem Singly Indexed Substances (CHEMSIS)
Clinical Toxicology of Commercial Products
    (CTCP)
Conference Papers Index (CPI)
Epilepsyline
International Pharmaceutical Abstracts (IPA)
National Coal Resources Data System (NCRDS)
Pest Control Literature Documentation
    (PESTDOC)
Pharmaceutical Literature Documentation
    (RINGDOC)
Pharmaceutical News Index (PNI)
Rapra Abstracts
Searchable Physics Information Notices (SPIN)
Smithsonian Science Information Exchange (SSIE)
Society of Automotive Engineers (SAE) Abstracts
Technotec Technology Exchange Data Base
Toxicology Data Bank (TDB)
Toxline

8.7 Licenses, Patents, and Trademarks

Claims/Chem
Claims/Citation
Claims/Uniterm
Claims/U.S. Patents
Elcom Data Base
European Patents Register (EPR)
Index to API Abstracts/Patents (APIPAT)
Inpadoc (IDB)
International Pharmaceutical Abstracts
Technotec Technology Exchange Data Base
Usclass
USPO/USPA
World Patent Index (WPI)

8.8 Technological Shifts and Trends

BHRA Fluid Engineering
Biosis Previews
Compendex
Conference Papers Index (CPI)
Dechema Thermophysical Properties
    (DETHERM-SDR)
Elcom Data Base
Energy Bibliography and Index (EBI)
International Pharmaceutical Abstracts
Rapra Abstracts
Searchable Physics Information Notices (SPIN)
Smithsonian Science Information Exchange (SSIE)
Society of Automotive Engineers (SAE) Abstracts
Specialized Textile Information (STI)
Technotec Technology Exchange Data Base
World Nuclear Power Plant

8.9 Miscellaneous and General

American Men and Women of Science
Britannica 3
Canadian News Index (CNI)
Canadian Press Newstex (CPN)
Chronolog Newsletter
CIS/Index
Congressional Record Abstracts (CRECORD)
Data Base Index (DBI)
Elcom Data Base
Eurofile
Federal Index (FEDEX)
Federal Register Abstracts (FEDREG)
Foods Adlibra
Food Science and Technology Abstracts (FSTA)
Geoarchive
Geological Reference File (GEOREF)
GPO Monthly Catalog Data Base
Harvard Business Review
Information Bank
Key Issues Tracking (KIT)
Magazine Index
Management Contents
Medline
National Newspaper Index (NNI)
National Technical Information Service (NTIS)
Newsearch
Newspaper Index (NDEX)
Nexis
Oceanic Abstracts
Pre-Med
PTS Prompt
The Source
State Publications Index (SPI)
Textile Information Treatment Users' Service
    (TITUS)
Trade and Industry Index
TROPAG (Tropical Agriculture)
Ulrich's International Periodicals Directory
Universal Serials and Book Exchange (USBE)
Wall Street Journal Highlights Online

9.1 Agriculture and Mining

Agline
Agricultural Research Projects (AGREP)
Agriculture Commodities Data Base (AGDATA)
Agriculture Data Bank
Agriculture Forecast
Agriculture Online Access
Coal Data Banks
Coal Data Base
Commonwealth Agriculture Bureaux Abstracts
Current Research Information System (CRIS)
EIS Non-Manufacturing Establishments
Evans Economics Agriculture Database
Farm and Industrial Equipment Institute (FIEI)
Fertilizer Forecast
Food Science and Technology Abstracts (FSTA)
Forest Products & Abstract Information Digests
    Service (AIDS)
Forestry Data Banks
Geoarchive
Geological Reference File (GEOREF)
Iron and Steel Forecast
Middle East Data Base (MEDAB)
MINSYS
National Coal Resources Data System (NCRDS)
Nonferrous Metals Forecast
Nutritional Abstracts and Reviews (NAR)
Pest Control Literature Documentation
    (PESTDOC)
PTS International Time Series
Range Management
TROPAG (Tropical Agriculture)
U.S. Census of Agriculture (1978)
World Agriculture Supply—Disposition

9.2 Consultants

American Men and Women of Science
Encyclopedia of Associations (EA)
Technotec Technology Exchange Data Base

9.3 Consumer Protection

Highway Safety Literature (HSL)
Medical Documents (MEDOC)

9.4 Conventions and Meetings

Encyclopedia of Associations (EA)

9.5 Educational Issues

AIM/ARM
Book Review Index (BRI)
Educational Resources Information Center (ERIC)
Federal Assistance Programs Retrieval System
    (FAPRS)
Foundation Directory
Grant Information System
Guidance Information System
Remark
U.S. Public Schools Directory

9.6 Foreign Trade

BI/Data
Canadian Socio-Economic Information
    Management System (CANSIM)
European National Source
Evans Economics IMF International Financial
    Statistics
Foreign Traders Index (FTI)
IMF Balance of Payments
Imports (Oil Imports)
International Energy Data Banks
Nikkei Energy Data Bank
Trade Opportunities Weekly
U.S. Exports

9.7 Health Care, Hospitals, and Medicine

Alcohol Information Retrieval System (AIRS)
Bioethicsline
Biosis Previews
CATLINE (Catalog Online)
Conference Papers Index (CPI)
Drug Info and Alcohol Use/Abuse
Epilepsyline
Excerpta Medica (EMBASE)
Foundation Directory
Medical Documents (MEDOC)
Medline
Pharmaceutical Literature Documentation
    (RINGDOC)
Pharmaceutical News Index (PNI)
Pharmaceutical Prospects
Population Information Online (POPLINE)
Pre-Med
Prospects
Sport
Toxicology Data Bank (TDB)
Toxline
Veterinary Literature Documentation (VETDOC)

9.8 Human Relations and the Behavioral Sciences

AIM/ARM
Alcohol Information Retrieval System (AIRS)
Book Review Index (BRI)
Labordoc
Medical Documents (MEDOC)
Social Scisearch
Sociological Abstracts

9.9 Import—Export

Evans Economic USA Database
Foreign Traders Index (FTI)
IMF Direction of Trade Statistics (DOTS)
PCS/Energy Database: DOE Monthly Petroleum
    Statistics Report
Steel Data Banks
Trade Opportunities Weekly
Traders
U.S. Iron and Steel Imports

9.10 Industrial Relations

PTS Indexes

9.11 Information Processing Technology

Auerbach Compar
Elcom Data Base
International Software Directory
Library and Information Science Abstracts (LISA)
Microcomputer Index
Online Chronicle

9.12 International News and Developments

Asian Data Bank
Australian Bureau of Statistics Data Base
    (ABSDATA)
Developing Countries Data Bank
Economics Abstracts International
Economists' Statistics
European National Source
Evans Economics International Database
EXSTAT
Fintel Company Newsbase
International Business Intelligence Program Index
International Financial Statistics (IFS)
Latin American Data Bank
Middle East Data Base (MEDAB)
Nikkei Economic Statistics
OECD Data Base
PTS International Forecasts Abstracts
PTS International Time Series
U.S. Political Science Documents (USPSD)
World Bank Debt Tables

9.13 Management Planning

ABI/Inform
Accountants' Index
Book Review Index (BRI)
Citibase
Citibase Weekly
Disclosure
DRI Financial and Credit Statistics (DRI-FACS)
Fintel Company Newsbase
Media General Data Base
Merrill Lynch Economics National Data Base
Middle East Data Base (MEDAB)
Newsbeat
PTS Indexes
PTS U.S. Forecasts Abstracts
Social Scisearch
Standard & Poor's News
U.S. Prices Data Bank
U.S. Regional
Value Line II
X/Market

9.14 Personnel Management/Human Resources

American Men and Women of Science
Labordoc
Regional Employment
Regional Industry

9.15 Real Estate and Building Trends

Artbibliographies Modern
Boeckh Building Cost System
Citibase
Citibase Weekly
Cost Forecasting Data Banks
Cost Programs
Dodge Construction Analysis System
EIS Non-Manufacturing Establishments
Evans Economics Regional Housing Service Data
    Base
Evans Economics USA Database
Market Program
Merrill Lynch Economics Regional Data Base
Orr System of Construction Cost Management
PCS/SPEC
Regional
Regional Data Associates (RDA)
Regional Forecast
U.S. Economic/CE
U.S. Model Data Bank

9.16 Service Industries and Businesses

Conference Board (CBDB)
EIS Non-Manufacturing Establishments
Evans Economics USA Database
Nabscan Data Base
Nielsen Retail Index
Regional
Site Potential

9.17 Small Business

EIS Non-Manufacturing Establishments
Farm and Industrial Equipment Institute (FIEI)
Nabscan Data Base
Site Potential

9.18 Transportation and Shipping

Accident/Incident Data System
Association of European Airlines Data Base (AEA)
Highway Safety Literature (HSL)
ICAO Traffic Statistics
INS-U.S. International Air Travel Statistics
Official Air Line Guide (OAG)
Regional Industry
Service Difficulty Reporting System (SDR)
Ship Abstracts (SHIP)
Society of Automotive Engineers (SAE) Abstracts
Transportation
Transportation Cost Service (TCS)
Tris-on-Line

9.19 Union/Labor Activity

Labordoc

9.20 Miscellaneous and General

Astis Online Database
Book Express
Book Review Index (BRI)
Britannica 3
Canadian News Index (CNI)
Canadian Press Newstex (CPN)
Chronolog Newsletter
CIS/Index
Compuserve
Congressional Record Abstracts (CRECORD)
Data Base Index (DBI)
Developing Countries Data Bank
Encyclopedia of Associations (EA)
Eurofile
Federal Assistance Programs Retrieval System
    (FAPRS)
Federal Index (FEDEX)
Federal Register Abstracts (FEDREG)
GPO Monthly Catalog Data Base
Guidance Information System (GIS)
Harvard Business Review
Information Bank
Key Issues Tracking (KIT)
Magazine Index
Management Contents
National Newspaper Index (NNI)
Newsbeat
Newsearch
Newspaper Index (NDEX)
Nexis
Population Information Online (POPLINE)
PTS Prompt
Range Management
The Source
Sport
Standard & Poor's News
State Publications Index (SPI)
Trade and Industry Index
Tradenet
Ulrich's International Periodicals Directory
Universal Serials and Book Exchange (USBE)
Wall Street Journal Highlights Online
Wharton Econometric Forecasting Databases

10.1 Acquisition and Merger Analysis

Bancompare
Canadian Bond Market
Compustat
Disclosure
Mergers and Acquisitions
PTS Indexes
Spectrum
Standard & Poor's News
Standard & Poor's Stock Guide Retrieval Service
X/Market

10.2 Business Diversification—New Ventures

Citibase
Compustat
Disclosure
DRI Financial and Credit Statistics (DRI-FACS)
DRI-SEC (Securities Data Bank)
FTCDATA

10.3 Company Profiles

Chemical Data Banks
Dunsprint
EIS Industrial Plants
EIS Non-Manufacturing Establishments
ICAO Traffic Statistics
PCS/Energy Database: Electric Utility Information
Pharmaceutical News Index
PTS Indexes
Standard & Poor's General Information File
Standard & Poor's News
X/Market

10.4 Competitive Development Activity

Best Executive Data Service (BEDS)
Defense Market Measures System (DM2)
Disclosure
FTCDATA

10.5 Energy Management

Coal Data Banks
Coal Data Base
DOE Energy Data Base (EDB)
Drilling Activity Analysis System (DAAS)
Dwight's Energydata
Electric Power Industry Abstracts (EPIA)
Energy
Energy Projects (ENG)
Energy Bibliography and Index (EBI)
Energy Calendar (ENC)
Energy Data Bank
Energyline
Energynet
Energy Programs (ENP)
Environmental Periodicals Bibliography
Fast Permit Reports (FPR)
Federal Energy Data Index (FEDEX)
Index to API Abstracts/Literature (APILIT)
Index to API Abstracts/Patents (APIPAT)
Imports (Oil Imports)
International Energy Data Banks
Iron and Steel Forecast
Middle East Data Base (MEDAB)
National Technical Information Service (NTIS)
Nikkei Energy Data Bank
OECD Quarterly Oil Statistics
PCS/Energy Database: API Monthly and Quarterly
    Drilling Reports
PCS/Energy Database: API Weekly Statistical
    Bulletin
PCS/Energy Database: DOE Energy Data Reports
PCS/Energy Database: DOE Monthly Petroleum
    Statistics Report
PCS/Energy Database: Electric Utility Information

PCS/Energy Database: Federal Energy Data
    System (FEDS)
PCS/Energy Database: Hughes Rig Count
PCS/Energy Database: Joint Association Survey on
    Drilling Costs
PCS/Energy Database: Reed Rock Bit Company
    Rig Census
PCS/Energy Database: State Energy Data System
    (SEDS)
Petroleum Abstracts (TULSA)
Petroleum Argus
Petroleum/Energy Business News Index (P/E
    NEWS)
Petroseries
Platt's Data Bank
Solar Energy Information Data Bank (SEIDB)
World Energy Industry

10.6 Growth Products and Industries

International Business Intelligence Program Index
Pharmaceutical News Index (PNI)
Pharmaceutical Prospects
PTS Indexes
Standard & Poor's General Information File
Standard & Poor's Industry Financial Data Bank

10.7 Long Range Plans

Bank of Canada Weekly Financial Statistics
Best Executive Data Service (BEDS)
Business Conditions Digest (BCD)
California Data Bank
Canadian Business Periodicals Index (CBPI)
Citibase
Citibase Weekly
Compustat
Conference Board
Disclosure
Dow Jones News/Retrieval Service and Stock Quote
    Reporter
DRI Capsule
DRI Financial and Credit Statistics (DRI-FACS)
DRI Industry Financial Service Data Bank
    (DRIFS)
DRI-SEC (Securities Data Bank)
EEI Capsule
Europrospects—European Economic Indicators
EXSTAT
IMF Direction of Trade Statistics (DOTS)
International Business Intelligence Program Index
PTS International Forecasts Abstracts
PTS International Time Series
PTS U.S. Forecasts Abstracts
Spectrum
Standard & Poor's Industry Financial Data Bank
Standard & Poor's News
U.S. Model Data Bank

10.8 Miscellaneous and General

Britannica 3
Business Credit Services
Canadian News Index (CNI)
Canadian Press Newstex (CPN)
Chronolog Newsletter
CIS/Index
Congressional Record Abstracts (CRECORD)
Data Base Index (DBI)
Developing Countries Data Bank
Eurofile
Federal Index (FEDEX)
Federal Register Abstracts (FEDREG)
GPO Monthly Catalog Data Base
Harvard Business Review

Information Bank
Key Issues Tracking (KIT)
Magazine Index
Management Contents
National Newspaper Index (NNI)
Newsearch
Newspaper Index (NDEX)
Nexis
The Source
State Publications Index (SPI)
Trade and Industry Index
Ulrich's International Periodicals Directory
Universal Serials and Book Exchange (USBE)
Wall Street Journal Highlights Online
Wharton Econometric Forecasting Databases

PRODUCER INDEX

ABC-Clio, Inc.
    2040 Alameda Padre Serra
    Box 4397
    Santa Barbara, California 93103
    (805) 963-4221

ADP Network Services, Inc.
    175 Jackson Plaza
    Ann Arbor, Michigan 48106
    (313) 769-6800

Alberta Agriculture
Market Analysis Branch
    3rd Floor, 9718 107th Street
    Edmonton, Alberta, Canada T5K 2C8
    (403) 427-5381

American Geological Institute
    5205 Leesburg Pike
    Falls Church, Virginia 22041
    (703) 379-2480
    (800) 336-4764

American Institute of Certified Public Accountants
National Automated Accounting Research System (NAARS)
    1211 Avenue of the Americas
    New York, New York 10036
    (212) 575-6393

American Institute of Physics
    335 East 45th Street
    New York, New York 10017
    (212) 661-9404

American Meteorological Society
    45 Beacon Street
    Boston, Massachusetts 02106
    (617) 227-2425

American Petroleum Institute
Central Abstracting and Indexing Service
    156 William Street
    New York, New York 10038
    (212) 587-9660

American Society of Hospital Pharmacists
International Pharmaceutical Abstracts
    4630 Montgomery Avenue
    Washington D.C. 20014
    (301) 657-3000

American Society of Metals
American Metals Information
    Metals Park, Ohio 44073
    (216) 338-5151

The Arbitron Company
    1350 Avenue of the Americas
    New York, New York 10019
    (212) 262-2600

Arctic Institute of North America
The University of Calgary
    2500 University Drive, N.W.
    Calgary, Alberta, Canada T2N 1N4

Arnold Bernhard & Co.
    711 Third Avenue
    New York, New York 10017
    (212) 687-3965

Arthur D. Little, Inc.
    Acorn Park
    Cambridge, Massachusetts 02140
    (617) 364-5770

Association of European Airlines
    B.P. 4
    350 Avenue Louise
    1050 Brussels, Belgium

AUERBACH: The Information Company
    6560 North Park Drive
    Pennsauken, New Jersey 08109
    (609) 662-2070
    (800) 257-8162

Barter Worldwide, Inc.
6575 Green Valley Circle, Suite 112
Culver City, California 90230
(213) 641-1000

BBM Bureau of Measurement
120 Eglington Avenue East
Toronto, Ontario, Canada M4P 1E3
(416) 486-5055

Bell & Howell
Micro Photo Division
Old Mansfield Road
Wooster, Ohio 44691
(216) 264-6666
(800) 321-9881

BHRA Fluid Engineering
Cranfield, Bedford
England MK43 0AJ
0234-750422

Billboard
1515 Broadway
New York, New York 10036
(212) 764-7300

BioSciences Information Service (BIOSIS)
2100 Arch Street
Philadelphia, Pennsylvania 19103
(215) 568-4016
(800) 523-4806

Bloodstock Research Information Services, Inc.
801 Corporate Drive, 3rd Floor
Post Office Box 4097
Lexington, Kentucky 40544
(606) 223-4444

E. H. Boeckh Company
Post Office Box 664
615 East Michigan Street
Milwaukee, Wisconsin 53202
(414) 271-5544
(800) 558-8650

Boeing Computer Services Company
177 Madison Avenue
Morristown, New Jersey 07960
(201) 540-7700

R.R. Bowker Company
Data Services Division
1180 Avenue of the Americas
New York, New York 10036
(212) 764-5100

Bridge Data Company
10050 Manchester Road
St. Louis, Missouri 63122
(314) 821-5660

Broadcast Advertiser Reports, Inc.
500 5th Avenue
New York, New York 10036
(212) 221-2630

Brodart, Inc.
On-Line Services
1609 Memorial Avenue
Williamsport, Pennsylvania 17705
(717) 326-2461
(800) 233-8467

Bunker Ramo Information Systems
35 Nutmeg Drive
Trumbull, Connecticut 06609
(203) 377-4141

The Bureau of National Affairs, Inc.
1231 25th Street, N.W.
Washington D.C. 20037
(202) 452-4200

Business International Corporation
One Dag Hammarskjold Plaza
New York, New York 10017
(212) 750-6300

CACI, Inc.
1815 North Fort Myer Drive
Arlington, Virginia 22209
(703) 841-7807
(800) 336-4752 X7807

California Library Authority for Systems and Services
(CLASS)
1415 Koll Circle
Suite 101
San Jose, California 95112
(408) 289-1756

Cambridge Scientific Abstracts
6611 Kenilworth Avenue
Suite 307
Riverdale, Maryland 20840
(301) 951-1327

Canada Law Book Limited
240 Edward Street
Aurora, Ontario, Canada L4G 3S9
(416) 773-6300

Canadian Daily Newspaper Publishers' Association
321 Bloor Street East
Toronto, Ontario, Canada M4W 1E7
(416) 923-3567

Canadian National Revenue Department
Deputy Minister of National Revenue
Ottawa, Ontario, Canada

Capitol Services International
415 Second Street, N.E.
Suite 200
Washington D.C. 20002
(202) 546-5600

Carrollton Press
1911 Fort Myers Drive
Arlington, Virginia 22209
(703) 525-5940

Cates, Lyons and Company
74 Trinity Place
New York, New York 10006
(212) 964-7002

CEA
French Atomic Energy Commission
Department des Programmes
26. rue de la Federation
75015 Paris, France
73 60 00

Centre de Recherches de Pont-a-Mousson
Service de Documentation Industrielle
BP No. 28 - Maidieres
54700 Pont-a-Mousson, France
(8) 381 60 29

Chase Econometrics/Interactive Data Corporation
486 Totten Pond Road
Waltham, Massachusetts 02154
(617) 890-1234

Chemical Abstracts Service
American Chemical Society
Post Office Box 3012
Columbus, Ohio 43210
(614) 421-6940
(800) 848-6533

Citibank
Citibase Economic Database
Post Office Box 5294 FDR Station
New York, New York 10150
(212) 559-5312

Commission of the European Communities
DG XIII
Batiment Jean Monnet, 8
Plateau de Kirchberg
BP 1907 Luxembourg
(352) 430 11

Commodities Research Unit
27 Red Lion Square
London, England WC1 4RL
(01) 242-9462

Commonwealth Agricultural Bureaux
Farnham House
Farnham Royal
Slough, England SL2 3BN
2814 2281

Comp-U-Card of America, Inc.
777 Summer Street
Stamford, Connecticut 06901
(203) 324-9261

CompuServe, Inc.
5000 Arlington Centre Boulevard
Columbus, Ohio 43220
(614) 457-8600

Computer Directions Advisors, Inc.
11501 Georgia Avenue
Silver Springs, Maryland 20902
(301) 565-9544

Computer Sciences Corporation
650 North Sepulveda Boulevard
El Segundo, California 90245
(213) 678-0311

The Conference Board, Inc.
Information Services Department
845 3rd Avenue
New York, New York 10022
(212) 759-0900

Control Data Corporation
Technology and Information Services
Post Office Box 0, HQV001
Minneapolis, Minnesota 55440
(612) 853-3575
(800) 328-1870

Cost System Engineers, Inc.
131 E. Exchange Avenue, Suite 222
Fort Worth, Texas 76106
(817) 625-1177
(800) 433-2153

Data Courier, Inc.
620 South Fifth Street
Louisville, Kentucky 40202
(502) 582-4111
(800) 626-2823

Data Resources, Inc.
29 Hartwell Avenue
Lexington, Massachusetts 02173
(617) 861-0165

DECHEMA (Deutsche Gesellschaft fur Chemisches
Apparatesesen e.V.)
Informationssysteme und Datenbanken (IuD)
Theodor Heuss Allee 25
Postfach 970146
D-6000 Frankfurt
Federal Republic of Germany
0611/75641

Demographic Research Company
233 Wilshire Boulevard
Suite 995
Santa Monica, California 90401
(213) 451-8583

Derwent Publications Ltd.
Rochdale House
128 Theobalds Road
London, England WC1X 8RP
(01) 242-5823

DIALOG Information Services, Inc.
3460 Hillview Avenue
Palo Alto, California 94304
(415) 858-3777
(800) 227-1960

Direction de la Documentation Francaise
29-31, Quai Voltaire
75007 Paris, France
33 (1) 261 50 10)

Disclosure, Inc.
5161 River Road
Bethesda, Maryland 20816
(301) 951-1300
(800) 638-8076

Doane - Western, Inc.
8900 Manchester Road
St. Louis, Missouri 63144
(314) 968-1000
(800) 325-9519

Donnelley Marketing
1515 Summer Street
Stamford, Connecticut 06905
(203) 348-9999

Dow Jones & Company, Inc.
Post Office Box 300
Princeton, New Jersey 08540
(609) 452-2000
(800) 257-5114

Drug Information Service Center
University of Minnesota
College of Pharmacy
Minneapolis, Minnesota 55455
(614) 376-7190

Dun & Bradstreet, Inc.
99 Church Street
New York, New York 10007
(212) 285-7000

Dwight's Energydata, Inc.
   1201 Exchange Drive
   Richardson, Texas 75081
   (214) 783-8002
   (800) 224-4784

Econintel Information Services, Ltd.
   37 Ludgate Hill
   London, England EC4M 7JN
   (01) 248-4958

Economic Information Systems, Inc.
   310 Madison Avenue
   New York, New York 10017
   (212) 697-6080

Edison Electric Institute
c/o Utility Data Institute, Inc.
   1225 Nineteenth Street, N.W., Suite 250
   Washington D.C. 20036
   (202) 887-1922

Encyclopaedia Britannica, Inc.
   425 North Michigan Avenue
   Chicago, Illinois 60611
   (312) 321-7000

Energy, Mines & Resources
CANMET, Technology Information Division
   555 Booth Street
   Ottawa, Ontario, Canada K1A 0G1
   (613) 995-4029

Engineering Index, Inc.
   345 East 47th Street
   New York, New York 10017
   (212) 644-7881
   (800) 221-1044

Environment Canada
WATDOC
   Inland Waters Directorate
   Ottawa, Ontario, Canada K1A 0E7
   (819) 997-1238

Environment Information Center, Inc.
   292 Madison Avenue
   New York, New York 10017
   (212) 949-9494

Eurocharts Ltd.
   Plantation House, 2nd Floor, E Section
   10/15 Mincing Lane
   London, England EC3M 3DB
   (01) 626-8765

European-American Bank & Trust Company
   10 Hanover Square
   New York, New York
   (212) 437-4300

European Association of Information Services (EUSIDIC)
   Post Office Box 85566
   97
   The Hague, The Netherlands

European Patent Office (EPO)
   Box 5818 Patentlaan 2
   NL-2280 HV Rijswijk
   Netherlands
   (070) 906-789

Europ-Oil Prices
   Star House
   104-108 Grafton Road
   London, England NW5 4BD
   (01) 485-8792

Evans Economics, Inc.
   1211 Connecticut Avenue, N.W.
   Suite 710
   Washington D.C. 20036
   (202) 342-0050

Extel Computing, Ltd.
   Lowndes House
   1-9 City Road
   London, England EC1Y 1AA
   (01) 638-5544

Extel Statistical Services, Ltd.
   37/45 Paul Street
   London, England EC2A 4PB
   (01) 253-3400

Farm and Industrial Equipment Institute
   410 North Michigan Avenue
   Chicago, Illinois 60611
   (312) 321-1470

Federal Aviation Administration
Flight Standard National Field Office
   800 Independence Avenue, S.W.
   Washington, D.C. 20591
   (202) 426-4000

Federal Deposit Insurance Corporation
   550 17th Street, N.W.
   Washington D.C. 20429

Federal Home Loan Bank Board
   320 First Street
   Washington D.C. 20552
   (202) 377-6000

Federal Reserve Board
   20th and Constitution Avenue, N.W.
   Washington D.C. 20551
   (202) 452-3000

Financial Post
Investment Databank
   481 University Avenue
   Toronto, Ontario, Canada M5W 1A7
   (416) 596-5692

Fintel Ltd.
   102-108 Clerkenwell Road
   London EC1M 5SA, England
   (01) 251-9321

Forest Products Research Society
   2801 Marshall Court
   Madison, Wisconsin 53705
   (608) 231-1361

The Foundation Center
   888 7th Avenue
   New York, New York 10106
   (212) 975-1120

FRI Information Services Limited
   1801 McGill College Avenue, Suite 600
   Montreal, Quebec, Canada H3A 2N4
   (514) 842-5091

Frost & Sullivan, Inc.
   106 Fulton Street
   New York, New York 10038
   (212) 233-1080

The Futures Group
   76 Eastern Avenue
   Glastonbury, Connecticut 06033
   (203) 633-3501

General Electric Information Services Company
401 N. Washington Street
Rockville, Maryland 20850
(301) 340-4000

Georgetown University
Kennedy Institute for Bioethics
Washington D.C. 20057
(202) 625-2371

Geosystems
Post Office Box 1024
Westminster, London, England SW1P 2JL
(01) 222-7305

GTE Information Systems, Inc.
East Park Drive
Mount Laurel, New Jersey 08054
(619) 235-7300

Gulf Publishing Company
Post Office Box 2608
3301 Allen Parkway
Houston, Texas 77001
(713) 529-4301

Harper & Row, Publishers, Inc.
Harfax Database Publishing
54 Church Street
Cambridge, Massachusetts 02138
(617) 491-2300

Harvard Business Review
Soldiers' Field
Boston, Massachusetts 02163
(617) 495-8600

House of Commons
Computer Systems Branch
Post Office Box 1005, South Block
Ottawa, Ontario, Canada K1A 0A6
(613) 593-5224

Hughes Tool Company
5425 Polk Avenue
Houston, Texas 77023
(713) 924-2222

IFI/Plenum Data Company
302 Swann Avenue
Arlington, Virginia 22301
(703) 683-1085

IMS America, Ltd.
Ambler, Pennsylvania 19002
(215) 643-0400

Industrial Bank of Japan
1-1 Yaesu
5-Chrome
Chuo-Ku
Tokyo 104, Japan
(03) 216-0251

Information Access Corporation
404 Sixth Avenue
Menlo Park, California 94025
(415) 367-7171
(800) 227-8431

Information Handling Service
Inverness Business Park
15 Inverness Way East
Englewood, Colorado 80150
(303) 779-0600
(800) 525-7052 X328

Information Resources Press
Horner & Company
1700 North Moore Street, Suite 700
Arlington, Virginia 22209
(703) 558-8270

Institute for Scientific Information
University City Science Center
3501 Market Street
Philadelphia, Pennsylvania 19104
(215) 386-0100
(800) 523-1850

Institut Textile de France
35 rue des Abondances
F-92100 Boulogne sur Seine
France
(01) 825 1890

Institution of Electrical Engineers
Station House Hitchin
Nightengale Road
Herts, England SG5 1RJ
0462/53331

Interactive Data Services, Inc.
22 Cortlandt Street
New York, New York 10007
(212) 285-0700

International Academy at Santa Barbara
Environmental Studies Institute
2074 Alameda Padre Sierra
Santa Barbara, California 93103
(805) 965-5010

International Civil Aviation Organization
Post Office Box 400
1000 Sherbrooke Street, West
Montreal, PQ, Canada, H3A 2R1
(514) 285-8064

International Food Information Service
Lane End House
Shinfield, Reading, England RG2 9BB
0734 8833895

International Labour Office (ILO)
CH-1211
Geneva 22, Switzerland
(22) 998684

International Monetary Fund
19th and H Street, N.W.
Washington D.C. 20431
(202) 477-7000

International Patent Documentation Center
INPADOC, Sales Department
Mollwaldplatz 4
1040 Vienna, Austria
0222/658784

A. T. Kearney, Inc.
222 Riverside Plaza
Chicago, Illinois 60606
(312) 648-0111

Komp Information Services, Inc.
811 Fountain Avenue
Louisville, Kentucky 40222
(502) 426-7754

Lawyers' Co-operative Publishing Company
50 Broad Street
Rochester, New York 14603
(716) 546-5530

Learned Information Ltd.
Besselsleigh Road
Abingdon
Oxford, England OX13 6LG
Oxford (0865) 730275

The Library Association
7 Ridgemount Street
London, England WC1E 7AE
(01) 636-7543

Library of Congress
Washington D.C. 20541
(202) 287-6100

Library of Congress
Cold Regions Bibliography Project
Science & Technology Div.
Washington D.C. 20541
(202) 287-5668

James R. LymBurner & Sons Limited
20 Victoria Street
Toronto, Ontario, Canada M5C 1Y1
(416) 862-0595

Management Contents, Inc.
2265 Carlson Drive, Suite 5000
Northbrook, Illinois 60062
(312) 564-1006
(800) 323-5354

Marshall and Swift Publication Company
1617 Beverly Boulevard
Post Office Box 26307
Los Angeles, California 90036
(213) 624-6451
(800) 421-8042

McClean-Hunter, Ltd.
481 University Avenue
Toronto, Ontario, Canada M5W 1A7
(416) 596-5693

McGraw-Hill, Inc.
1211 Avenue of the Americas
New York, New York 10020
(212) 997-1221

Mead Data Central
200 Park Avenue
New York, New York 10017
(212) 883-8560

Media General Financial Services
301 East Grace
Richmond, Virginia
(804) 649-6736

Mediamark Research Inc.
341 Madison Avenue
New York, New York 10017
(212) 599-0444

Merrill Lynch Economics, Inc.
1 Liberty Plaza
165 Broadway
New York, New York 10080
(212) 766-6200

Microcomputer Information Service
Santa Clara, California
(408) 984-1097

Micromedia Limited
144 Front Street West
Toronto, Ontario, Canada M5J 2L7
(416) 593-5211

Ministere de l'Environment du Quebec
Place Innovation
2360 Chemin Ste-Foy
Quebec, Quebec, Canada G1V 6H2
(418) 643-2795

MJK Associates
122 Saratoga Avenue, Suite 11
Santa Clara, California 95050
(408) 247-5102

Money Market Services, Inc.
490 El Camino Real
Belmont, California 94002
(415) 595-0610

NABSCAN
486 Lexington Avenue
New York, New York 10017
(212) 557-1843

National Association of Insurance Commissioners
350 Bishops Way
Brookfield, Wisconsin 53005
(414) 784-9540

The National Center for Research in Vocational Education
The Ohio State University
1960 Kenny Road
Columbus, Ohio 43210
(614) 486-3655
(800) 848-4815

National Computer Network of Chicago, Inc.
1929 N. Harlem Avenue
Chicago, Illinois 60635
(312) 622-6666

National CSS, Inc.
187 Danbury Road
Wilton, Connecticut 06897
(203) 762-2511

National Electrical Manufacturers Association
2101 L Street, N.W., Suite 300
Washington D.C. 20037
(202) 457-8400

National Library of Medicine
Toxicology Information Program
8600 Rockville Pike
Bethesda, Maryland 20209
(301) 496-6193

National Planning Association
1606 New Hampshire Avenue, N.W.
Washington D.C. 20009
(202) 265-7685

National Standards Association, Inc.
5161 River Road
Washington D.C. 20016
(301) 951-1310
(800) 638-8076

A. C. Nielsen Company
Nielsen Plaza
Northbrook, Illinois 60062
(312) 498-6300

NIKKEI (Nihon Keizai Shimbun)
Databank Bureau
1-9-5 Ohkmachi Chiyoda-ku
Tokyo, Japan 100

Official Airline Guides, Inc.
2000 Clearwater Drive
Oak Brook, Illinois 60521
(312) 654-6000

ONLINE, Inc.
11 Tannery Lane
Weston, Connecticut 06883
(203) 227-8466

Organization for Economic Cooperation and Development
International Energy Agency
2. rue Andre-Pascal
75775 Paris Cedex 16
France
(01) 524-8200

The Oryx Press
2214 North Central at Encanto
Phoenix, Arizona 85004
(602) 254-6156

Paine, Webber, Jackson & Curtis, Inc.
140 Broadway
New York, New York 10005
(212) 437-2121

Paint Research Association
Waldegrave Road
Teddington, Middlesex, England TW11 8LD
(01) 977-4427

Petroleum Information Corporation
Box 2612
Littleton, Colorado 80201
(303) 825-2181

Policy Review Associates, Inc.
7315 Wisconsin Avenue, Suite 727E
Bethesda, Maryland 20014
(301) 762-8008

Predicasts, Inc.
11001 Cedar Avenue
Cleveland, Ohio 44106
(216) 795-3000
(800) 321-6388

Print Measurement Bureau (PMB)
11 Yorkville Avenue, Suite 502
Toronto, Ontario, Canada M4W 1L2
(416) 961-3205

Production Systems for Architects & Engineers, Inc.
1735 New York Avenue, N.W.
Washington D.C. 2006
(202) 626-7550
(800) 424-5080

QL Systems, Ltd.
797 Princess Street
Kingston, Ontario, Canada K7L 1G1
(613) 549-4611

Quotron Systems, Inc.
5454 Beethoven Street
Los Angeles, California 90066
(213) 398-2761

Reed Rock Bit Company
6501 Navigation Boulevard
Houston, Texas 77011
(713) 924-5200

Regional Data Associates
194 Nassau Street
Princeton, New Jersey 08540
(609) 924-4611

The Research Association for the Paper and Board, Printing
and Packaging Industries
Randalls Road, Leatherhead
Surrey, England KT22 7RU
929810

Robinson-Humphrey Co., Inc.
2 Peachtree Street, N.W.
Atlanta, Georgia 30303
(404) 481-7176

Royal Tropical Institute
Department of Agricultural Research
Mauritskade 63
NL 1092 AD Amsterdam, The Netherlands
(020) 924949

Rubber and Plastics Research Association of Great Britain
Shawbury, Shrewsbury, Shropshire
England SY4 4NR
(0939) 250383

Rutgers University
Center of Alcohol Studies
Information Services Division
Post Office Box 969
Piscataway, New Jersey 08854
(201) 932-3510

SDC Search Service
2500 Colorado Avenue
Santa Monica, California 90406
(213) 820-4111 X5104

Securities Data Company
62 William Street, 6th Floor
New York, New York 10005
(212) 668-0940

Security Pacific National Bank
SPNB CALIFORNIA DATABANK, H8-3
Post Office Box 2097, Terminal Annex
Los Angeles, California 90051
(213) 613-5381

Selling Areas - Marketing Inc.
541 North Fairbanks Court
Chicago, Illinois 60611
(312) 329-6800

I.P. Sharp Associates
145 King Street West
Toronto, Ontario, Canada M5H 1J8
(416) 364-5361

Ship Research Institute of Norway
Post Office Box 6099 Etterstad
Oslo 6, Norway
02/68 92 80

Shirley Institute
Manchester, England M2O 8RX
061/455-8141

Simmons Market Research Bureau, Inc.
219 East 42nd Street
New York, New York 10017
(212) 867-1414

Smithsonian Science Information Exchange
300 Madison National Bank Building
1730 M Street, N.W.
Washington D.C. 20036
(202) 634-3933

Society of Automotive Engineers
400 Commonwealth Drive
Warrendale, Pennsylvania 15096
(412) 776-4841

Sociological Abstracts, Inc.
Post Office Box 22206
San Diego, California 92122
(714) 565-6603

Solar Energy Research Institute
1617 Cole Boulevard
Golden, Colorado 80401
(303) 231-1000

Source Telecomputing Corporation
1616 Anderson Road
McLean, Virginia 22102
(703) 734-7500 X 546
(800) 336-3366

Sport Information Resource Centre (SIRC)
Coaching Association of Canada
333 River Road
Ottawa, Ontario, Canada K1L 8B9
(613) 746-5357

SRI International
333 Ravenswood Avenue
Menlo Park, California 94025
(415) 326-6200

Standard & Poor's Compustat Services, Inc.
7400 South Alton Court
Englewood, Colorado 80112
(303) 771-6510

Standard & Poor's Corporation
25 Broadway
New York, New York 10004
(212) 248-2525

Strategic Information Systems, Inc.
1 Harrison Road
Kinnelon, New Jersey 07405
(201) 838-3944

Telerate Systems, Inc.
1 World Trade Center
104th Floor
New York, New York 10048
(212) 938-5200

Three Sigma Research Center, Inc.
1875 Palmer Avenue
Larchmont, New York 10538
(212) 671-4200

Time Share Corporation
630 Oakwood Avenue
West Hartford, Connecticut 06110
(203) 522-0136

Townsend-Greenspan & Co., Inc.
1 New York Plaza
New York, New York 10004
(212) 943-9515

Transporation Research Board
National Research Council
2101 Constitution Avenue, N.W.
Washington D.C. 20418
(202) 389-6611

TRW Business Credit Services
1 City Boulevard
Orange, California 92668
(714) 937-2000

TRW Information Services Division
Seventh Floor
505 City Parkway West
Orange, California 92668
(714) 937-2000

Universal Serials and Book Exchange
3335 V Street, N.E.
Washington D.C. 20018
(202) 529-2555

University Microfilms International, Inc.
300 North Zeeb Road
Ann Arbor, Michigan 48106
(313) 761-4700
(800) 521-0600

University of North Carolina
Carolina Population Center
University Square - East 300A
Chapel Hill, North Carolina 27514
(919) 933-3006

University of Pittsburgh
University Center for International Studies
4G22 Forbes Quadrangle
Pittsburgh, Pennsylvania 15260
(412) 624-1234

University of Rochester
Department of Pharmacology
601 Elmwood Avenue
Rochester, New York 14642
(716) 275-3146

University of Tulsa
Information Services Division
Jersey Hall, Room 138
1133 North Lewis Avenue
Tulsa, Oklahoma 74110
(918) 939-6351 X295

University of Utah
Eccles Health Sciences Library, Building 89
Salt Lake City, Utah 84112
(801) 581-5269

Urban Decision Systems, Inc.
Post Office Box 25953
Los Angeles, California 90025
(213) 820-8931

U.S. Census Bureau
Washington D.C. 20233
(301) 763-7273

U.S. Census Bureau
Foreign Trade Division
Washington D.C. 20233
(301) 763-4150

U.S. Department of Agriculture
NAL Building
Beltsville, Maryland 20705
(301) 344-3755

U.S. Department of Commerce
Bureau of Export Development
Commerce ITA/1033/FTI
Washington D.C. 20230
(202) 377-2980

U.S. Department of Commerce
Trade Facilitation Information & Services Division
ITA/1033/FTI
Washington D.C. 20230
(202) 377-2988

U.S. Department of Education
National Center for Education Statistics
400 Maryland Avenue, S.W. Room 3009
Washington D.C. 20202
(202) 436-6729

U.S. Department of Education
National Institute of Education
ERIC Processing and Reference Facility
4833 Rugby Avenue, Suite 303
Bethesda, Maryland 20014
(301) 656-9723

U.S. Department of Energy
12th Street and Pennsylvania Avenue, N.W.
Washington, D.C. 20461
(202) 556-6061

U.S. Department of Energy
Energy Information Administration (EIA)
1726 M Street, N.W.
Washington D.C. 20461
(202) 633-5602

U.S. Department of Energy
International Analysis Division
Technical Information Center
Post Office Box 62
Oak Ridge, Tennessee 37830
(615) 596-1155

U.S. Department of Energy
2101 L Street, N.W.
Washington D.C. 20037
(202) 457-7141

U.S. Department of Health and Human Services
National Center on Child Abuse and Neglect
Children's Bureau
Post Office Box 1182
Washington D.C. 20013
(202) 755-0590

U.S. Department of Labor
Bureau of Labor Statistics
441 G Street, N.W.
Washington, D.C. 20212
(202) 523-1092

U.S. Department of Transporation
400 Seventh Street, S.W.
Washington D.C. 20590
(202) 426-4000

U.S. Environmental Protection Agency
Air Pollution Technical Information Center
EPA (MD 18)
Research Triangle Park, North Carolina 27711
(919) 549-2460

U.S. Environmental Protection Agency
Information Project
The Ohio State University
1200 Chambers Road, Room 310
Columbus, Ohio 43212
(614) 422-6717

U.S. Environmental Protection Agency
Office of Toxic Substances
Industry Assistance Office
401 M Street, S.W. MS-TS799
Washington D.C. 20460
(800) 424-9065
(202) 554-1404

U.S. Federal Deposit Insurance Corporation (FDIC)
550 17th Street, N.W.
Washington D.C. 20429
(202) 389-4701

U.S. Geological Survey
Office of Energy Resources
115 National Center
Reston, Virginia 22092
(703) 860-6086

U.S. Government Printing Office
Library Division
Superintendent of Documents
Records Branch, STOP: SSMR
Washington D.C. 20401
(202) 275-3302

U.S. National Highway Traffic Safety Administration
400 Seventh Street, S.W., Room 5108
Washington D.C. 20590
(202) 426-2768

U.S. National Institutes of Health
National Institute of Neurological and Communicative
Disorders and Stroke
9000 Rockville Pike
Bethesda, Maryland 20014
(301) 496-6691

U.S. National Library of Medicine
8600 Rockville Pike
Bethesda, Maryland 20209
(301) 496-6217

U.S. National Technical Information Service
Office of Data Base Services
5285 Port Royal Road
Springfield, Virginia 22161
(703) 487-4600

U.S. Office of Management and Budget
Executive Office of the President
Washington D.C. 20500
(202) 395-3000

Washington Representative Services, Inc.
4040 North Fairfax Drive, Suite 110
Arlington, Virginia 22203
(703) 243-8912

Water Research Centre
Communications Group
Medmenham Laboratory
Henley Road, Medmenham, Marlow
Bucks, England SL7 2HD
049/166 531

The Welding Institute
Abington Hall
Abington, Cambridge, England CB1 6AL
Cambridge 0223-891162

Wharton Econometric Forecasting Associates, Inc.
3624 Science Center
Philadelphia, Pennsylvania 19104
(215) 386-9000

Wood Gundy Limited
Royal Trust Tower
Post Office Box 274, T-D Center
Toronto, Ontario, Canada M5K 1M7
(416) 362-4433

World Energy Industry Information Services
A Division of Business Information Display, Inc.
4202 Sorrento Valley Boulevard, Suite J
San Diego, California 92121
(714) 452-7675

VENDOR INDEX

ADP Network Services, Inc.
175 Jackson Plaza
Ann Arbor, Michigan 48106
(313) 769-6800
Bancompare; BCD; Boeckh Building Cost System; Bridge Data Stock & Options Real Time Information System; CBDB; Citibase; Compubond; Compustat; CPI/PPI; CTS; Europrospects; Exstat; Fastock II; FDIC Report; Flow of Funds Accounts; IFS; Nielsen Retail Index; Savings and Loan; SITE II; SITE Potential; STP/LTP; U. S. Economic; U.S. Financial; Value Line II.

BELINDIS
Belgian Ministry of Economic Affairs
Rue J.A. de Mot. 30
1040 Brussels, Belgium
32 (2) 233-6737
Economics Abstracts International.

Billboard
1515 Broadway
New York, New York 10036
(212) 764-7300
BIN.

BLAISE
The British Library
2 Sheraton Street
London, England W1V 4BH
(01) 636-1544
Bioethicsline; Health Planning and Administration; Toxline.

Bloodstock Research Information Services, Inc.
801 Corporate Drive, 3rd Floor
P.O. Box 4097
Lexington, Kentucky 40544
(602) 223-4444
Horse Data Bank.

E. H. Boeckh Company
Post Office Box 664
615 East Michigan Street
Milwaukee, Wisconsin 53202
(414) 271-5544
(800) 558-8650
Boeckh Building Cost System.

Bridge Data Company
10050 Manchester Road
St. Louis, Missouri 63122
(314) 821-5660
Bridge Data Stock & Options Real Time Information System.

Brodart, Inc.
On-Line Services
1609 Memorial Avenue
Williamsport, Pennsylvania 17705
(717) 326-2461
(800) 233-8467
Book Express.

BRS, Inc.
1200 Route 7
Latham, New York 12110
(518) 783-1161
(800) 833-4707
ABI/Inform; Agricola; American Men & Women of Science; Auerbach Compar; BBIP; Biosis Previews; Book Express; CA Search; CDI; Compendex; CULP; Dow Jones News/Retrieval Service and Stock Quote Reporter; Drug Info and Alcohol Use/Abuse; EDB; EIS Digests of Environmental Impact Statements; Energyline; Enviroline; ERIC; FEDEX; Fintel Co. Newsbase; GPO Monthly Catalog; Harfax; Harvard Business Review; Health Planning and Administration; IRP; IRIS; Management Contents; Medline; Medoc; NTIS; PNI; Pollution Abstracts; Pre-med; PTS Indexes; PTS Prompt; SSCI; SSIE; SPI; Ulrich's International Periodicals Directory; USBE.

Bunker Ramo Information Systems
35 Nutmeg Drive
Trumbull, Connecticut 06609
(203) 377-4141
Telequote III.

Business Information Services
Control Data Corporation
500 West Putnam Avenue
Greenwich, Connecticut 06830
(203) 622-2000
American Profile; Bankanal; Compustat; CPI/PPI; Disclosure II; Dri Capsule: EEI Capsule; EIS Industrial Plants; EIS Non-manufacturing Establishments; Eurabank; Evans Economics Data Bases; Exshare; Exstat; FAPRS; Financial Institutions Data Base; IFS; IIDB; ORR System; Site II; SITE Potential; X/Market.

Chase Econometrics/Interactive Data Corporation
486 Totten Pond Road
Waltham, Massachusetts 02154
(617) 890-1234
Agriculture Forecast; BCD; California Data Bank; CBDB; Compustat; CPI/PPI; Energy; Exshare; Exstat; FDIC Report; Fertilizer Forecast; Financial; Financial Forecast; Flow of Funds Accounts; Foreign Exchange Rate Forecast; IFS; IMF Balance of Payments; IMF Dots; Inflation Planner Forecast; Insurance Forecast; Iron and Steel Forecast; Metals Week; Non-ferrous Metals Forecast; Passenger Car; Regional Data Banks; U.S. Economic/CE; U.S. Iron and Steel Imports; Value Line II; World Agriculture Supply-Disposition; World Bank Debt Tables.

Chemical Abstracts Service
Post Office Box 3012
Columbus, Ohio 43210
(614) 421-6940
(800) 482-1608
CAS Online.

CIS, Inc.
Suite 401
2135 Wisconsin Avenue, N.W.
Washington D.C. 20007
(202) 298-6200
(800) 424-2722
Chemlaw; CTCP.

CISI
35. boulevard Brune
75680 Paris Cedex 14, France
33 (1) 539-2510
World Nuclear Power Plant.

CISTI
National Research Council Canada
Ottawa, Ontario, Canada K1A 0S2
(613) 993-1210
Biosis Previews; CA Search; Coal Data Base; Compendex.

Citishare
Box 1127
New York, New York 10043
(212) 559-0787
Citibase; Citibase-Weekly.

CompuServe, Inc.
5000 Arlington Centre Boulevard
Columbus, Ohio 43220
(614) 457-8600
Citibase; Citibase-Weekly; Compuserv; Comp*U*Star;Compustat; FDIC Report, Microquote; Quick Quote; Savings and Loan; SITE II; SITE Potential; Standard and Poor's General Information File; Value Line II.

The Computer Company
1905 Westmoreland Street
Richmond, Virginia 23230
(804) 358-2171
Oil Imports; INS-U.S. International Air Travel Statistics.

Computer Directions Advisors, Inc.
11501 Georgia Avenue
Silver Spring, Maryland 20902
(301) 565-9544
Spectrum.

Computer Sciences Corporation
650 N. Sepulveda Boulevard
El Segundo, California 90245
(213) 615-0311
Citibase; LSH, NCRDS; SITE II; SITE Potential.

COMSHARE, Inc.
Post Office Box 1588
3001 S. State Street
Ann Arbor, Michigan 48106
(313) 994-4800
Citibase; IFS; SITE II; SITE Potential.

The Conference Board of Canada
25 McArthur Road, Suite 100
Ottawa, Ontario, Canada K1L 5R3
(613) 746-1261
Citibase.

Control Data Corporation
Post Office Box 0 HQV 001
Minneapolis, Minnesota 55440
(612) 853-8100
(800) 328-1870
AIRS; Citibase; EIS Industrial Plants; EIS Non-Manufacturing Establishments; FEDWIR; Technotec Technology Exchange Data Base; Traders.

Cornell University
Computer Services
G-02 Uris Hall
Ithaca, New York 14853
(607) 256-4981
CBDB.

Data Resources, Inc. (DRI)
29 Hartwell Avenue
Lexington, Massachusetts 02173
(617) 861-0165
Agriculture Data Bank; Asian Data Bank; BEDS;
California Data Bank; CANSIM; CBDB; Chemical
Data Banks; Coal Data Bank; Commodities Market
Data Bank; Compustat; Consumer Economic Service
Data; Cost Forecasting Data Banks; Developing
Countries Primary Source Data Bank; Dodge
Construction Analysis System; DRI-FACS; DRIFS;
DRI-SEC; Energy Data Bank; European National
Source; FIEI; Forestry Data Banks; IFS; IMF
Balance of Payments; IMF DOTS; International
Energy Data Banks: Latin American Data Bank; New
York City Model Data Bank; Nikkei Economic
Statistics; Nikkei Energy Data Bank; Paper and Pulp
Data Bank; Platt's Data Bank; SITE II; SITE
Potential; Standard and Poor's Industry Financial
Data Bank; Steel Data Banks; TCS; Transportation;
U.S. Central Data Bank; U.S. County Data Bank;
U.S. Model Data Bank; U.S. Prices Data Bank; U.S.
Regional; Value Line II.

Datacentralen
Retortvej 6-8
DK-2500 Valby
Denmark
45 (1) 468122
27122 dcdk
Agrep.

Datacrown, Inc.
770 Brookfield Road
Ottawa, Ontario, Canada K1V 6J5
(613) 731-6910
Citibase.

DATA-STAR
199 High Street
Orpington, Kent
England BRG OPF
(44) 689-38488
ABI/Inform; Biosis Previews; Fintel Co. Newsbase;
Harfax; Management Contents; Pre-med; PTS
Indexes; PTS Prompt.

Dialcom, Inc.
1109 Spring Street, Suite 410
Silver Spring, Maryland 20910
(301) 588-1572
Financial Post Investment Data Bank; Securities.

DIALOG Information Services, Inc.
Orgn. 5280
3460 Hillview Avenue
Palo Alto, California 94304
(415) 858-3810
(800) 227-1960
ABI/Inform; Adtrack: Agricola; AIM/ARM; Aptic;
Aqualine; Artbibliographies Modern; ASFA; BHRA
Fluid Engineering; BI/Data ITS; Biography Master
Index; Biosis Previews: BRI; CA Search; CDI;
Chemlaw; Chemsearch; Chemsis; Child Abuse and
Neglect; Chronolog Newsletter; CIN; CIS/Index;
Claims/Chem; Claims/Citation; Claims/Uniterm;

DIALOG Information Services, Inc. (*continued*)
Claims/U.S. Patents; Commonwealth Agricultural
Bureaux Abstracts: NAR; Compendex; CPI; Crecord;
CRIS; Disclosure II; DM 2; Dun's Financial Profiles;
EA; EDB; Economics Abstracts International; EIS
Industrial Plants; EIS Non-manufacturing
Establishments; Energyline; Energynet; Enviroline;
EPB; ERIC; Excerpta Medica; FEDEX; FEDREG;
Foods Adlibra; Foundation Directory; FSTA; FTI;
Geoarchive; GEOREF; GPO Monthly Catalog; Grant
Information System; Harfax; Health Planning and
Administration; Inpadoc; International Business
Intelligence Program Index; International Software
Directory; IPA; IRIS; ISMEC; LISA; LRI; Magazine
Index; Management Contents; Medline; MGA;
Microcomputer Index; Newsearch; NNI; NTIS;
Oceanic Abstracts; Online Chronicle; PIRA; PNI;
Pollution Abstracts; Population Bibliography; PTS
Indexes; PTS International; PTS Prompt; PTS U.S.;
Rapra Abstracts; Remarc; Sociological Abstracts;
SPIN; SSCI; SSIE; Standard and Poor's News;
Standards and Specifications; STI; Surface Coatings
Abstracts; Trade and Industry Index; Trade
Opportunities Weekly; Tris-on-line; TSCA Chemical
Substances Inventory; U.S. Exports; USPSD; U.S.
Public Schools Directory; WAA; Weldasearch.

DIMDI
Weisshausstrasse 27
Post Office Box 420580
D-5000 Cologne 41
Federal Republic of Germany
(49) 221 4724-1
Agrep; ASFA; Biosis Previews; Commonwealth
Agricultural Bureaux Abstracts: NAR; Excerpta
Medica; Toxline.

Dow Jones & Company, Inc.
Post Office Box 300
Princeton, New Jersey 08540
(609) 452-2000
(800) 257-5114
Disclosure II; Dow Jones News/Retrieval Service and
Stock Quote Reporter; Media General Data Base;
Wall Street Journal Highlights; Wall $treet Week;
Weekly Economic Survey; Weekly Economic Update.

Dun & Bradstreet, Inc.
99 Church Street
New York, New York 10007
(212) 285-7669
Dunsprint.

ECHO Service
Commission of the European Communities
DG XIII
Batiment Jean Monnet
B.P. 1907
Luxembourg
(352) 43011 X2923
Agrep; Eurofile.

ESA-IRS
8-10 Rue Mario Nikis
F-75739 Paris Cedex 15
France
Aqualine; Biosis Previews; CA Search;
Commonwealth Agricultural Bureaux Abstracts:
NAR; Compendex; CPI; Energyline; Eurofile; PNI.

ESA-QUEST
Via Galileo Galilei
00044 Frascati, Italy
(06) 94011
Compendex; FSTA; ISMEC; Oceanic Abstracts;
Rapra Abstracts.

European Patent Office
Post Box 5818 Patentlaan
2 NL-2280 HV Rijswijk
Netherlands
(070) 906-789
EPR.

FRI Information Services Limited
1801 McGill College Avenue, Suite 600
Montreal, Quebec, Canada H3A 2N4
(514) 842-5091
Bondata; Financial Post Investment Data Bank; IFS.

G.CAM
Tour Maine-Montparnesse
33, Avenue du Maine
F-75755 Paris Cedex 15
France
(33) 1 538-1051
Citibase.

General Electric Information Services Company
401 North Washington Street
Rockville, Maryland 20850
(301) 340-4000
BI/Data; Boeckh Building Cost System; Citibase;
Currency Exchange Data Base; DAAS; Dwight's
Energydata; EMIS; FAPRS; FPR; FTCDATA;
Industrial Bank of Japan; NEMA; ORR System;
Petroleum Argus; Pharmaceutical Prospects;
Prospects; SITE II; SITE Potential.

Geosystems
Post Office Box 1024
Westminister, London, England SW1P 2JL
(01) 222-7305
MINSYS.

GID-SIT
Herriotstrasse 5
Postfach 710370
D-6000 Frankfurt am Main 71
Federal Republic of Germany
(49) 611 66871
Commonwealth Agricultural Bureaux Abstracts:
NAR; Detherm-SDR.

GTE Information Systems, Inc.
East Park Drive
Mount Laurel, New Jersey 08054
(609) 235-7300
GTE Financial System One Quotation Service;
Newsbeat; Standard and Poor's Stock Guide Retrieval
Service.

IMS/Marketronics
19 West 44th Street
New York, New York 10036
(212) 869-8810
(800) 223-7942
MRI; SMRB.

Informatech
3467 Rue Durocher
3rd Floor
Montreal, Quebec, Canada H2X 2C6
(514) 845-2206
Envirodoq.

Informatics, Inc.
6011 Executive Boulevard
Rockville, Maryland 20852
(301) 770-3000
(800) 638-6595
Citibase; HSL.

Information Handling Services
15 Inverness Way East
Englewood, Colorado 80150
(303) 779-0600
(800) 525-7052 X 328
Tech-net.

Interactive Market Systems, Inc.
19 West 44th Street
New York, New York 10036
(212) 869-8810
(800) 223-7942
BAR; MRI; Nielsen Retail Index; Nielson Station
Index; Nielson Television Index; SAMI; SMRB; TGI.

Lawyers' Co-operative Publishing Company
50 Broad Street
Rochester, New York 14603
(716) 546-5530
AUTO-CITE.

Management Science Associates, Inc.
5100 Centre Avenue
Pittsburgh, Pennsylvania 15232
(412) 683-9533
BAR; MRI; Nabscan Data Base; Nielson Retail
Index; Nielson Station Index; Nielson Television
Index; SAMI; SMRB.

Market Data Systems, Inc.
3835 Lamar Avenue
Memphis, Tennessee 38118
(901) 363-0500
Bridge Data Stock & Options Real Time Information
System.

Marketron
21031 Ventura Boulevard, Suite 1020
Woodland Hills, California 91364
(213) 347-6400
SMRB.

Market Science Associates, Inc.
777 Third Avenue
New York, New York 10017
(212) 751-4980
BAR; Nielsen Station Index; Nielson Television
Index; SAMI.

Marshall and Swift Publication Company
1617 Beverly Boulevard
Post Office Box 26307
Los Angeles, California 90036
(213) 624-6451
Cost Programs; Market Program.

Massachusetts Institute of Technology
Information Processing Services
Room 39-466
Cambridge, Massachusetts 02139
(617) 253-4102
Citibase.

Mead Data Central
200 Park Avenue
New York, New York 10017
(212) 883-8560
AUTO-CITE; Britannica 3; Disclosure II; Lexis;
NAARS; Nexis.

MJK Associates
122 Saratoga Avenue, Suite 11
Santa Clara, California 95050
(408) 247-5102
CDIS.

National Computer Network of Chicago, Inc.
1929 N. Harlem Avenue
Chicago, Illinois 60635
(312) 622-6666
Optdat.

National CSS, Inc.
187 Danbury Road
Wilton, Connecticut 06897
(203) 762-2511
California Data Bank; CSS/Quotes+; Dun's
Financial Profiles; Flow of Funds Accounts;
Marketbase; Merrill Lynch Economics Data Bases;
Onsite; Tradeline.

National Library of Medicine
8600 Rockville Pike
Bethesda, Maryland 20209
(301) 496-6217
Bioethicsline; Catline; Epilepsyline, Medline; Popline;
TDB; Toxline.

The New York Times Information Services, Inc.
1719-A Route 10
Parsippany, New Jersey 07054
(201) 539-5850
AMI; Disclosure II; The Information Bank; KIT;
Medab.

A.C. Nielsen Company
Nielsen Plaza
Northbrook, Illinois 60062
(312) 498-6300
Nielsen Retail Index.

Norwegian Centre for Informatics
Post Office Box 350 Blindern
Oslo 3, Norway
02 695880
Ship Abstracts.

On-Line Research, Inc.
151 Railroad Avenue
Greenwich, Connecticut 06830
(203) 661-1395
U.S. Census.

Pergamon-InfoLine
12 Vandy Street
London, England EC2A 2DE
(01) 377-1225
CA Search.

Proprietary Computer Systems, Inc.
16625 Saticoy Street
Van Nuys, California 91406
(213) 781-8221
Citibase; PCS/Energy Data Bases; PCS/Spec.

QL Systems Limited
797 Princess Street
Kingston, Ontario, Canada K7L 1G1
(613) 549-4611
ACWS; ASFA; ASTIS Online Database; CBPI;
CENV; CNI; CPN; ENC; Eng; ENP; HOQ; WAA.

Quotron Systems, Inc.
5454 Beethoven Street
Los Angeles, California 90066
(213) 398-2761
Quotron 880.

Rapidata, Inc.
20 New Dutch Lane
Fairfield, New Jersey 07006
(201) 227-0035
CBDB; Citibase; Citibase-weekly; FINSTAT; IFS;
IMF Balance of Payments; Telerate Historical
Databases; ZDDB.

SDC Search Service
2500 Colorado Avenue
Santa Monica, California 90406
(203) 820-4111 X6194
(800) 421-7229
ABI/Inform; Accountant's Index; Agline; Agricola;
APILIT; APIPAT; Banker; Biosis Previews; CA
Search; CASSI; CBPI; CDI; CIN; CIS/Index; CNI;
Cold Regions; Commonwealth Agricultural Bureaus
Abstracts: NAR; Compendex; Crecord; CRIS; DBI;
EBI; EDB; Elcom Data Base; Energyline; Enviroline;
EPIA; ERIC; FEDEX; FEDREG; Forest Products:
AIDS; FSTA; GEOREF; GPO Monthly Catalog;
Grant Information System; ISMEC; Labordoc; LISA;
Management Contents; NDEX; NTIS; Oceanic
Abstracts; P/E News; Pestdoc; Petroleum Abstracts
(Tulsa); PTS Prompt; Range Management; Ringdoc;
SAE Abstracts; Safety; SSCI; SSIE; Sport; Titus;
Tropag; TSCA Chemical Substances Inventory;
USCLASS; U.S. Government Contract Awards;
USPO/USPA; USRFP; VETDOC; Votes Data Base;
WPI.

Securities Data Company Time-Sharing
62 William Street, Sixth Floor
New York, New York 10005
(212) 668-0940
Mergers and Acquisitions; New Issues of Corporate
Securities; New Issues of Municipal Debt; Private
Placements.

I.P. Sharp Associates
145 King Street West
Toronto, Ontario, Canada M5H 1J8
(416) 364-5361
ABSDATA; Actuarial Data Base; AEA; Agdata;
Bank of Canada Weekly Financial Statistics;
BI/Data; Canadian Bondmarket; Canadian
Department of Insurance; Canadian Stock Options;
CANSIM; CPI/PPI; Currency; DRI Capsule:EEI
Capsule; Economist's Statistics; Eurocharts
Commodities; Exstat; Financial Post Investment Data
Bank; ICAO Traffic Statistics; IFS; Imports;
INS-U.S. International Air Travel Statistics;
MRATE; NPA/Economic; OAG; OECD; Petroleum
Argus; Petroseries; Securities; TSEINDEXHIST;
U.S. Stock Options Data Base; World Bank Debt
Tables.

SIA Computer Services
Ebury Gate
23 Lower Belgrave Street
London, England SW1W ONW
(01) 730-4544
Citibase; World Nuclear Power Plant.

Solar Energy Research Institute
1617 Cole Boulevard
Golden, Colorado 80401
Solar Energy Information Data Bank.

Source Telecomputing Corporation
1515 Anderson Road
McLean, Virginia 22102
(703) 734-7500 X546
(800) 336-3366
Comp*U*Star; The Source; Tradenet.

Spidel Societe pour l'Informatique
98. boulevard Victor Hugo
92115 Clichy, France
33 (1) 731-1191
BIIPAM.

STSC, Inc.
7316 Wisconsin Avenue
Bethesda, Maryland 20014
(301) 657-8220
Citibase.

Sun Information Systems
280 King of Prussia Road
Radnor, Pennsylvania 19087
(215) 293-8055
Citibase.

Telesystemes-Questel
40. rue de Cherche Midi
75006 Paris, France
(33) 1 544-3813
CA Search; EPR.

Telmar Media Systems, Inc.
90 Park Avenue
New York, New York 10016
(212) 949-4640
BAR; MRI; Nielsen Station Index; Nielsen Television
Index; SAMI; SMRB; TGI.

Time Sharing Resources, Inc.
777 Northern Boulevard
Great Neck, New York 11021
(516) 487-0101
Citibase; Compustat; CPI/PPI; Flow of Funds
Accounts; Savings and Loan.

TRW Information Services Division
1 City Boulevard
Orange, California 92668
(714) 937-2700
Business Credit Services; Credit Data.

TCS 30 Tower Lane
Avon, Connecticut 06001
(203) 674-1141
GIS.

Tymshare, Inc.
20705 Valley Green Drive
Cupertino, California 95014
(408) 446-6000
Citibase; SAMI/SOLO; SITE II; SITE Potential.

Uni-Coll Corporation
3401 Science Center
Philadelphia, Pennsylvania 19104
(215) 387-3890
CPI/PPI; Flow of Funds Accounts; Wharton
Econometric Forecasting Data Bases.

United Telecom Computer Group
5454 W. 110th Street
Overland Park, Kansas 66211
(913) 341-9161
AIDS; Compustat; DRI Capsule: EEI Capsule; SDR;
SITE Potential.

Warner Computer Systems, Inc.
245 East 40th Street
New York, New York 10016
(212) 697-0110
Compustat; FDIC Report.

World Energy Industry Information Services
A Division of Business Information Display, Inc.
4202 Sorrento Valley Boulevard, Suite J
San Diego, California 92121
(714) 452-7675
World Energy Industry.